G000310737

A Far Country

A Far Country

TRAVELS IN ETHIOPIA

by Philip Marsden-Smedley

CENTURY
London Sydney Auckland Johannesburg

First published in Great Britain in 1990 by Century
An imprint of Random Century Ltd
20 Vauxhall Bridge Road, London SW1V 2SA

Century Hutchinson Australia (Pty) Ltd
20 Alfred Street, Milsons Point, Sydney, NSW 2061, Australia

Century Hutchinson New Zealand Ltd
PO Box 40-086, 32-34 View Road, Glenfield, Auckland 10, New Zealand

Century Hutchinson South Africa (Pty) Ltd
PO Box 337, Bergvlei 2012, South Africa

Set in Linotronic Palatino by SX Composing Ltd, Rayleigh, Essex
Printed and bound in Great Britain by Mackays of Chatham Ltd, Chatham, Kent

British Library Cataloguing in Publication data

Marsden-Smedley, Philip
A Far Country: Travels in Ethiopia
1. Ethiopia. Description and travel
I. Title
916.3'047

ISBN 0-7126-2566-6

ዳዊትና፡ የእስራኤልም፡ ቤት፡ ሁሉ፡ በቅኔና፡ በበገና፡ በመሰንቆም፡ በከበሮም፡
በነጋሪትና፡ በጸናጽል፡ በእግዚአብሔር፡ ፊት፡ በሙሉ፡ ኃይላቸው፡
ይጫወቱ፡ ነበር።

1 Chronicles 13:8. Amharic text.

We have still the broken materials of that first world and walk upon its ruins; while it stood, there was the seat of *paradise* and the scenes of the *golden age*.

Thomas Burnet
The Sacred Theory of the Earth

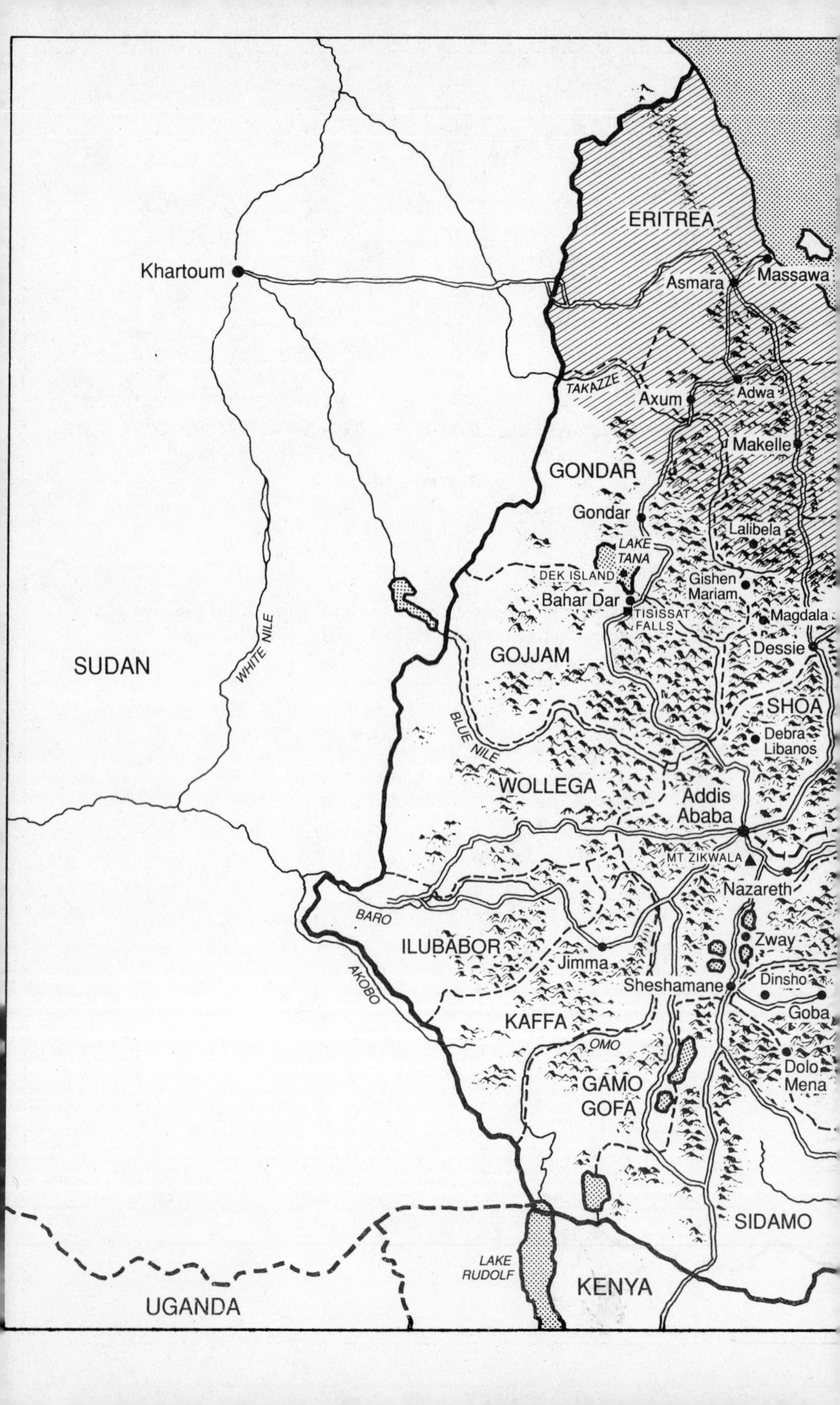

ERITREA
Massawa
Asmara
Khartoum
TAKAZZE
Axum
Adwa
Makelle
GONDAR
Gondar
Lalibela
LAKE TANA
DEK ISLAND
Gishen Mariam
Bahar Dar
TISISSAT FALLS
Magdala
Dessie
GOJJAM
SUDAN
WHITE NILE
SHOA
BLUE NILE
Debra Libanos
WOLLEGA
Addis Ababa
MT ZIKWALA
Nazareth
BARO
ILUBABOR
Zway
Jimma
AKOBO
Sheshamane
Dinsho
Goba
KAFFA
OMO
Dolo Mena
GAMO GOFA
SIDAMO
LAKE RUDOLF
KENYA
UGANDA

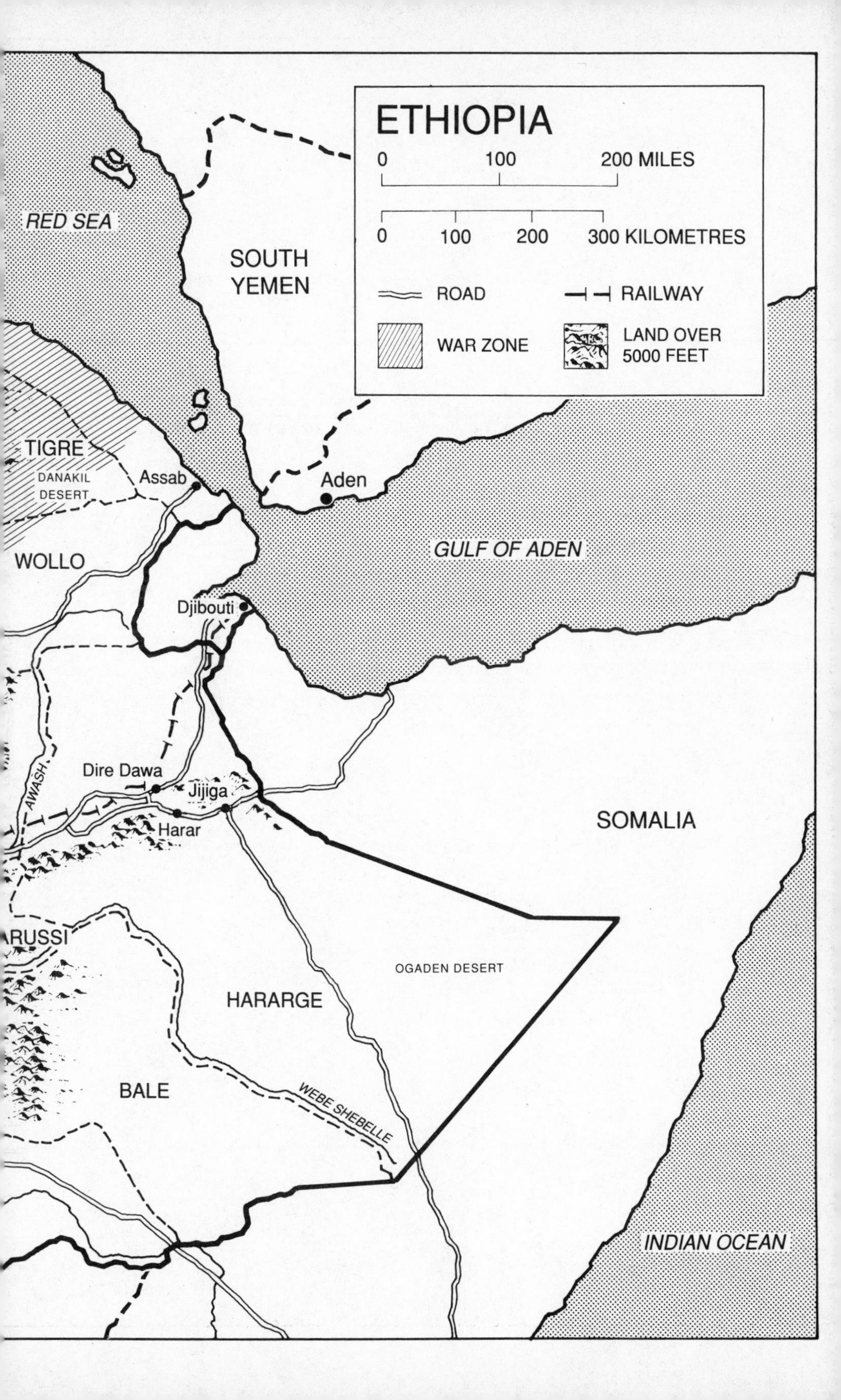
ETHIOPIA
0
100
200 MILES
0
100
200
300 KILOMETRES
ROAD
RAILWAY
WAR ZONE
LAND OVER 5000 FEET
RED SEA
SOUTH YEMEN
TIGRE
DANAKIL DESERT
Assab
Aden
WOLLO
GULF OF ADEN
Djibouti
AWASH
Dire Dawa
Jijiga
Harar
SOMALIA
RUSSI
OGADEN DESERT
HARARGE
BALE
WEBE SHEBELLE
INDIAN OCEAN

Author's note:
I have had to disguise the identities of many people in this book. I hope they know who they are, and will accept my thanks for their help.

1

In the early part of the fourteenth century, the Dominican Friar Jordanus de Sévérac ran a mission at Quilon, on the southern tip of India. All the other missionaries had been killed by Muslims, but the friar heard from merchants a story that brought him a little solace.

They told him of the 'Third India' where, at a certain place, dragons would congregate to fly. The skin of the dragons was studded with jewels. So heavy were the stones that the beasts could manage only a few beats of their scaly wings before plunging into a river, whose spring was in Paradise. Then the people of that country – Ethiopians – would run down to the river and pluck the jewels from the dragons' skin to take to their emperor. This emperor was the greatest ruler in the world, and presided over fifty-two kings. But what caught the attention of the lonely friar was that the emperor's people were all Christians. He realized the merchants were speaking of Prester John.

Most literate Europeans knew about Prester John. They knew about his letter, written to the great Christian courts in the twelfth century. They knew he would help them rid the Holy Sepulchre of the Muslims, and they knew his kingdom was a miraculous place full of unicorns and pygmies, and precious stones, a land of plenty somewhere beyond Jerusalem. But no one knew exactly where it was.

First estimates had linked Prester John with the great kings of Asia, with Yeh-lu Tashih or Genghis Khan. Marco Polo makes him a Tartar, but the Tartars weren't Christian. Then there was the mysterious cult of St Thomas, and the Nestorians in India – they were Christians, of sorts, but had no great ruler.

When Friar Jordanus retold the merchants' story in his *Mirabilia Descripta*, people began to accept that Prester John's kingdom might not be in Asia at all but further to the south, in the vast, hot regions of Ethiopia.

Rumours were already circulating in Europe about Ethiopia, from dark-skinned monks in Jerusalem, from envoys in Genoa. These men said they lived in a land of great mountains, split by gorges and dashing rivers. And they spoke of an emperor, who could just be Prester John. For by this time, in the mid-1300s, Ethiopia's rulers had been Christian for exactly one thousand years.

The day I arrived in Addis Ababa the synod elected a new patriarch of the Ethiopian Orthodox Church. The old one had died a month or so before. So the bishops assembled and for a week they gossipped and ruminated at the patriarch's palace. Then in a secret ballot, they picked Abuna Merkorios, previously the Archbishop of Gondar.

But I passed the palace with no more than a glance at its dove-grey basalt walls and tall arched windows. I walked down to the crossroads at Arat Kilo and round to Piazza.

Addis Ababa is built on the side of a hill. The lowest point of the city – the airport – is about 6000 feet above sea level, while the benign, wooded peaks of the Entoto Hills rise another 2000 feet above that. In the thin air I stopped for breath and watched the sky darken at the top of the city. Clouds spilt over the peaks and billowed upwards.

In the language of most Ethiopians, Amharic, there are two words for cloud: *demenoch* are rain clouds, *gum* a foggy mass which is damp, but has no rain. The clouds above Entoto were black and heavy, and were *demenoch*. Soon they had blocked out the afternoon sun and were growling with thunder.

A sudden wind tugged at the banana leaves beside the road, and chased scraps of litter along the kerb. Curtains of dust rose before it, and people quickened their step, hurrying into the shanty, shouting to each other and hitching up their collars. As the first drops dappled the pavement, I ran for the eaves of an office block and joined a crowd pressed beneath it for shelter.

The rains had been good that year. People were saying they couldn't remember when there'd been more rain. Now towards the end of the wet season, the gorges that run down from the Entoto Hills were muddy and swollen. In front of me Churchill Avenue was awash. The rain fell in columns, a jungle of glassy stalks so thick that no one could do anything but wait. One or two cars with their headlights on tried to creep through it, but others had stopped, with crippled wipers and misted-up windows. A mongrel splashed across the road, and in the semi-darkness the thunder seemed to shrink the city to a single room, echoing from wall to wall.

When the storm was over, I walked out again into Churchill Avenue. The rain had eased, and a gossamer of mist hung over the tarmac and the tin roofs, and the air was muggy with damp and the smell of rotting meat.

I could see beyond the city, on to the saturated plain below. Down there the clouds had already broken up and a bright green mantle spread down towards the edge of the plateau, to the Rift Valley: south towards the sun.

To the ancients, Ethiopia was an open-ended region to the south of the known world. Out of the African interior came tall men with black faces, traders and slaves, and the Greeks called them 'Aethiops' meaning 'burnt face'. Their land was inaccessible, obscure, where the physical world ended and the imaginary one began.

For Herodotus, it was 'where the south declined towards the setting sun . . . the last inhabited land in that direction'. In *Prometheus Bound*, Aeschylus pointed to Ethiopia as 'a land far off, a nation of black men . . . men who live hard by the fountain of the sun where is the river Aethiops.'

Its images became either fantastic – unbearably hot, it was the home of men with eyes in their chests and man-eating bulls and serpents that ate first-born daughters; or moral – to Homer it was a place of justice and piety, and there was a belief, held by the Greeks and later the Byzantines, that the 'blameless Ethiopians' were the first to worship the gods.

And there were sensual associations. The Egyptians equated Ethiopia with the Land of Punt, the source of ivory and spices, incense and gold, the exotic trade that flowed up the Red Sea. But the Egyptians also knew Ethiopia from the west, beyond the swamps of the Sudd, as the uncharted regions of Cush. That made it the source of something much more vital: the waters of the Nile.

At some time around the birth of Christ, the idea of Ethiopia came down to earth and fastened itself around the Kingdom of Axum, and the Red Sea port of Adulis; Ptolemy located it there in AD 150. And following their conversion in AD 330, Axumite kings found references to Ethiopians in the Bible – after that they didn't mind the name, and started to use it themselves.

When it came to teaching the principle of holy war to his followers, Mohammed told them to spare Ethiopians 'for it has fallen to them to receive nine-tenths of the courage of mankind.' Now the map of Islam shows the Ethiopian highlands as an island of dissent, not far south of Mecca.

In Europe, traces of the classical myth remained, and lingered to seep into medieval thinking: Ethiopia on the empty edge of the map, south of Jerusalem, the Land of Prester John: hope beyond the shadow of Islam.

And in other ages Ethiopia has meant different things, giving just enough away to lure the imagination, a biblical kingdom, mountainous and isolated, not generous with her secrets. Ethiopia has parallel histories: her own history, and the history of the way she is seen.

I remember a February afternoon a few years before the famine of the mid-1980s, reading about the early Church in Africa. By the seventh century, I was told, one in seven Africans were Christian, the result of St Mark's ministry to Alexandria. Then the Arab horsemen swamped the faith with the teachings of Mohammed, riding along the North African coast and up into Spain. The Christians in Africa were reduced to isolated communities, and declined until the advent of European missionaries. Except in Ethiopia. Until the revolution in 1974, Ethiopia was the oldest Christian country in the world.

After that, Ethiopia crept up on me. I stumbled on information, found 'Ethiopia' catching my eye on a page. The name became a lodestar in my reading, and in countless indexes I searched for references, between Estonia and Etruscans, Essenes and Evans-Pritchard. Often, where I'd expected a chapter, in general histories of the Christian Church, books of African art, there was a single reference – or nothing at all. And soon I found the same facts recurring and realized that Ethiopian scholarship was, like its subject, somehow cut off from the mainstream.

I discovered in me the scar of schoolbook Africa, the place whose history began when Europe set out to explore it. But here was the only African country to have defeated a colonial power – and a civilization second only to Egypt in its antiquity.

A pageant of dimly-remembered associations emerged – Dr Johnson's *Rasselas*, the tiny figure of Haile Selassie and the Rastafarian belief that he was a god, Rimbaud who stopped writing poetry when he was nineteen and went to live in Ethiopia, Evelyn Waugh who based *Scoop* and *Black Mischief* on his own travels there.

The only history of the country I could find was published in 1935. It had five illustrations. I remember the drawing of Lalibela's rock churches, and Ortelius's map of Prester John's kingdom, and the last picture out of focus, badly cropped, an aerial photograph of a part of the plateau: a table-top mountain surrounded by shadowy cliffs and wooded valleys.

As my research widened, so the mountain seemed to grow, and its flat summit, striped with plots of teff-wheat, became a mysterious lost world and I wanted to be there. But one thing more than any other persuaded me to go: at that time I knew no one, friend or acquaintance, who had visited Ethiopia.

Someone gave me the name of a former British ambassador to Addis Ababa, a man who had enjoyed the rare intercession between two royal courts. But his Ethiopia, he imagined, had gone. 'You're a bloody fool,' he told me. 'Don't you realize the country is now run by Marxist bandits?'

My grandmother knew of a scholar who had left Ethiopia during the bloody years of the late seventies. Dr Pankhurst was delighted at my interest. He filled my luggage with presents for his friends and gave me a sheaf of letters of introduction.

But in Addis Ababa the letters yielded only surprise. Travel was out of the question. I met an American academic at the university who had been waiting six months to get out of the capital. An English woman who had lived in Ethiopia for thirty years told me the best thing I could do was to book a flight home. Perhaps, after all, the ambassador had been right.

For ten days I hung around government offices, harassed each contact in turn, and got nowhere. Then in desperation I returned to the first man I had seen. I told him if I went home now, all I could say about his country was that it was ugly and repressive.

But if he let me travel, I could do much to advertise Ethiopia's beauty and antiquity. I told him my opinion carried weight in my own country, and he got me the permits in a couple of hours.

I went to Lake Tana and spent some time on the islands. I slept in villages where they grew everything they owned. In some places I asked when the last foreigner had been, and they shrugged and said 'Never.'

One evening, shortly before I left the lake, I sat on the shore and watched the cranes and hornbill fly over the water to roost. It had been raining but the sun had slipped beneath the cloud-bank and lit up the far peaks. And I knew then that I would have to come back to Ethiopia, that it had become more remote, more alluring.

Afterwards, those days on the islands took on the bright tones of an idyll and I forgot the discomfort and the problems of getting there. I read all I could and dreamed only of returning.

2

The synod was still sitting when I went to the Church Office, behind the patriarch's palace. In the compound, groups of cassocked priests stood chatting beneath the juniper. Beside them was a stack of orange freight containers stamped with ASSAB.

The Reverend Tadessa had a spartan office, and wore a dark suit and bright-striped tie. He walked out from behind his desk and gripped my hand. 'Welcome, welcome!'

On the wall was a faded black-and-white portrait of the former patriarch. Tadessa pointed to a chair and started to explain about the election. 'You have come at a good time. On Sunday we have the inauguration service. Seven o'clock at Selassie Cathedral. We do it twice: once inside, and then outside so everyone can see.'

I explained my interest in Ethiopia.

'We have a proverb,' he said and leaned back in his chair. 'To know Ethiopia, the Church is the gate.'

'What about travel?' I hoped he might help me get permits.

Tadessa sat forward and put his hands together on the desk. When he spoke it was almost in a whisper. 'After the war with the Italians, for many years you could travel freely. Now, you understand, we have er . . . peace problem in the north. No one can travel – everything now is a problem.'

We talked a little more and as I stood to leave he said: 'You will come on Sunday to the service, won't you?'

'Of course.'

And he smiled and took my hand, and held it as we walked across the bustling compound to the gate.

Sunday morning was bright after a night of heavy rain. I walked up through the city shortly after dawn. The wet streets shone, and on patches of waste ground wild dogs still squabbled over the night's bones. Tawny eagles and kites wheeled overhead. The road steepened and became filled with phantom figures leaning into the hill, their white cotton shawls pulled tight against the cold.

A muddy path led up to the church. Spread on sheets along its flank, vendors had arranged piles of tapers and various small devotional texts, and soapstone crosses. They vied for space with lepers, and beggars with goitre. One man sat in the middle of the path exchanging a joke with a friend through the legs of the crowd, his scrappy beard open in a smile. He had a child in his lap. But when I looked closer I saw it wasn't a child: it was his scrotum, swollen with elephantiasis.

Behind the path a grove of juniper scattered the sun over the headstones of the thirty-eight Patriots, resistance leaders during the Italian war.

Selassie Cathedral is dedicated not to its patron, Emperor Haile Selassie, but to *selassie*, the Amharic for 'trinity'. The Emperor commissioned the building early in his reign, and it was barely finished when the Italians reached the capital in 1936. The west front had been added later in a sort of pre-fab baroque and was hung for the ceremony with Ethiopian tricolours. The courtyard below buzzed with priests in white robes.

Inside the cathedral a priest led me towards the front of the nave. 'Here,' he whispered, and pointed me to the space reserved for the crew of Ethiopian TV. I squatted among coils of flex, and in front of me a man in a tan leather jacket and white shoes played with a light-meter.

Soon afterwards, the Archbishop of Gondar sauntered out of the chancel and took his place opposite me, on a makeshift throne beneath the pulpit. Above his head hung an embroidered reproduction of Leonardo's *Last Supper*.

A priest walked up to the microphone on the chancel steps and announced in English: 'We will start the ceremony with a song.' And a slow chant began.

The man in white shoes ordered a pair of arc-lights to be turned on. The archbishop blinked and held his hand in front of his eyes.

Further up, the nave was lined with a row of empty chairs for the visiting bishops. It stood like a fragile sea wall against the flood of faces behind it. More and more pushed in through the high doors. But soon the guards closed them, and the noise of the crowd subsided.

The first to take his place was the bespectacled Anglican Bishop of Bury St Edmunds, distinctive in his white ruffled soutane. He stooped donnishly and shuffled between the chairs, frowning at some imagined dilemma of protocol. I felt suddenly very concerned for him, and for a moment he looked lost, glancing around at the empty places beside him. But soon he was joined by a tubby Greek Orthodox bishop and a pair of whispering cardinals in zucchetta and crimson robes. They seemed more at ease and smiled like cocky prefects at a school asssembly, their bright cassocks and heavy chains less conspicuous in this Eastern church than the Anglican's austerity.

The arc-lights were swung towards them, away from the archbishop. I watched him take out a red handkerchief and mop his brow. I realized then that I had met him before.

He had granted me a brief audience on my previous visit. I had waited in a cold room with blue-daubed walls and a concrete floor. I saw him sneak behind the building to change into his episcopal robes. When he spoke to me it was through an interpreter, and I remembered the studied show of ceremony. He told me to go to my country and teach them of the Ethiopian Church, like Moses bringing the tablets down from Sinai. I recalled a tall shy man, with a certain presence, but I was surprised to see him here, about to take the supreme office of his Church.

Nothing ever happens in Addis Ababa without rumour, and already I had heard mutterings of the synod's 'rigged elections', and 'the government's choice'.

His Grace, Abuna Merkorios, was about to be crowned as the fourth patriarch of the Ethiopian Orthodox Church. Until 1950 an archbishop had always been sent from Alexandria, from the Coptic Church. But it was an isolated post and rarely could the archbishop speak Amharic. There were frequent quarrels between Ethiopia and Alexandria, and the Copts often used the post to get rid of a troublesome bishop. The Ethiopians used to pay little heed to the Copt and the Ethiopian's own Abbot of Debra Libanos acted as chaplain to the Crown, and was recognized by most people as primate.

In his reordering of the country Haile Selassie agreed with the

Coptic Church to rationalize their role and in 1955 the first native Ethiopian patriarch took his place at the World Council of Churches.

I glanced at the programme. The short biography of Merkorios showed an exemplary path up through the church hierarchy: religious instruction from an early age, four years studying *kene* (church poetry), eleven years studying and teaching music, two years hermitage, a bishop for nine years. His diocesan achievements in Gondar sounded heroic: 185 churches renovated, 43 new ones built, new church schools, grinding mills, textile mills, water pumps and church halls. The list rang with the new-dawn zeal of a May Day report.

Merkorios was approached by two Ethiopian bishops – the Bishop of Sudan and the Bishop of Djibouti. The man in white shoes had taken off his leather jacket, but he looked agitated and shifted from foot to foot.

The bishops placed the crown on Merkorios's bald head. Applause broke from the congregation and the new Patriarch stood and read a speech. Around the chancel, groups of Ethiopian bishops and senior clergy leaned on ivory-topped prayer sticks. The Bishop of Bury St Edmunds sat down and toyed with his episcopal ring; he looked tired.

At 10 a.m. the bells rang, and guards threw open the double doors. A slow procession started down the aisle: the Patriarch under his heavy crown, the bishops in his wake, and ahead of them the TV cameraman walking backwards with his own train of flex and jostling attendants, and the director in his white shoes.

Outside the party reassembled. Bishop Xaven Chinchinian, the Armenian Bishop of Africa, rose and made a speech in French. He extolled the great antiquity of their Churches, and the deep communion between their Monophysite creeds. After each sentence he paused for a translation to be made into Amharic.

In turn the other Orthodox Churches presented gifts and delivered their messages of goodwill, from Greece, Russia, Alexandria and Malabar; then the cardinals and a pastor from the World Council of Churches, and the Bishop of Bury St Edmunds. The Patriarch sat at a table draped in a gold-embroidered cloth. As each gift was put in front of him he gave a faint smile.

From the table a red carpet flowed down the steps and across the stone pavings of the courtyard. The crowd jostled up to the edge of the yard, pressing forward, threatening the truncheoned soldiers. Some younger spectators had climbed up on to the four statues of the Apostles for a better view.

I stood in the yard with the officials and TV crew, and watched a group of clergy step forward and form two columns, one on either side of the carpet. They wore robes and white breeches, and carried prayer sticks and sistra: these were the *debtara.*

Debtara are an essential part of the Ethiopian Church. Their role has been likened to that of the Levites in the Temple, responsible for readings and chants and music – and dance. One of them now took up a large wooden kettledrum and hung it from his shoulder. The others started a low chant and shuffled towards each other, dipping their prayer sticks. The drum sounded and the dancers backed away. They raised their voices and shook sistra. Their movements quickened with the drumming. They abandoned the unison of the chant and started to shout and sway independently; in the crowd women ululated in response.

It was a compelling sight, with the rhythmic steps and the thicket of canes, then a sudden double beat of the drum, a change in tempo or a long note held by the *debtara.* Everyone sat up a little. An eastern bloc diplomat in the front row turned and smiled at his wife. A Korean beside him, previously asleep, started, looked around and reached for a small camera.

At that moment too the sun broke through a huge muddy cloud that had shed a few drops of rain since we emerged. The sun umbrellas bloomed above the heads of the crowd and in the front row the Bishop of Addis Ababa put on a pair of very dark, metal-rimmed sunglasses. He turned and said something to Tsana Markos, the acting patriarch, and they both grinned. The Bishop of Bury St Edmunds also seemed absorbed by the dance, leaning forward, chin in hand, almost smiling.

Only the new Patriarch in the centre of it all, shadowed beneath an ornamental braid umbrella, and beneath the heavy red diadem, seemed unmoved, his expression of majesty a little forced, his countenance a little too stern. He looked like a reluctant beauty queen at a rural carnival, hoisted on to a slow float and pulled through the crowd.

At 12.30, without warning, he got up and started to walk down the steps, sending the marshalls into a panic of beating and shouting. The front row of spectators was breached and the Patriarch got into an old green Land Rover.

In the lobby of one of the big hotels I met an American field officer from the UN. 'So, you just arrived in Addis?' He had a West Coast accent.

'Yes, a few days ago.'

'And what are you doing?'

'Research – I'm hoping to travel.'

'Yeah? Where do you want to go?'

'Harar, Gondar, Lake Tana, the south, maybe north to Dessie and Lalibela.

He shook his head. 'Well, good luck to you! But I can't think they'll let you go. They don't like foreigners snooping around here.'

'I know.'

'What about permits?'

'I've got to wait in Addis until I sort them out.'

He nodded in sympathy. Then his eyes lit up as he remembered something. 'You don't play poker, I suppose? We have a game tonight.'

When we drove down towards the old airport that evening, the darkness seemed to shroud the city, to make it more distant. A film of eucalyptus smoke hovered around the treetops, and slops of orange light fell on the muddy fringes of the road. Bare bulbs hung in open doorways, but most of the shanty glowered in the late dusk, a forbidding web of walkways and mud-walled shacks.

A hooded guard swung open a sheet metal gate to reveal a two-storey villa. Inside, the UN poker school filled the scattered sofas and chairs. Each man had a beard. They looked like frontiersmen, and I listened to them talk in the cool American tones that can be used equally well for war or a ball game.

The latest crisis to grip the aid community was a flood of refugees along the northern Somali border. News had filtered slowly up to Addis Ababa. 'Obviously left in a hurry – no warning. There are people in the camp who were just visiting friends. And a lot of professionals too, doctors, lawyers – don't normally find those guys in refugee camps. They usually make plans of their own.'

'What's the main problem?'

'Water, I heard. Guess we'll have to tank it in.'

'Gondar's got problems again with its water supply.'

'Yeah? I thought the Koreans were going to build a dam up there.'

'Why can't they just pipe it up from Lake Tana. Plenty of water there.'

'The fall's too great.'

'You know, in Tigré – all those new dams? They're full already. Just completed and along come the biggest rains in years. They're a real success story.'

'I hear the locusts have copulated in Eritrea.'

'This early? That means they'll swarm and come south by December.'

Later we gathered round a table covered in green baize. When we started the game, conversation ceased. They had a practised repertoire of games: stud and pantaloon, Jacob's ladder and Texas flip, and one or two house games like Philby's crutch and leg-over, named after 'a hard fellow in Aden'.

At about eight we stopped to eat, a buffet of spiced meat sauces and salads and fruit. We drank wine and talked again, away from the table. An economist from the World Bank told me that Ethiopia was prompt with repaying debts, too prompt sometimes for her own good. 'I think it's a matter of pride.'

We resumed play, and again attention focused on the game. The dealer called the games and the players grunted bets, but otherwise there was just the sound of chips and cards on the green baize. The ashtrays filled up and in the end the economist was the biggest loser; I won enough to pay my tutor for a couple of Amharic lessons. At half past eleven we settled up and drove back through deserted streets to beat the midnight curfew.

Sylvia Pankhurst, the mother of Dr Pankhurst, had heard Mussolini's bellicose speeches in the mid-1920s, and knew it would all end in war. So when he invaded Ethiopia in 1935, she stepped up her anti-fascist campaign in Britain. She helped sway public opinion against Italy, and welcomed the exiled Haile Selassie when he arrived at Waterloo Station. She moved to Addis Ababa after the war, and was given a full state funeral when she died there in 1960.

Helen, her granddaughter, was doing some work on 'gender relations'. She had been in the field a little way north, but was now in Addis Ababa picking up supplies.

'Look,' she said on the phone, 'I have to see an air hostess. She has brought me some stationery from London. But then we'll go and see Afewerk Tekle. You'd be interested to meet him.'

We found the air hostess's house down a muddy grass track. She opened the door in a pink dressing gown and rubbed her eyes. She had a tall, voluptuous beauty, an exportable kind of beauty for the national airline: sprigs of straightened hair, fine bones and skin not too dark, just the right shade of varnished teak. I had seen her buoyant looks on posters, walking arm-in-arm with other smiling hostesses away from an EAL Boeing, which dwarfed them with its cathedral proportions. The posters hung in tea houses and bars all over the city and in offices and private houses, a little piece of home-grown glamour. Ethiopian Airlines promises a narrow corridor to the outside world, and every girl dreams of being an air hostess.

Afewerk Tekle lived in a white stuccoed villa. He is one of Africa's leading artists. He held his chin high, hung only his own paintings on the wall, and talked with the elegant gesticulations of those used to being listened to.

He'd just been asked to join a party going on a tour of the Far East. On Sunday he was to fly in a chartered plane to North Korea. With him were going the Prime Minister and three other ministers: Housing, Energy and Mines, and Construction. He feigned annoyance at being given such short notice. 'How should I know whether to wear my national costume, or how many of my decorations to take? I do not want to be seen to upstage our hosts.'

A maid brought a tray of tea and roasted corn.

At the far end of the room, the north light fell through the window on to a sheepskin rug, which covered a dais for his sitters. Beside it was a completed work on an easel. I recognized it as an abstraction of his stained-glass work.

A more figurative work hung behind it, of the war: a young soldier clutched a rifle to his chest; behind him the desert was broken with the impact of shells, and the broken husks of tanks. An improbable dogfight took place in a spare bit of sky by the boy's temple.

And I remembered something I had seen that morning, as I passed the barracks down by the old airport. Another painted image, cruder, but in the same bright colours. A soldier in modern battledress was emerging from the ghostly figure of a warrior. He was an old Amhara warrior, with spear and shield, and a head-dress of flowing lion's mane. Beneath the picture were the slogans: REVOLUTIONARY MOTHERLAND OR DEATH! and EVERYTHING TO THE WARFRONT! It was easy to forget that, in the north, the country was fighting a civil war.

Later, crossing the road in the centre of town, Helen and I were pursued by a boy holding out his hand. He was bare-footed but otherwise looked robust. He twisted his face into well-rehearsed expressions of pathos.

'Why do you beg?' Helen bent down suddenly, and pointed at the boy. 'You are healthy. Why don't you go to school?'

The boy was taken aback. 'But I have no mother.'

'And I suppose your father has run off, and you have no brothers and sisters, eh?'

The boy knew he was beaten, and conceded a hint of a smile before running away.

I sat with a pot of insipid tea in the bar of a government hotel, and waited to meet a doctor, the friend of a friend.

The hotel offered a bland cosmopolitan comfort with low lighting and low imported sofas. The young urban rich wallowed in them, in their casual sweaters and gold jewellery, rarely talking. A party of tired professionals mumbled in another corner. Between the stasis of office life and the simplicity of their homes, the sofas were a sanctuary for these people. Ethiopians with money, those that remain in the country, find spending it a problem. Few imports find their way up on to the high plateau, and those that do come with a duty tag of 200 per cent or more.

I was joined by a group of three youngish men. One of them said, 'Hello sir, can we sit with you?'

'Of course.'

'I am a film cameraman, and these are my friends.' He flicked his hand at each of his companions. 'He is a TV presenter, and this one – he is an expert in catastrophe.'

I never discovered what this meant as Dr Mesfin arrived and we left immediately for his house. We drove there down a road so pitted that I had to grip the seat with both hands. Dr Mesfin talked.

He had five children, he told me, his three youngest were at home now. They were studying at the Lycée.

'Where are the older ones?'

'The eldest – he is twenty – is in Washington, and I have a seventeen-year-old daughter studying in Paris. In a few years the younger ones will join her there.'

'Will they come back?'

He shrugged and paused, turning the car through his gates. 'I think not.' He stopped the car outside the house and turned off the engine. 'I would rather they were happy there than unhappy here.'

Inside, his remaining daughters lined up to meet me and smiled as they bowed and shook my hand. Mesfin and I sat in two chrome-framed chairs on corduroy cushions. The girls fetched us drinks. His wife joined us, an elegant, demure woman who sat apart from us on a stool and listened while Mesfin told me about his hospital.

This was middle-class life in Ethiopia, struggling to maintain pre-revolutionary standards. The youngest girl was fourteen, as old as the revolution itself. I wondered whether she would stay in Ethiopia when it came to the choice, and found myself hoping she would want to.

Mesfin told me a story of an incident during his training. 'We were given a lecture about parasites. Africa, the lecturer told us, is infested with parasites – parasitical diseases are one of the continent's major problems. In the class with me were students from Ghana and Nigeria. Afterwards they said, "How can we accept this colonial prejudice against Africa? What do you think, Mesfin?" I was surprised – it hadn't occurred to me. So I said: "I don't feel slighted – I am an Ethiopian, not an African."'

Later he put on a video of a BBC documentary made the previous year about the threat of recurring famine. It had been made by Jonathan Dimbleby. Dimbleby had made another film in 1974. Then he had shown pictures of starving people in northern Ethiopia, and set them against a wedding-feast for the Emperor's daughter, and the imperial dogs being fed. The film is seen as the turning-point in the creeping revolution. Apparently the Emperor knew nothing of the famine. I asked Mesfin what Ethiopians thought about foreigners coming here and telling them about their problems.

'We were shocked! You've seen how we give money to the poor.'

But it sounded like a statement. Every now and then I had the sense that I was only being told what I wanted to hear. There was a false bottom to communication that had nothing to do with my faltering Amharic. Ethiopians have a notorious reticence. Some subjects – famine, the war, the Red Terror of '77, are too sensitive for polite conversation. They are private, family matters, not to be discussed with outsiders. And, when the last famine became world news, it was embarrassment and shame that was felt most acutely by educated Ethiopians. Aid workers and journalists, who highlight the problem, are not always welcome.

But there is also the traditional xenophobia of an isolated people. In the past, the foreigners who have climbed up to the plateau have rarely profited Ethiopia. If it wasn't the Italians wanting an East African empire, it was the Portuguese in the seventeenth century urging the Monophysite Christians to abandon their heresies and turn to Rome. And before that it was the shadow of Islam, a constant threat from the lowlands, for which the mountains seemed the only foil.

Mesfin asked one of his daughters to eject the completed video and in its place appeared the live broadcast of a documentary about nineteenth-century Ethiopia. History is safe territory, free from the responsibility of the living, and a reinforcement of the rigid sense of Ethiopian identity. So we chatted away amicably about the Magdala campaign when the British victory caused Emperor Theodore's suicide, and war with the Mahdi in the 1880s, until the threat of the curfew brought back the present, and I rose to leave.

3

At the Institute of Ethiopian Studies, there is a stuffed lion at the top of the stairs. In the reading room the books stand in glass-fronted cases. I peered in at the small section of travelogues and reminiscences, and found my own interests spelt out in their zealous titles: *Africa's Last Empire, The Hidden Empire, The Roof of Africa, Fountain of the Sun, The Land of Prester John, The Land of Sheba, Cradle of Mankind*.

The university term had not yet started and the high-backed chairs were empty. Above them the ceiling was edged with beaded mouldings and supported a brass chandelier. The pale blue walls seemed to contain an air of former grandeur, for this high room used to be the Emperor's court, and the whole building his first palace.

A french window in one wall opened on to the roof of the *porte cochère*. Here the slight figure of Haile Selassie would appear over the parapet, surveying an oval of tall palms and ornamental gardens and ponds. I stood there and looked down on a scene little changed: a team of gardeners weeding the beds, pushing wheelbarrows which squeaked, arranging sprinklers. Hundreds of small birds, sparrows, bright yellow sunbirds and bee-catchers, trilled and flew around the shrubs like bustling courtiers. And in the middle was a strange imperial edifice – a free-standing spiral staircase in stone, topped by the Lion of Judah itself. On official days the *kantiba*, Addis Ababa's mayor, used to climb its steps and address the Emperor. The imperial stone lion, unlike most in Addis Ababa, was intact.

Away to the right the drive disappears beneath a tunnel of cedar boughs, to the gates. The gates open on to the circus at Sidist Kilo, and face a hospital, previously Haile Selassie Hospital. After the revolution the name was dropped and now in red letters above the ground-floor windows has been painted: YEKATIT 12 HOSPITAL.

As well as its own language and script, Ethiopia has a different system of time. The clock begins at dawn: 6 a.m. is twelve o'clock in Ethiopia; 8 a.m. is two o'clock. The new year is in September and there are thirteen months: twelve of thirty days, and one of five. And they still use the Julian calendar, eight years behind the Gregorian calendar.

So Yekatit 12, 1929 in Ethiopia is equivalent to 19 February, 1937, one of the blackest days in the hundred-year history of Addis Ababa. The day before, a pair of Eritreans had walked up the drive, beneath the young cedars to the palace. It had been taken over by Graziani, viceroy of Mussolini's Africa Orientale Italiana. There was an Italian holiday to celebrate the birthday of the Prince of Naples. A group of dignitaries had assembled on the steps, Italian and Ethiopian beside each other, united for the day. In front of them was a crowd of beggars and the poor, waiting to receive alms. The Eritreans stepped up and lobbed ten hand grenades towards the steps.

The cross-bearer of the Coptic Archbishop was killed. Among the injured was Graziani himself, who suffered 365 shrapnel wounds. Italian soldiers fired into the crowd of beggars. Later on, in the city centre, the Blackshirts were told by their Federal Secretary, 'For three days I give you *carte blanche* to destroy and kill and do what you like to the Abyssinians.'

The licence unleashed months of pent-up fear and hatred – the Italians were far from home, among a remote and hostile people. Houses and shops were looted and burnt, fugitives tripped up and beaten to death. In Addis Ababa the Italians killed thousands of Ethiopians, and more around the country. Bodies were scattered in the streets, and the city's streams ran with blood.

A more methodical search for the culprits of the attack led, at one point, to the monastery of Debra Libanos, a few hours north of Addis Ababa. The abbot had excused himself from the ceremony, and it was rumoured that one of the Eritreans had fled to the monastery afterwards.

Three months later, on 20 May, Debra Libanos celebrated the feast of its founder, Ethiopia's greatest native saint, Tekla Haimanot. In the mid-morning, after the all-night service, the monks came out into the sunlight. They paraded around the church, dancing behind the *tabot*, the replica of the Ark of the Covenant that embodies the sanctity of each church.

After the ceremony the local commander, Colonel Garelli, stood and ordered the arrest of the monks. All three hundred were shot, as were twenty-three laymen suspected of conspiracy. The *debtara* were shot the following week.

Graziani reported to his command in Rome: 'Of the monastery at Debra Libanos . . . there remains no trace.'

I took the dawn bus to Debra Libanos, over the Entoto Hills, into the wide plain beyond, squeezed between an old monk and a girl with a baby. The child wailed and the girl opened her dress and suckled it.

Debra Libanos is in the same province as Addis Ababa. Some people I had asked said that meant no permits were needed, one or two had said I must have permits – most seemed unsure. I trusted to luck, and at the checkpoint on the edge of the city, the soldiers yawned and waved us on.

In the crisp morning air the windows soon fogged up and I leaned across the dozing monk to wipe the glass. Flat unfenced fields stretched beneath the mist in a green and yellow patchwork, broken only by the smudges of tracks and farmsteads: brown thatched roofs, brown mud walls.

About three hours north of Addis Ababa, the plateau plunged into the Blue Nile Gorge, here about a mile deep. We left the main road and followed an unmetalled route along the ridge until it dipped down to a narrow finger above the Jema river. At the end of the road, the bus stopped beside the shining dome of a church.

A guard showed me into a hut strewn with fresh grass. The abbot sat behind a table signing papers, an elegant figure in a black cassock. He read my letter, then looked up and smiled.

'I think I saw you at Selassie Cathedral, at our Patriarch's service. You were there?'

'Yes.'

'Come, I will show you a room.' We pushed through a low door into his own garden where his banana trees circled a plot of sorghum. Around it was an L-shaped single-storey building with red wooden doors. One of these hung open and an old man was leaning against the jamb, reading and muttering a text in the sun.

'He is a visiting bishop – from Sidamo. These rooms we keep

for special visitors.' The abbot showed me into a dark cell. He threw open the shutters and a cloud of startled fleas plunged into the dust.

'I'm very honoured,' I said, and he beamed.

Then he took me to the church and, bowing, left me there while he returned to his work. Outside, its stone walls rose to a plain parapet and flat cruciform roof, and the bell-shaped dome. But somehow it was all wrong, ill-proportioned; the transepts seemed truncated, the dome too heavy and its finial – a golden cross – grotesquely large. The vaulted nave inside was too short for its height and had the inert emptiness of a municipal building.

An elderly monk approached, old enough to have been one of the first novices here after the massacre.

'Which is your country?' he asked.

'Britain.'

His few remaining teeth were long and yellow. 'Yes, you have an English face. Tell me, are there churches there? Is it a highland country, or lowlands?'

'We have churches, maybe as many as you. But our mountains are much smaller.'

He looked down and tried to picture it. Then he remembered something and asked, 'Oh, I wonder, do you know Asfa Wossen there? Is he alive still?'

Asfa Wossen has crowned himself Amha Selassie, Emperor of Ethiopia. He lives in London, in Portland Place. He was the Emperor's eldest son, but not his favourite. That honour belonged to Makonnen, Duke of Harar. But he was killed in the early 1960s in a car crash at Mojo, on the way from Addis Ababa to Harar. If he'd lived, Ethiopia's recent history might have been very different.

I reassured the monk about Asfa Wossen and left the church for the mid-afternoon sun.

Below the church the ground fell away to another broad ledge. Here I stumbled on a necropolis in a grove of thorn scrub. Cramped plots lay behind iron railings. There were headstones of marble and alabaster inscribed with Amharic epitaphs, and angels bearing festoons and busts of the Sacred Heart.

The pediment of each headstone was marked by a small enamel

oval: a sepia photograph. Some were grinning portraits in suit and tie, others stern figures in military uniform or the white jodhpurs made fashionable by the Emperor; one man was remembered sitting at a desk, his pen poised over a document.

To be buried here at Debra Libanos was the final accolade for a nobleman, a deathbed plea to his family, even a condition of the will. But for the bereaved family it often meant a tedious trudge through the mountains, sometimes for days, to be faced with the abbot's fee for the plot.

The ornate, classical graves seemed to have come in with independence in 1941, a legacy of the Italian Occupation. The photographs showed proud men, the agents of the Emperor's quest for progress. I wondered if they shared his vision, or if they sensed at all that modernization would mean their downfall. By 1974 their kin had lost all power – no one could offer any organized resistance to the revolution; the Emperor had become a lonely, isolated figure, his wife and favourite son dead, his palace echoing with rumours of the inevitable change.

Since 1974 there had been few additions to the graveyard, and most had suffered from neglect. Ivy curled around the cracked stones and some of the ledgers had broken open to expose the bones.

Dotted among the graves, like ghosts, were the poor and deformed, hunched against the pediments or hobbling towards me for alms, and beyond them like the soldiers at Calvary, was a group of boys throwing craps on top of a sarcophagus.

When Evelyn Waugh spent a night here in 1930, his companion, Professor W, feigned illness to avoid the food the monks gave them. But when they were alone in their tent, they tucked into a hamper they had brought. They ate olives and tinned grouse, and drank lager.

I went to bed that night early, after a bowl of plain rice. The air was full of the rattle of crickets. From the cliffs above the monastery came the sound of a waterfall and I could hear the occasional curt barks of a baboon.

Later I was woken by the cold, and a troop of bugs crawling across my chest. A bell tolled midnight close at hand; I lit the candle beside my bed and read.

Just before sunrise I woke again, this time to the sound of thunder. It rolled down the gorge like falling rock. The rain started to patter on to the metal roof, then rose to a crescendo. I pushed open the shutters, and saw the pink strands of dawn wiped across the clouds. The waterfall now gushed over the cliffs as a muddy torrent, and from the corrugated gulleys of the zinc roof, streams of water crossed the window, as straight as the bars of a prison cell.

Negussie had been at the monastery for five years, sent there by his family when he was nine. He had a round boyish face with impressionable eyes, but his brow was already creased from constant frowning.

'Why did you come here, Negussie?'

He looked away and said, 'Mental problem.'

His family were farmers in Bale, a few hundred miles to the south. They had no money for hospital and had despaired of their listless son. It was the local priest who had suggested taking the waters of St Tekla Haimanot at Debra Libanos.

So they had put the boy on to the Addis bus with a parcel of food and some money, and a letter to the abbot which said he should be taken on as a novice.

'But now it is difficult for me,' Negussie said. 'Sometimes I beg.'

He had offered to show me the sacred springs, and banged on my door soon after dawn. We crossed brooks the colour of smoked glass and entered the forest at the foot of the cliff. There were people bathing and collecting the holy water wherever it seeped through the rock.

'Can we get up the cliff?'

Negussie frowned. 'But why? There is nothing up there.'

But we found a narrow path through the rocks, and climbed up to the lip of the plateau. On top women rested loads of firewood before the descent, and in the distance stretched the great basin of the Blue Nile; below the cliff, the silvery dome of Debra Libanos shone lifelessly from the forest.

A group of men was carrying rocks of tufa towards the edge. 'They are making the path,' said Negussie. 'Recently three men came here at night, and lost the path. They fell down the cliff and died.'

He looked down at the ground and shuffled his feet. I could see he didn't like this place.

'Will you show me Tekla Haimanot's cave?' I said.

Negussie cheered up and led me back down the cliff. We reached an iron gate that blocked the cave's entrance. 'Let me tell you the story of Tekla Haimanot.' He paused, and when he spoke again seemed more assured. 'Tekla Haimanot came to this place to pray. After twenty years his leg fell off and he prayed on one leg for seven years and died. He was buried in this cave for fifty-seven years and then taken to the church.' He pointed along the cliff, and then started to run. 'Wait here! I will ask the hermit if we can look inside.'

He ran up a small path beside the shrine to a tiny hut. Above it plumes of moisture rose from the rock, and across the gorge the far cliff glowed an opaque grey in the mist.

The hermit appeared, muttering. He approached the gate of the shrine at a crouching trot, bearing before him the rusty blade of a shovel. On it was a pile of smouldering charcoals and crystals of incense resin.

He bent to kiss the gate and pulled a key from around his neck. Inside, it was no more than a damp crypt, the floor dotted with an archipelago of tins and plastic beakers. The hermit tipped the spade into a censer beside a makeshift altar. On the altar rested an image of the Virgin and a faded chromolithograph of Christ, and in the middle the stylized figure of Tekla Haimanot.

He stood against a plain green background with a long face and wide eyes. His right leg was broken off at the knee and lay by his side. Each side of him was a row of bodkins arranged to wake him should he fall asleep during his seven-year vigil. And from his shoulders there fanned a pair of wings which fell in scallops of striped feathers to his thigh.

Of the stories that have wrapped themselves around Tekla Haimanot, one has him being thrown by Satan off the cliff of Debra Damo in Tigré, Ethiopia's sixth-century monastery. The saint is saved by the Archangel Gabriel who equips him with the wings to break his fall.

But his principal role was of more historical importance: that of kingmaker.

St Tekla Haimanot lived in the thirteenth century under the Zagwé dynasty. The Zagwé came from different stock and did not have quite the ethnic legitimacy of the Axumite rulers who preceded them. In 1270 the last Zagwé king was denied sanctuary and killed in a church.

The saint is seen as providing the licence for the new Emperor Yekkuno Amlak and his offspring to replace the Zagwé dynasty as the true imperial line. How he did this makes the tradition of Ethiopian kingship one of the most intriguing anywhere. It also reveals much about the singular nature of the Ethiopians – regardless of current ideology.

Tekla Haimanot pulled together the threads of an oral tradition and commissioned the *Kebra Nagast*, the Book of the Glory of Kings, written in the early fourteenth century by Isaac the Poor Man. When the British looted the book after the Battle of Magdala in 1868, Emperor Yohannis wrote to Queen Victoria and demanded its return. It is now back in Ethiopia.

The *Kebra Nagast* is the mythical charter of the Ethiopians and their now defunct monarchy. It tells the Ethiopian version of the story of Solomon and Sheba:

In Jerusalem, the new city of the Israelites, King Solomon was visited by Makeda, the Queen of Sheba. Before she left, the king held a banquet in her honour. They had ten courses of heavily spiced food. Afterwards Solomon turned to the queen and asked her to spend the night in his chamber. She agreed, provided he did not take her by force. Solomon said that she too must not take anything from him. When they retired, a bed for the queen was set apart from Solomon and a bowl of water placed beside it. Solomon took to his bed Sheba's servant-girl, a union from which stemmed the Zagwé dynasty.

During the night Sheba woke with a thirst and drank some water. Solomon claimed she had broken her oath, and that he was entitled to her, and thus was conceived the true line, the Solomonic dynasty.

Later that night Solomon had a dream which troubled him greatly; it involved two brilliant suns. The first dropped from heaven and stayed for some time over the land of Israel and then flew off to Ethiopia where it dwelled forever, shedding a light over the people there. Solomon waited to see if it would return, but it did not. Then a second sun rose over the land of Judah and its light was even brighter than the first. The sun paid the Israelites no heed and they, in turn, avoided its rays. But eventually the Israelites could take it no more and attacked the sun with staves, trying to extinguish it. Instead it escaped to illuminate the rest of the world, in particular Ethiopia and Rome. Solomon told Makeda of the dream saying that it heralded great blessings for her country.

The first sun was the Tabernacle of the Lord, the Ark of the Covenant. This was taken later from the Temple by Menelik I, their son, the first Solomonic king, when he returned to Ethiopia. It is now, the Ethiopians claim, in St Mary's Church at Axum, and a replica of it forms the *tabot*, the emblem of each church. When I asked about its actual existence the Ethiopian clergy seemed baffled and evasive, as if the question misses the point; it is one of the mysteries, and transcends the need for evidence.

But some of the laity told stories of quests to see it. Last century a party of looters found a secret passage that led to the chamber of the Ark in Axum. At the far end of the passage they reached a door. They opened the door and the monk-guards chased them out. When they emerged from the darkness, the looters found their feet covered in gold dust. Another story had two Italian soldiers during the Occupation reaching the inner chamber, but this time the monks killed them.

It is tempting to suppose that the *Kebra Nagast* initiated the Ethiopian claim to have the Ark, perhaps attributing a more general tradition specifically to Ethiopia. But one hundred years before it was written, Abu Salih, an Armenian recording the history of the Church in Egypt, said that:

> the Ethiopians possess the Ark of the Covenant, in which are two tables of stone, inscribed by the finger of God with the commandments, which he ordained for the children of Israel.

Their claim to having the Ark, which is a unique claim – Jewish history loses track of it after the sacking of the Temple in the sixth century BC – makes the Ethiopians in their own eyes the chosen race and Axum the heir of Zion.

It also confirms Ethiopia as the most Judaic of all the Christian nations.

The second sun was Christ. Ethiopia's conversion is dated at AD 330, more than a hundred years before St Patrick arrived in Ireland. A contemporary historian, Rufinus, tells the story.

The ship of a Syrian philosopher was sailing up the Red Sea from India, when it was boarded by natives. Its crew were put to the sword. Only two boys were spared, Frumentius and Aedesius. They were taken in by the emperor's court at Axum, and when they were grown, their wisdom earned them high rank and Frumentius ruled the country in lieu of the young regent, Ezana. When Ezana came of age, the two Syrians left the country. Aedesius went back to Tyre, while Frumentius went to Alexandria where he was consecrated by the great Coptic Patriarch Athanasius as the first Bishop of Axum. He returned to the emperor and converted a great number of the people.

When the Emperor Ezana himself was converted is not recorded. But we know that he did become Christian from the coins of his reign: early ones bear the pagan symbol of a sun and crescent moon, later ones show a cross.

The period of the greatest spread of Christianity began in the fifth century. The arrival of the Nine Saints, Monophysite refugees from the Council of Chalcedon, heralded a period of new monasteries, of proselytizing, and saw the translation of the Bible into Ge'ez.

By the middle of the sixth century, the Axumite Empire was a significant Christian power. Its territories spread north, across the Red Sea, up into Southern Arabia. At its zenith, the Axumites marched on Mecca, on a mission to destroy the Ka'aba. King Abraham rode at the head of a huge retinue on an elephant, but the campaign failed. The date was AD 570, the Muslim Year of the Elephant, the year the prophet Mohammed was born.

Negussie said he'd take me to Mass that afternoon, as long as I fasted beforehand. I left my boots outside the church and joined the monks at the front of the nave. A *debtara* handed out prayer sticks, and from somewhere deep in the hidden section of the church, I heard high chanting and the boom of a drum.

A robed priest read a series of pericopes in Ge'ez. None of the laity understands Ge'ez, but after the readings the priest – and an acolyte with umbrella and fly-whisk – carried the book around the congregation to be kissed. A pair of speckled pigeons flew in through the door and settled on a parapet inside the dome.

I leaned on my prayer stick. I felt dizzy from hunger and stared through the swirls of incense in a semi-trance. The monks stood unmoving, their statuesque faces set in timeless smiles.

After a few hours a *debtara* drew back the curtain of the sanctuary and a priest brought out the sacrament. The people lined up and drank from the chalice. One woman fainted and the flapping of the pigeons – now mating in the dome – echoed like a gale around the church.

The next morning was bright and cold. I stood with Negussie by the gate of the church waiting for the bus. Suddenly he said, 'Please send me a passport from your home. Your government is good – won't they give me a passport?'

'But you are going to be a monk.'

He looked away. 'Maybe, but this is not a good country. I would like to go to your country.'

A priest pulled up in a Mercedes Land Cruiser bearing the motif of the Ethiopian Orthodox Church Aid Division (EOC DICAD). He handed two plastic bottles to a boy and offered me a lift back to Addis Ababa.

'We have been visiting one of the Church's development projects,' explained Abba Girma as the boy returned with the bottles. 'Holy water,' he explained. Then he turned to his driver, who was leaning against the car with a cigarette. '*Enhid!* Let's go!'

To Negussie I gave a few parting words and some money for his help. For a moment his face broke into a smile and I wished I could do more.

We drove back through the village of Debra Libanos and up on to the ridge. A troop of gelada baboons was crossing the road, untroubled by our approach.

Girma turned to me and said without warning, 'What hope do you see for mankind?'

'It's a big question,' I said. 'What about you?'

He narrowed his eyes and looked down into the gorge which fell in giant steps to the river, a distant thread meandering through its own alluvium. 'I read once in a book that Einstein was asked, "What will happen after the Third World War?" and he replied, "I don't know, but I know what will be used as weapons in the Fourth." "What's that?" "Stones," said Einstein.'

Girma smiled to himself and then said, 'You see sometimes I see all this progress going so fast – and where to?'

'What about progress in Ethiopia? Is the revolution progress?'

He paused. 'I like the idea of communism. It is like what Paul proposed in the Epistles: no property owned. Look at Debra Libanos – there the monks are real communists!' He laughed, as though it had not struck him before.

'But Ethiopia is poor. Do you think the people should pursue wealth?'

'Oh yes!'

'Might they become godless?'

'Well, we have a saying in Ethiopia: Civilization without God is Satan's Way.'

'But what about the rich man and the eye of the needle?'

'There are many good merchants in the Bible. Job and Abraham were both rich men.'

I knew how the Ethiopian priests loved to prolong this biblical banter, so I said, to conciliate, 'Yes, the Bible is full of contradictions.'

'It is not!' he snapped. 'If you read it carefully, you will see there is only one way!'

We fell into silence.

After the revolution, the Church was stripped of its constitutional role and placed on the same footing as Islam. In the uncertain early days the two faiths coexisted under the red flag in a climate of tolerance. But after two or three years the revolution took hold and Mengistu launched the Red Terror to assert the authority of the Dergue. More than a hundred members of the Dergue had been shot to reduce it to a loyal core of about twenty. Aimed at counter-revolutionary factions more public purges concentrated on imprisonment and conspicuous executions. The Church did not escape and many of the hierarchy, including the patriarch, were arrested.

Addis Ababa at that time echoed with a combination of gunfire and suspicion. Church attendance rose, and on feast days you couldn't even get into the church compounds. In the traditions of the Ethiopian Church, at least, there remained some sense of continuity.

Apologists for the Church and its ambiguous role in a Marxist state, point at President Mengistu and say, 'His wife is a devout Christian. She can be seen taking part in services at least twice a week – and their children are baptized and go to Sunday School.'

We passed parties of shepherds and children selling faggots of eucalyptus for firewood. The driver braked hard and reversed the car towards a flock of sheep. He got out and grabbed the front leg of an animal, haggling with its owner. But in the end he left it and we drove on. Ethiopian New Year was approaching and in Addis Ababa it was important to have an animal to kill for the feast. The farmers knew this and kept the prices high.

4

Opposite the main post office in Addis Ababa is a pedestrian square named *Diglachen* or 'Our Victory'. Fountains spout in ponds between the steps, and on the banks flourish ornamental borders representing the red flag and the Ethiopian flag. In the centre of the square the Eternal Flame burns on a low plinth. Now on a warm afternoon it flickered with confidence. But often during the cloudbursts I had wondered whether it went out; people assured me it did not.

Behind the Flame a triangular obelisk tapered up to a red star, lit at night in vulgar neon. On either side a large bas-relief spelt out to the ten or twenty people now standing before them the epic struggle of their revolution. In each a bust of Mengistu hovered above columns of figures, all of them larger-than-life. One picture showed the utopian paradise the revolution would bring: farmers, teachers and builders marching through a landscape teeming with tractors and new buildings. The front markers held up their hands and released a flock of doves into the red flag.

The other image reminded visitors of what the revolution had purged. A brigade of grim-faced troops marched in mechanical symmetry out of a collage of destruction. Behind they left skinny beggars and toiling peasants, and a skeletal mother suckling her child. This group, huddled together to add mass to its suffering, surrounded a rotund figure on horseback: the Old Order looking dispassionate.

I walked past the fountains and back down the steps into Churchill Avenue. A marching band was rehearsing for the Revolution Day parade. Behind it ambled a Sunday afternoon crowd. I slipped down a side road away from them, and went to see Billy.

The morning had ended in a fleeting barrage of rain, and puddles stood beside the frayed edges of the tarmac. From side-streets came streams still bubbling over the mud. As I passed, bare-footed children shrieked with glee, *'Ferenj! Ferenj!'*

Private cars were prohibited on Sundays. Only an occasional diplomatic car, or a licensed blue taxi, or an aid vehicle dashed along the crowded roads. Sundays belonged to pedestrians, and they wandered from place to place, arm-in-arm with friends, or stood in smiling groups.

I walked briskly across the city and arrived at Billy's gate struggling for breath in the thin air. He greeted me like an old friend.

Billy had been born in Ethiopia in the 1950s, the son of an Irish mother and an Italian restaurateur. His hybrid background rested easily on strong shoulders. He was a lion-hearted man who loved Ethiopia. But often he talked as though he were trapped there.

'I lived in Europe for a couple of years and, OK, I had a good time, but it was so small. And people are unfriendly, even in Ireland where I have a big family. I felt I had to be in Africa, so I came back and started my own family here.' He spoke emphatically, using his large hands. But at the fringes of his voice there wavered an audible sadness.

For him the revolution had divided the elysian days of his youth from darker times more recently. A few years earlier his father had knelt to pray at the grave of a friend and scratched his cheek on a railing. He died of tetanus soon afterwards and Billy took over responsibility for the restaurant. More than anything else, he missed the expeditions taken with his father in the late 1960s, hunting warthog in the Rift Valley.

On the surface not much had changed. He still went hunting and had started to take his young son, and the family still owned the restaurant. They lived fairly well. But for those like Billy with private capital, life had become a battle to keep it – most had been successful but now found themselves living against the grain in an authoritarian state, tied down like Gulliver by a mesh of lilliputian restrictions.

The memory of the Red Terror and lingering injustice were more embittering. Billy rubbed his eyes. 'You know, in '77 you could see bodies just lying on the street. They had signs nailed in their backs: "Traitor to the Revolution!" They had to stay there a week sometimes before their families could collect them for burial. Then they were charged 100 birr and 5 birr bullet tax.'

Anger flashed across Billy's face. He slapped the table with the flat of his hand. 'Shit, you know these people have been frightened ever since!'

A man with no legs sold tickets at the National Museum. Inside the building I found the first Amharic typewriter, and beside it a studio shot of its proud inventor. Ethiopia has the oldest surviving written culture in Africa; this man had managed to get the 236-letter Amharic alphabet on to a single keyboard – still used in every office – by having separate keys for the six vowel suffixes, and two letters to a key.

Elsewhere were dusty cases of imperial costumes, and in another room, more of Afewerk Tekle's paintings.

Downstairs, a Jamaican in a black beret bent to peer at the bones of Lucy. He was a drummer, and had taken time off from an African tour to visit Ethiopia. Lucy was from Hadar in the Danakil Desert. She lived about three million years ago, and is one of the most complete early hominids yet found.

Lucy was found in 1975 by Don Johanson. (Someone was playing 'Lucy in the Sky with Diamonds' in the camp shortly afterwards.) He chose for her scientific name *Australopithecus afarensis,* and this name has caused more problems. Palaeontologists cannot agree her exact place in our ancestry, and further digging has been prevented by the Ethiopian government.

Hadar, and the Omo Valley in southern Ethiopia have been added to places like the Olduvai Gorge in Tanzania, and Lake Turkana in Kenya to suggest that the African Rift Valley is the place where the early hominids became man. In our post-Darwinian world East Africa has replaced Eden as the place of mythical origin, the antediluvian Paradise, where the first man incurred the wounds of the Fall to pass down to his descendants.

The ticket officer was basking in his wheelchair when I came out. He pointed through the gates towards Sidist Kilo: 'The Emperor's lions – you must see the lions!'

I found the beasts looking sorry and ill-fed behind the bars of a cage, in a small municipal garden.. The Emperor Haile Selassie, the Lion of Judah himself, loved his lions. When he made his official tour of Europe in 1924 as regent, he took six with him; he presented four to the French, and two to George V. And in his last years there was one that skulked around the palace and would attend him on some public appearances, getting older and weaker with the régime.

'Please sir, can I join you?' A young man fell into step beside me.

'Of course.'

We found a bench in the corner of the garden, and he pointed towards the lions. 'The Emperor, you know, believed in magic.'

'Are you sure?'

'Oh yes, he believed there was a dragon in one of the lakes to the south and built a palace there.'

I knew this was fanciful. 'What about President Mengistu?'

He looked around automatically before speaking. Then he leaned towards me. 'The President, he is like the Emperor.'

'He believes in magic?'

'No, no, but he lives at the palace. When he gives degree ceremony, he sits in the Emperor's throne.'

I had heard this, but had been told too that he had chosen a small house in the palace grounds, and privately lived a very simple life.

'Do you have a job?' I asked.

'No job. I am a student. But now it is holiday time and I have no money. But look, I have written a letter.'

He pulled out a piece of squared paper addressed, in English, 'Dear Sir . . .'

'I will send it to foreign aid companies to ask for a job. Is it good?'

'Yes, it is good.' I corrected some of his English, and handed it back. Then I asked him about morale among the students.

'Sometimes there is problem,' he said. 'There was a demonstration last term.'

I confirmed the story later. A group of students had gathered on the campus. The official reason was that their grants had not kept up with the price of food, but apparently it revealed a deeper current of dissent. It was not tolerated for long and a small unit was sent in from the barracks. The leaders were detained and there were reports of injuries in the scuffle. But no more complaints were heard.

On 13 September 1974 a Volkswagen pulled up outside the Jubilee Palace and three soldiers went inside. Some minutes later they came out, escorting a small man in a suit. This was the fall of the Lion of Judah, Haile Selassie, Ethiopia's 225th emperor.

Exactly fourteen years later, at 9 a.m., I watched six black Mercedes slide into Revolution Square and pull up beneath a grey rostrum. I saw one minister get out of each car in the uniform of government: a blue safari suit, made in Korea. They climbed up the steps and took their places on the dais. The gilt and velvet throne in front of them was still empty.

The 'square' was a large half moon of tarmac at the foot of the city's slopes. In the middle of its straight edge a now permanent rostrum had been built against a high-rise government office. The office dealt with immigration and refugees. Opposite it rose a gentle semi-circular grass bank, split by stone kerbs into terraces.

From where I sat, on one of these, the capital's skyline was still shaped more by natural features than by the buildings: the random glass-and-concrete buildings were offset by patches of eucalyptus and dwarfed by the Entoto Hills above.

All around the mock stadium marshalls jostled the crowd into position, the marching bands rested their instruments on the ground and a military policeman in front of me trod his cigarette into the dust. All of us waited for the President.

When everything was still, nine motor cycles swept down Menelik Avenue and into the square. In their midst was Mengistu. He sat in the back of an open-topped Cadillac, an early 1960s model, very large and metallic green, its chromium rear fins glinting like knives in the sun.

A public address system echoed across the terraces: 'President of the People's Democratic Republic of Ethiopia, Commander-in-Chief of the Revolutionary Army, Colonel Mengistu Haile-Mariam arrives, watched by hundreds of thousands of people here to celebrate the great event . . .'

He got out of the car, a slight figure in neat green uniform. The show worked well – his step across the podium had a clipped authority that was not regal, yet undoubtedly real. For all the flags and the bands and the officials already assembled, and the thousands (not hundreds of thousands, ten perhaps) of spectators, the square of red velvet where he now sat seemed, just for a moment, to be the heart of the country.

Next to me a large woman stopped talking for the first time since I had arrived and pushed a parasol over her shoulder. The President rose to make his speech.

Last year the Revolution Day celebrations had been on a grander scale, to herald the transfer of power from the Provisional Military Government to the National Shengo, a voted assembly. Tanks and artillery were paraded and there was a fly-past by a squadron of Mig fighters. Since then, there had been some alarming defeats in Eritrea and Tigré, and in May the government had launched its counter-offensive. The new slogan appeared in public places: 'EVERYTHING TO THE WARFRONT!' The Motherland was threatened and the imported ideology was dropped for something more potent: old-fashioned nationalism.

This year Mengistu spoke for only twenty minutes (his six-hour speeches were something of a legend) and there were no surprises: more calls to arms, a little economic encouragement and a restatement of agricultural policies, all delivered in staccato, monotonic Amharic.

'Ethiopia *Tikdem*!' He ended the speech with the slogan that ends all broadcasts and official letters. It means, roughly, 'Ethiopia first!'

The parade started with two flag bearers. One held the green, yellow and red tricolour, the other the plain red flag. Around the square the same two flags fluttered from high poles. Then came a squad of goose-stepping soldiers and a group of children with balloons. The city's Urban Associations were required to produce a troop each and these appeared in squares, the first all with green flags, then yellow, then red, then more children dressed in white and wearing green hats, yellow hats and red hats.

The woman next to me started chattering again, and interest in the parade seemed to falter. Overhead soared a pair of tawny eagles. The militia trooped past, represented by three goose-stepping platoons: the army in khaki, the air force in blue and the navy in white, and then it was over and the woman bowed to me and said goodbye.

I looked back at the rostrum but the President had disappeared, and there was no sign of his Cadillac.

One evening there was some shouting from the *kebelle* yard below my room. The *kebelles,* 'Urban Associations', are the local arm of the party and keep people at bay by controlling the supply of various goods, and reporting dissent, an effective system of favour and sanction.

The *kebelles* also assist in finding recruits to send to the north, to the front. I imagined that that was what the shouting was about. I looked down to see a man being held by a couple of guards. He was screaming something about Mengistu. Five others stood round him. One of them raised a gun at him, and the others stepped back. He stopped screaming and they took him into a hut.

Later I told a teacher what I had seen. We were driving to a bar near the National Theatre. He said, 'Yes, the city is quite tense. I spoke to a friend today whose sixteen-year-old son has disappeared. He checked all the hospitals, but – nothing. The poor man was desperate.'

I had felt that the tension in Addis had eased in the last few years. People in public places talked more candidly, there were fewer soldiers on the streets and the curfew was less fiercely marshalled. The government, I assumed, had passed some threshold of maturity, and now had a grumbling covenant with its people. Yet I knew also how deceptive Ethiopia can be: assumptions shattered by glimpses behind the veil, the hidden truths.

The Ethiopians have turned their love of hidden truth into entertainment. The teacher took me to a traditional bar, where a wiry man scratched at a single-string fiddle and composed *samenna wark* couplets.

The minstrel, known as an *azmari,* came over and made up a wry verse about a foreigner and a wolf. Others in the bar chuckled and looked at me as they picked their teeth. I remember the dim orange light from the lamps and the equivocal smile of the *azmari.* I remember the way, when he sang, that his body stiffened, and allowed only the sawing of his bow-arm across the strings, but I didn't understand his verse.

Samenna wark means 'wax and gold'. The goldsmith fashions a wax model and makes a cast around it. He heats the cast and the wax runs out through a hole. Then he pours in the gold and lets it set. So the poet, the *azmari,* constructs verse with a preliminary 'wax' meaning, in which is concealed a more profound 'gold' meaning.

Donald Levine, in an ethnography of Ethiopia called simply *Wax and Gold*, traces the practice to *kene*, the mystical tradition of church poetry. He quotes this example of *samenna wark:*

> The son of a hermit, high rank to display,
> Made love with Christ's wife today;
> When she fed him leaves he wasted away.

The 'wax' meaning is clear: a man of low rank seduced a noblewoman to earn prestige, but she fed him poison leaves. But the hermit's son or companion is also hunger, and the 'wife' of Christ is fasting. So the 'gold' meaning is that the hermit's hunger is heightened by its union with fasting, and becomes holier, but that when he eats, the hunger goes.

Other *azmaris* use pun, in which Amharic is rich, or biblical allusion. But all rely on ambiguity, the more subtle and heavily-laden the better. But if an *azmari* gets lost and mixes a metaphor his audience will shout: 'hermaphrodite!'

The tradition of *samenna wark* has spread from the Amhara heartland and offers a clue to the privacies of Ethiopia, the dry jokes, the rumours, and the pervasive suspicion that in every action there is some hidden motive.

Later, just before curfew, I peered over the wall of the *kebelle.* There was no sign of the dissident, but I could see armed guards beside the gate. One of them ran over and shouted, 'Hey, what is it! What do you want!'

'Nothing, nothing.' I held up my hands as I backed away. But he followed me with his rifle until I was well out of sight.

5

In the *azmari* bar, I had told the teacher I was planning to go to Harar. 'In which case,' he had said, 'you must speak to my friend, Mohammed. He is from Harar.'

We met outside the university canteen. The feathery leaves of a mimosa hung over the table and spotted it with shadows; sparrows pecked crumbs from the dust. Mohammed sat neatly, in a well-cut blazer. He stared at me with disarming assurance. 'So, you are going to Harar. You know it was a forbidden city for Christians.'

'Yes, until Richard Burton went there in 1854.'

'And I suppose you are interested in the French poet?'

'Rimbaud – yes, I am.'

'Well, when you get to Harar, go and see Father Emile – he knows about the poet.'

We turned to talking about America. Mohammed said, 'Since the Second World War there has been I think material abundance. But it has opened a cultural vacuum. The Americans must concentrate on leaving their children something cultural.' He added, unsmiling, 'They must forget all this hippy, gippy business. If they are not careful, America will collapse.'

Such was the view, I imagined, of countless young Muslims; Mohammed gave the impression that it was his own.

'And Britain is dying too. It is so insecure – afraid of challenges always, from Europe, from all the old colonies and their neighbours. Your news reports are full of Britain defending itself.'

'You listen to the BBC?'

'I used to, but I stopped about two or three months ago. All the danger everywhere – it is not the whole picture.'

'And what about Ethiopia?'

He continued in the same unflappable tone. 'Now we have a better social structure, we need to inject the dynamism. In some ways Ethiopia is getting stronger.'

One thing intrigued me. Harar was an ancient Muslim city-state on the eastern edge of the plateau. For hundreds of years it had been an independent emirate, and one of Islam's holy cities, a great *Sunni* teaching centre. Only recently did the Christian Amhara cross the Rift Valley and annex it to Ethiopia. I asked Mohammed, 'Do you see yourself as an Ethiopian?'

'Of course! It makes no sense to talk of regions that were or were not part of Ethiopia. All this area' – and he swept his hand across the table to denote the Horn of Africa – 'has been a mix of peoples for thousands of years. I am a Harari and a Muslim. My local culture is the most important to me. But after that I am an Ethiopian. Ethiopia is many races, but one people.'

Ethiopia's present borders contain an empire. In the 1880s and 1890s – at the same time as Europe was carving up the rest of Africa – Emperor Menelik II consolidated his power in the highlands, then doubled the size of the country with conquests in the south and east. He forfeited the northern province of Eritrea, but kept the Europeans at bay with deft diplomacy – and military success: nowhere else in colonial Africa was a European power as soundly defeated as the Italians were at Adwa in northern Ethiopia in 1896; nowhere else did an African power remain independent from Europe.

But it is now the Eritreans and Tigreans – in the ancient heartland of Ethiopia – who are fighting the war for independence. The Harari, newer members of the empire and Muslim, seem more content. They have hung up their weapons and are now among the richest Ethiopians, running a network of businesses in Addis Ababa, Harar and Dire Dawa.

Menelik marched down the Rift Valley from Addis Ababa in 1887. He met the Harari force at Chelenko and, in less than fifteen minutes, the ancient Muslim stronghold was defeated. There is a joke that the Harari did not want to leave their shops for any longer.

At the Mapping Agency opposite Adwa Park, I had some problems getting the maps I wanted.

I wandered from one office to another, up and down concrete stairwells, through battleship-grey corridors. I presented my papers and was asked, 'What is the purpose of your visit to Ethiopia? Why do you want these maps?'

I signed a pledge saying that no one was to see the maps, and that no one was to know I had them. And twice I had to dash out to another part of town to get a counter-signature. At one point I realized the effort to get the maps had surpassed their probable value; at that point they took on a symbolic importance.

At two minutes to four I reached the map room itself, in the basement. An officer was locking the door. She explained that the cashier had gone home, and dropped the keys into her bag. My mission had failed. Half in humour and half in anger, I invoked the Archangel Mikhael in Amharic.

She smiled and reopened the door.

When I got back to my room I spread the maps out on the floor. They were 1:250000 – the 1:50000 were being reprinted – and showed the land around Harar. To the north was a band of close contours below the Rift Valley, to the south the same contours spread wider and wider into the Ogaden Desert. And in the bottom left-hand corner was a credit: US Geological Survey 1968.

That evening in the bar of the Ghion Hotel I met a friend from one of the aid agencies. We sat on short stools, carved from hagenia, and drank Meta beer.

James was a Scot and had projects in the south – in Sidamo. He called them 'integrated rural development projects', adding sardonically, 'That means we do everything – education, medicine, agricultural schemes, water, the whole lot.'

He had been here in 1985 organizing relief in northern Wollo. 'Do you know,' he said, 'what struck me most about those famine victims? I have worked in the Sudan. When there is a food shortage there, they riot. I have seen a food riot in Khartoum – it is not pleasant. But in Wollo, where the famine was far, far worse, they just sat outside the camp. It was as if they had decided: we've done all we can, walked to the feeding camp, and now it's up to God whether we live or die.'

He took another gulp of beer. 'I don't think they ever understood why we were trying to help them. They probably didn't even think about it. Some people considered their ingratitude was arrogance. But I think it was just that life wasn't as important to them as we all imagined.'

As we left, James said, 'Jenny from the UN is going to Harar, on her way to the refugee camps. I'll tell her to look out for you.' Then he added, 'Did you hear about the air crash at Bahar Dar yesterday?'

I hadn't. It was one of two 737s that Ethiopian Airlines used for domestic flights. Shortly after take-off from Bahar Dar, *en route* north to Asmara, the plane had had a bird strike. The pilot managed to turn and lift the wheels. He made a belly landing in a field, in the flat hinterland of Lake Tana. The mud had absorbed a lot of the impact, but the nose came to rest in a ravine, and the hull broke open in flames.

Official reports said thirty people had died, but rumours suggested there were few survivors.

On the phone, I told Billy I was going to Harar.

'When are you going?'

'Tomorrow. First thing.'

'How did you get permits?'

'Through NTO.'

'Yeah, well be careful. I was attacked by a group of thugs in Harar last year. They would have killed me if I hadn't screamed at them in Amharic. They thought I was a Russian.'

'I'll be careful,' I said.

The dawn came slowly behind La Gare, first with a moonlight blue on the wooden freight cars, then a bright strip beneath the cloud in the southern sky. In the carriage it was cold; a girl took her place opposite me and pulled a *gabbi* tight around her face. She propped her head against the wall and fell asleep.

In 1897 the French started work on the railway as a gift for Menelik. It was to run from their colony in Djibouti up to Addis Ababa, giving Ethiopia access to the sea. But by the time the first train pulled into Addis Ababa in 1917, Menelik had been dead for three years. The engineering wasn't easy, but disputes slowed the work more than the landscape; the last 23 kilometres took two years. And now it is still the only railway in the country.

From Addis Ababa it falls fast towards the Rift Valley, then follows it north-west towards Dire Dawa. Low cloud hung over the hillocks and young cowherds waded through the tall, dewy grass beside the track.

Somewhere after Nazareth, in the bright mid-morning, a middle-aged Somali pointed her hennaed hand towards me.

'Do you like this country?'

'Of course. That's why I'm here.'

'Do you like Ethiopian women?'

'Well, yes.'

She paused and looked away, lifting her chin. A girl in her late teens sat next to her, an orange veil only partly concealing her plump, ordinary face. The Somali placed her hand roughly on the girl's knee, and turned back to me.

'Do you want my daughter?'

Opposite me the girl in the *gabbi* woke up. She pushed the cotton cloth away from her face and smiled. She had the high-boned good looks of the Amhara.

The Somali woman continued, grunting across the aisle. 'I have eight daughters. This is the only one left.'

'Where are the others?'

'In America. Los Angeles.'

I pictured seven luckless Californians, and wondered how I could escape.

'Thirty camels,' she said.

I saw my chance. 'Ten.'

'Twenty.'

'Fifteen's my limit.'

The woman scoffed, but she was smiling, and beyond her, out of the window, a pair of startled oryx disappeared into the bush.

The train arrived in Dire Dawa long after dark. Before it had stopped, crowds of passengers had dashed forward, jumping up on to the steps to secure a place. I struggled through them and out into the dark square in front of the station. After Addis Ababa the heat was close, and a few minutes walking pressed the clothes to my skin, and stuck them there.

'Have you been to Dire Dawa before?'

I looked round to see the Amhara girl from the train. 'No.'

'Come, I'll show you.'

We walked into the town, passing open doorways which spilt pools of light on to the road. We ate in an old Greek café, and drank in a bar full of smugglers. We laughed when an old man was thrown from the bar for singing badly, and then the smugglers bought us drinks. When we came out it was late and the hot streets were empty.

'It's almost curfew,' I said. 'I'd better get to the Ras Hotel.'

'But I cannot stay at a government hotel.'

I said I was sorry, then watched her disappear beneath the plane trees, her *gabbi* pulled up over her head – a slight, tender figure running for a taxi.

The next day I left the muggy heat of Dire Dawa in a bus and climbed south into smooth scrub-covered mountains. The bus cleared the edge of the scarp and there was the plateau again, with its luminous green teff fields. We approached Harar from above and stopped outside the Duke's Gate.

Harar is no more than a mile long, and about half that across. Yet it has a density which is both palpable and oppressive. Within its walls over eighty mosques jostle with camel-coloured houses. A labyrinth of alleys, eroded to bedrock by the rains, squeezed its way between the buildings, and I don't remember anywhere a flat surface or right angle. It was as though the outer walls had contracted, squashing the town.

I crossed Feres Magala, the old Horse Market, an untidy circus on the bald knoll of the city, and went down to the main mosque. Behind it, in a sandy compound overlooking waves of blue hills, I found the Catholic missionary putting away a motor cycle.

'Come in. Come in,' said Father Emile, and showed me into a low house beside the compound. On the far side I could see the slate gables of a chapel.

'I have been here twenty-five years,' he said, removing his cap as he crossed the threshold, 'or maybe thirty – I don't know.'

He spoke in distant muttering tones that seemed only just to escape his diminutive frame, indistinct, like the years of his mission. Diffuse grey light stole through the bars of the window and lit the side of his face, and stubble covered his chin and the gullies of his cheek. Around his neck he wore a small pectoral cross on a string of wooden beads.

'But always I learn something new about Harar.' He pronounced the town's name without its H, and carefully as though it were a cherished abstract noun.

'What can you tell me about the walls?'

'The walls . . . *ah oui*, the walls.' His blue eyes narrowed behind tortoiseshell glasses and he paused, plumbing for the information, his lips shaping inaudible clues.

The city's walls had been the creation of the Emir Nur in the 1550s. Nur was the nephew of Ahmed Gran, the 'Left-handed', whose name in the Christian highlands is still spoken with contempt.

The Ottoman invasion of Egypt in 1516 had brought with it the conviction of Muslim supremacy, and the spirit of *jihad* flooded down the Red Sea. In Harar Gran had his eye on the Christian highlanders, the stubborn infidels who had held out for so long. During the 1530s he would ride out each year with a band of Turkish fusiliers, down into the Rift Valley and up the far scarp, into the northern highlands.

The raids were carried out during Lent. At this time the Christians were at their weakest, sticking to a fast of one meal a day: a little bread and vegetables after the evening service. Gran and his zealots burnt churches and pillaged their treasures. They put Christians to the sword and sacked Debra Libanos and the capital at Axum.

In 1539, the year Henry VIII destroyed the Abbey at Glastonbury, Gran breached the defences at the mountain-top monastery of Gishen Mariam. No account survives of the monastery before Gran's attack but an extraordinary costume of myth surrounds the mountain. It is certain that Ethiopian emperors used to imprison their sons there, and Gran killed them. The Ethiopians claimed to have buried half of the True Cross under its cruciform summit (Gran didn't find it). And according to *Purchas His Pilgrimage*, there was the world's greatest library there, and gold 'as the sands of the sea and the stars in the sky'. (Ethiopia seemed to be embodied in this place – capricious myth, spectacular mountains and the quirks of divine kingship; I decided I must reach this mountain.)

Ahmed Gran did more to threaten the survival of the ancient civilization than any other power before or since, and destroyed much of the heritage of over one thousand years of Christianity. But he did not quell the faith.

Eventually Gran was killed, in battle by troops of the Ethiopian Emperor Claudius. The new Emir of Harar, Nur, claimed Gran's widow, Bati Del Wanbara. But she told him first to avenge her husband's death.

Emir Nur killed Claudius on Good Friday and returned with his severed head to Harar. For two years Bati hung the head from a tree opposite her house, then she sold it to an Armenian.

Nur built the wall from local tuff and bound it with crude plaster. It averages about 15 feet in height, is spaced with rounded towers and has survived fairly well. Originally it was intended to redefine the town, and revive the conquering spirit of Gran. But its function became defensive as the surrounding Galla tribes gained in strength. From the end of the sixteenth century, the Harari slipped into a period of loose morality and internal squabbles, and never recovered the power of Gran.

'And now,' said Father Emile, 'we have piped water from the lake at Alemaya. The water table has risen and the walls are rotting. We used to bring the water up from the valley by hand.' He looked out of the window. 'Oh, the children – *les enfants sont arrivés*!'

Outside, a group of young Harari had gathered, with schoolbooks and pencils waiting to go to the mission school.

'The teacher needs this room. Can you come again tomorrow?'

He walked with me to the gate. A little of his reserve dropped and he asked, 'Tell me, do you live near Stonehenge?'

'Quite near,' I said. 'I was brought up in Somerset, and used to drive past it.'

His face lit up. 'Ah! I went there when I visited England. Quick – come!'

He led me back into his house, and through one of two doors that led off the main room. A plywood bureau divided his bedroom from a makeshift study. In the corner was a pyramid of tin chests and there were tottering stacks of books on the desk and the floor.

'Look, I have made a bibliography of Harar,' he said and showed me a fawn exercise book in which countless articles and reference books had been arranged beneath subject headings: AMHARA – ARCHAEOLOGY – ARCHITECTURE – BURTON, RICHARD. . . .

'But look – here,' and he turned to face the inside wall. A large glossy poster – the only picture in the room – showed Stonehenge against a deep black background. Behind the stones shone a bright gibbous moon.

Father Emile stood before the picture muttering, 'Ah yes – Stonehenge. . . . It is the solstice I think. Here, I have a pamphlet.' He stooped to recover something from one of the piles of papers, and showed me diagrams of speculative geometry around the site with his own notes scribbled beside it.

'You have been there recently?' he asked.

'I've been past it. But it's like a fortress now, surrounded by barbed wire.'

He grunted quietly, 'Pah!' and looked back at the pamphlet and the web of imaginary lines.

Outside the mission gates I met Ali. He was leaning against the wall opposite in a denim jacket and desert boots.

'You are a friend of Father Emile,' he said, more as a statement than a question. 'I sometimes work with him.'

We went to Feres Magala and played draughts beside the square. Ali had a lugubrious manner, and slouched in front of the board pondering each move, as if it was a pleasure to be savoured.

He won the game with ease and then said, 'I haven't played that since I was in prison.'

Prison, he explained, had happened to a great number of his contemporaries in the early years of the revolution. He was a student then, and had been locked up for a year with a random group of fellow students. Many of those who survived had gone to America. Ali had stayed behind, unable to raise the foreign currency. He was bright and spoke good English, picked up from the US Peace Corps who had a project near Harar in the late 1960s.

'Do you have a job?' I asked.

He shrugged and looked away. 'No. I cannot get a job until I have done my national service. And I won't do that. Maybe I will go back to college – this year I failed to get in. I will try again next year. I would like to have a family, but how can I marry without profession?'

It seemed that he had long ago accepted the hopelessness of his position. He was one of a broken generation, emasculated, a demographic vacuum that cushioned those in power. Those who got out of the country struggled rootlessly in exile, clinging to unreal views of home. They had come of age in the last uncertain years of the Emperor, to join a growing number of educated Ethiopians impatient to accelerate the changes his reign had started. To those who reached the top of the pile in the mid-1970s, Ali's generation of students posed the greatest threat. Many of the new rulers must have recalled how much their own militant convictions owed to their years as students. After the failed coup of 1960, students from the university were behind frequent calls for land reform and political change. In 1972, two thousand were arrested or expelled.

After the revolution, in April 1977, just before sensitive May Day celebrations in Addis Ababa, five hundred students were shot. They had been holding a 'counter-revolutionary' demonstration. The incident heralded the beginning of the Red Terror. It was shortly after this that Ali was arrested.

Later I walked up to the Old Gate. Spice-traders squatted in the portal and outside was a bustle of people doing different things: begging, haggling, some on the point of fights, others laughing beside bundles of firewood or chicken baskets. Beyond them was the open-air market. I wound through it and sat outside a café.

I heard someone say in English, 'I saw you in the market. Where are you from?'

I looked up at a dressy Ethiopian girl. 'Britain.'

'So am I,' she said, without irony. 'I'm visiting my family. They live just near here.'

Hirut had lived in London for ten years or so. She was not, she insisted, an exile, and came and went from Ethiopia freely. But it was clear she missed the Harar of her childhood.

Her father, an Amhara, had died shortly before the revolution, one of Harar's famous sons. He had been buried at Selassie

Cathedral after a full state funeral and three days of official mourning. At one time the Emperor had made him Governor of Harar, but he had resigned when he found the system too corrupt.

Hirut's family lived in the house built by the Italian governor. 'After liberation in 1941, the Emperor said my father could choose any house as a reward for his resistance work with the Patriots. The Italians had put in a small water-tank that could be heated with coals,' she said. 'But my father didn't let us use it. He would say, "If you get used to hot water, you'll miss it when you go to live somewhere else."'

'And now you live in Hampstead.'

'Yes!'

She remembered too the banana trees that grew in the compound, and the custard apples, and peaches the size of grapefruit. 'Boys from the town would come and throw stones over the wall to try and get the fruit.' But her father in his study used to hear the rocks bouncing on the Tuscan roof tiles. He would bellow from his office and the boys would run away.

'Oh, and the sugar cane!' Hirut clutched her stomach and beamed. 'We used to eat so much – and now I have a problem eating sugar!'

She pointed to a spot of high ground beyond the market. 'Over there used to be a famous house. Korra Bellimay it was called. Always there were people there, coming and going. When I was a girl, I used to hear the drums beating at night, and chanting – some sort of Sufi song. Each year they made a sorghum porridge in a petrol drum, and left it out for the hyenas. It was a superstition. Some years the leader of the hyenas would turn away, and none of them would eat. And that meant it would be a bad year.'

The son of the house had been a friend of her brother. 'He was a smart, educated man, full of jokes. He was appointed to Haile Selassie's government as a very young man. He always wore western suits, and would bring us presents when he came over. Oh, he was a charming man.' Hirut shook her head and looked away.

One year in the late 1970s, shortly after the Somali war, she came to Harar to see her family. Those were the days when she heard nothing but bad news, and she longed for the bloodshed to end, whatever the outcome. That year she heard that her brother's friend had been beaten to death; there were so many factions no one was sure who had done it.

As a foreigner in Ethiopia, regulations demand that you stay in the government-owned hotels. Out of Addis Ababa this meant one of a chain at the half-dozen or so main towns. In Harar I had gone straight to the Ras, the only state hotel in the town. It was in the new Amhara district outside the walls, opposite the crumbling, horseshoe palace of Lij Yasu.

But I couldn't see myself staying there more than a night. Like all government hotels, it attracted the worst elements of the town, arrogant officials and local sophisticates. It was not a place to talk freely. Foreigners are charged about 15 per cent more than Ethiopians. When I objected to the principle of this, I was told, 'No sir, we don't charge you more. It's just that we offer locals a discount.'

The evening was cold, but not too cold to sit outside after a meal of tepid pasta, served without grace in an empty dining room. At half past nine a UN Land Cruiser pulled up below the veranda. A woman got out and her Ethiopian driver parked on the forecourt.

'I'm Jenny,' she said, extending her hand. 'I saw James last night in Addis. He told me you'd be here.'

'How was your journey?'

'Terrible. We came across the Addis bus half-way down a cliff. We had to ferry two people to hospital. The driver was killed, and I should think two or three others. The ones we took to hospital were conscious but badly cut up – one had a broken leg. Very messy.' She peered into the hotel. 'Oh God, not another Ras!'

The next morning her party left for Jijiga and the Somali refugee camps. I went to find Father Emile.

On the southern slope of the town is the old Muslim market – moved outside the walls – to allow cars, says the local government. But few cars can get through the narrow alleys. Father Emile pointed at the empty space, and said, 'I remember this place when you could hardly move for traders.'

He led me out of the square, muttering distantly, and back into the alleys. Smirking infants cried, '*Abba! Abba!*' and ran away. Through half-open doors, I glimpsed a series of loamy yards festooned with washing, and Harari women scrubbing clothes on their doorsteps. The pale ochre of the buildings was the same ochre as the ground. But the women's robes, dyed lime green and saffron and printed with floral patterns, were a bold rebellion of colour.

I followed the father through a low door. He paused and took off his corduroy cap. 'Here,' he announced, nodding towards a two-storey building with twin gables and a dark panelled façade, 'is the house of Rimbaud.'

6

Arthur Rimbaud spent more time in Harar than anywhere else in his adult life. He was twenty-six when he passed the tomb of Sheikh Abdul, and rode up the hill to the Erer Gate, but he looked much older. The intensity of his early years had left his hair scratched with grey and furrowed the desert-scorched skin around his mouth.

Seven years earlier he had finished the long prose poem, 'Une Saison en Enfer' with a statement of intent, '*il me sera loisible de posséder la vérité dans une âme et un corps.*'

He took the poem to Paris with high hopes of a publisher and recognition. But Rimbaud's name was mud, following his liaison with Verlaine, which had ended a few months earlier with Verlaine shooting at the younger poet. The coterie of writers who made up the Parisian literary establishment rejected him and he returned to his mother's farm in Charleville to burn the poem. At nineteen, his life as a poet was over.

The second half of his life, though it produced no literature, was just as remarkable. Disillusioned, he isolated himself, and spent his remaining years in dogged reaction against his younger self.

For six years he lived as a peripatetic, walking through Europe, twice crossing the Alps on foot, and living off charity. Once he joined a Dutch ship bound for Java and served three weeks as a soldier before deserting. He found a British ship and ended up back in Charleville.

But eventually he grew sick of Europe, with its bourgeois comforts and sentimental faith, and he headed east again. Like the Parnassian poets who had snubbed him, he saw the Orient as a place of vitality. He dreamed of finding somewhere that would reawaken his old energies, somewhere new.

The East was also the place for quick wealth, and Rimbaud became a merchant. In Aden he met M. Bardey who appointed him to open up trade links with Harar. In November 1880, Rimbaud crossed the Red Sea and rode up to 'East Africa's Timbuktu'.

The Feres Magala was then an active market. Rimbaud established the new agency on its northern edge. He lived above the shop, in a sturdy two-storey building. A photograph he took of it shows small windows, and rubble walls reinforced with cedar beams. It was demolished after Menelik's invasion and in its place a storehouse was built, now the saloon where Ali and I had played draughts.

I was drinking coffee there one morning. A vine covered the wooden columns of the veranda, and filtered the early sun with its leaves; I could still hear a muezzin.

Father Emile came into the square on his motor bike, hunched forward, his cap pulled down tight to his ears. I waved and he pulled up.

'Oh, yes. Some coffee, just coffee, I think.' He sat down and put his cap on the table. A group of Galla crossed the square, strung out in a line like a family of ducks.

Father Emile pointed to the hill that rose above the town. 'You see there, that is Hakim Hill. People say that Rimbaud had a hut there. He would walk up in the afternoon to read.'

'And to write?' Fantasies have grown up among Rimbaud's followers of later, undiscovered poems.

'Ha! Maybe, maybe.'

'So he is remembered here.'

'Oh, yes. He was a popular man among the Harari, a respected merchant. He had *la juste balance*, always honest in business.'

'Too honest,' I said.

'Yes, perhaps.'

I found a small hotel near the Feres Magala. They said nothing about the restrictions and showed me a room without a window. The door opened on to a trellised balcony, and I could watch the main street below. Wooden steps – little more than a ladder – led to the ground floor, and the bar.

The bar was very dark. All day a crepuscular light seeped out through a couple of orange lampshades. On the walls, painted a glossy dark blue, hung three pictures: a painting of Bruce Lee, and two tourist posters of Axum and Lalibela, both places closed because of the war. In the late afternoon the low sun crept through gaps in the shutters and stretched across the bitumen floor.

Ali came into the bar. He sat down at my table saying, 'I waited for you again outside the French mission.' He was restless and wide-eyed and grinned demonically. He had been chewing *cha'at*, and his fingers drummed the table between us. *Cha'at* is a mild stimulant for which Harar is the world's principal source. The Muslim Harari condemn the Christians for bringing alcohol to their town, but see nothing wrong in an untreated local plant. On Sundays the *cha'at* ceremony is performed, it seems, by every Muslim male in the town. Then they recline on rafts of cushions and chew the alkaloids from the leaf with a bovine persistence. They play cards and drink tea, waited on by tacit wives and daughters.

By the evening the effects wear off and the younger ones are agitated. Long-term use stretches the nerves and they wander the dim streets, twitching and lunging; at this time, alcohol is tolerated if only as a narcotic.

'I need some *tej*,' Ali said.

So we went just outside the walls to a *tej* house where I bought him a bottle of the local mead. He drank it quickly and subsided into a harmless, benevolent drunkenness.

'Tomorrow,' he announced, slipping down into his chair, 'I will show you the hyenas.'

Later we went back through the gates to the hotel. When Harar was independent, the gates were closed each evening at dusk to keep out the hostile Galla, and the keys handed to the emir. At night I found the town's insularity emphasized, and in the darkness felt more conspicuous, more of a stranger.

A couple came into the bar and sat down at our table. He had a moustache and a huge warrior's frame and was shadowed by a frail-looking girl who didn't say a word; he told us he was from Tigré. Ali scowled at him until he bought some whisky for us all.

'Excuse me,' a man said to me from the next table. 'I think you are historian. I have seen you in the town. I can give you any date or information. I am Aderri. Menelik, you know, unified all Ethiopia. But before he came to Harar, no hotels, no bars, no prostitutes. Now . . .' He scowled and swept his hand around the room.

Soon we were joined by the Tigrean's brother and a friend of his girlfriend, and more whisky appeared. They all said they had come to see me, wondering who I was and what I was doing.

'Did you hear about the bus crash?' the Tigrean asked me. 'Thirty-four people died. . . .'

A wiry man came into the room wearing white Italian shoes and a buff raincoat that flapped behind him like a skirt. He sat at the table next to us and pulled out a small pistol. He glanced across at me and then ordered a drink.

'My brother had a friend in one of the buses,' the Tigrean continued. His brother was having an argument with Ali. The noise from our table was getting louder, and I became concerned that I was attracting too much attention.

But then a group of Cuban soldiers swayed in. The man in white shoes packed away his pistol and left.

The Tigrean leaned towards me, gesturing to the soldiers, and whispered, 'Bastards!'

'Are any of your family still in Tigré?' I asked.

'My mother, yes. I left because of the fighting. My father is dead. . . .' His voice trailed away, and he looked up.

'*Selam! Selam!*' A wild-eyed man clasped my hand and pulled up a chair. 'British, they said. You are British – a great people! I fought against the Italians in the war. . . . Now we need British and Americans again,' and he glanced at the soldiers and muttered, 'Not them.'

'You don't like Cubans?'

'What!' he hissed. 'They are socialist – socialism's like a rotten apple!'

In the far corner one of the soldiers wrestled a barmaid on to his lap. His hand crept under her skirt, and she squealed and wriggled free. The latest Ethiopian song was played again and again from a muffled tape recorder. Drinkers came into the bar, alone or in pairs, ordering coffee, beer, looking for whores. I heard a shout from the corner for Johnnie Walker whisky. A single shot cost more than my room and those who ordered it tended to be government officials. I turned and looked towards the corner: two men were picking their teeth and watching our table and the party of soldiers.

The Tigrean turned to me and said suddenly, 'We think you should go to bed.'

'I'll wait until curfew – there's still half an hour.'

But he repeated his advice, and then said, 'Come outside.'

I followed him out on to the street. Two vagrants were squatting against the hotel wall, arguing. When we appeared they stopped and asked for money. The Tigrean ignored them.

'There are people in there saying bad things about you. They are saying – what are you doing here, and that you are a spy.'

So I went up and sat outside my room, beside a window in the trellis. I felt powerless and angry. The evening had been tinged with suspicion. I knew the problems of being talked about and knew that word would reach the *kebelle* chiefs. I wasn't a tourist or an aid worker, and was on my own and asking people questions. Of course I was a spy! I resolved to be more careful.

At midnight a truck pulled up below the window and the Cubans scrambled on to the tailboard. They drove off to their base outside the walls, and left only silence, and the dark shapes of beggars along the wall.

The air was heavy, but a light breeze blew against my face, bringing hope of rain. I sat there long after the streets had emptied. My room was airless and smelt of diesel, so I slept against the sill.

From 1875, the Egyptians occupied Harar, the eastern outpost of an empire originally intended to cover all the lands of the Blue Nile. But power was being shuffled along its banks: the Mahdi had stranded Gordon in Khartoum, the Ethiopian highlands had proved defiant, and preparations were being made for a conference in Berlin – Europe was about to divide up Africa. In Cairo the British told the khedive he was broke, and in 1884 he withdrew his troops from Harar.

M. Bardey realized this meant stable trading in Harar was at an end. He called Rimbaud back to Aden, and employed him in his office. But Rimbaud was soon restless, and started to look around for an opportunity to increase the 12,000 francs he had saved.

Late in 1885 he met Pierre Labatut, who ran guns into the Ethiopian highlands, and was married to an Ethiopian. Rimbaud agreed to put his savings into a run, for a promised net return of 8000 francs. In December the two Frenchmen crossed the Red Sea to buy the rifles and prepare for the expedition. But Labatut became ill and returned to France. Cancer was diagnozed and soon afterwards he died. So Rimbaud joined forces with Soleillet, a seasoned explorer. But Soleillet died too, suddenly in the street during a trip to Aden. Another French arms caravan, led by Barral and Savouré, had crossed the desert some months earlier, but on their return from the highlands they were set upon by the Afar; their mutilated corpses were only identified by the gleam of a gold tooth of one of the women.

So Rimbaud was forced to lead his own caravan, without experienced help, and to cross some of the world's most savage terrain. With daytime temperatures reaching 120 degrees, the party lumbered across the Danakil Desert, harried constantly by the Afar. Labatut had been able to reach Ankober in two months. Rimbaud's caravan took four. And when he arrived he was told that his client was away campaigning – in Harar.

While Rimbaud was crossing the desert Menelik had marched a force of 30,000 men down the Rift Valley. He was aware that now the Egyptians had left, Harar was at risk from occupation by France, or even by Britain or Italy. At Epiphany, Ethiopian Christmas, in 1887, he met the Harari troops at Chelenko.

Leaving a garrison force in the town, Menelik returned to Entoto above the plains that were soon to become Addis Ababa, his 'New Flower'. At the king's old capital, Ankober, Rimbaud loaded his guns back on to mules and marched the two days south.

Menelik was not the simple tribal chief that Rimbaud imagined. He had learnt how to hold his own with Europeans, be they adventurers like Rimbaud, or wily envoys representing the interests of their governments. Nor were guns, in the flush of his victory, as precious to Menelik as they had been in Labatut's day. Those left by Barral and Savouré before they died could equip his new garrison in Harar.

At his court in the Entoto Hills, the king received Rimbaud wearing a Quaker's hat mounted on a white cloth which he tied behind his neck. First he threatened to impound the guns. Then he told the Frenchman to take them back to the coast. Finally he agreed to buy them, but at a fraction of Rimbaud's price.

Rimbaud was not yet free to leave. Menelik called in Labatut's debts and held Rimbaud responsible. Creditors filed through the court making petty claims and Labatut's widow appealed for all of what remained.

When he rode down from the Entoto Hills into the Rift Valley, the first European to travel from Addis Ababa to Harar, Rimbaud held a letter of credit – covering only 40 per cent of his original capital.

Menelik's acquisition of Harar had avenged centuries of harassment from the Muslim city. He appointed his cousin and favourite general Ras Makonnen as governor, and turned his attention to becoming the King of Kings, Emperor of Ethiopia.

Ras Makonnen cut a new gate in the walls and ran a boulevard down to the Feres Magala. There he pulled down the mosque and erected a church in its place. For some years just the minaret remained, rising above the town's flat roofs like the mast of a sunken ship.

This was how Rimbaud found the town after his journey from Entoto. It was three years since he had last seen it, and it smelt: the Christians were not so strict about sanitation and the town's air was heavy with putrefying waste.

Rimbaud presented his letter to Ras Makonnen. Later they were to become friends, but on this occasion Rimbaud collected his meagre dues and headed for the coast, wanting to move on, hoping for a better place beyond the Red Sea.

Ras Makonnen (the father of Haile Selassie) was described by Rimbaud as looking more like a priest or scholar than a great military commander. Yet it is as a warrior that he survives in Harar. On the main road leading down to the walls is an equestrian statue of Makonnen, the work of Afewerk Tekle. He is in the full dress of a Shoan warrior, with lion's mane and battle spear, and has a view over the Military Academy. Beneath the statue, on a grey afternoon, I watched an assembly of *debtara* form two lines and prepare to dance.

Maskal in Amharic means 'cross'. The festival commemorates the Finding of The True Cross (thousands of pilgrims at this time climb to the cruciform peak of Gishen, where the Ethiopian portion of the Cross is buried). But like Easter in Europe, *Maskal* embellishes a pagan festival to celebrate the beginning of fine weather, the end of the rains.

The object of the day was a tall pyre of eucalyptus boughs spotted with marigolds and hung with garlands of bougainvillaea. It stretched high above the crescent of onlookers around it, above even the tip of Makonnen's spear. Children sat at the feet of the crowd, staring wide-eyed at the bonfire.

A man beside me pointed towards a mural on the walls of the academy. It showed the heads of Marx, Engels and Lenin in line, so that only Marx revealed a full profile.

'You know what we say about them,' he said.

'What's that?'

'The three wise men – with only one ear!' And he slapped a hand to his mouth in mock remorse.

The *debtara*'s dance ended when Abuna Samuel, the local bishop, rose to give his address. He called for his people to strive towards God, and to think always of the poor and sick, and how they can be helped. When he had finished he marched down to the pyre. Three times he walked round it, waving his hand-cross at the foliage. But it seemed a ham procession, a transparent attempt to sanctify what clearly had little to do with Christianity, and soon there was a shout and a flaming torch was tossed over the heads of the crowd. The bishop hurried away, leaving the soldiers in charge.

Two more torches appeared and caught a shard of dry kindling. But most of the wood was green, and the flames flickered and died.

So a drum of petrol was carried into the circle and a man with wild eyes ran round the fire, splashing fuel on to the leaves.

This time the flames shot upwards. The crowd shouted encouragement. Now the hero of the hour, the wild-eyed man dispensed with his ladle and emptied the drum into the fire.

The effect was immediate. A storm of black smoke hid everything for a moment, then cleared as the boughs became a flaming tower. There was a strangled crackling as the leaves dried instantly and burned. Women screamed and fell over themselves to get away; the children closest could only turn their faces from the heat. But the soldiers stood their ground, smiling.

A group of clouds collected behind Makonnen's horse and soon heavy rain had doused the fire. More petrol was found, but the excitement had gone. Most of the onlookers had taken shelter beneath the dripping arcade of a nearby building, or were dashing through the rain back towards the town.

After the rain I went with Ali down through the Felana Gate to see the hyenas. A lifeless patch of compacted mud stretched from the walls into the darkness. I could make out the scattered carcasses of cattle, and could smell the circus smell of animals and rotting meat.

At a price, there was a man who would perform various tricks with the hyenas when they came to feed. He had names for them and would squat on the ground and let them eat from his hand.

'Ahmed! Omar!' he cried, tearing a ham from a carcass beside him. Then he barked and yelped and ran around; clearly *cha'at* was part of his preparation.

Two animals climbed out of a gully and padded towards him. He knelt down and howled like a lycanthrope, but the hyenas seemed uninterested. They stopped, and one turned and slipped away.

Something seemed wrong with the performance. Ali explained.

Shortly after dawn that day a Galla woman had been attacked as she walked back from the town to her village. The woman's face was badly mauled and the hyena's powerful jaws had broken her own jaw in two places. She had been carried straight to hospital, and the hyena had been shot, its body the meat now being fed to its fellows.

I felt suddenly repulsed by the scene, as though the attack was the result of the casual interest of visitors like myself.

So we left and went back through the gates, through shadowy lanes and up to Feres Magala where we played *carembola,* a form of billiards, in a crowded bar. The next morning I heard that at nine o'clock – the time we had left the hyenas – the Galla woman had died from her wounds.

By *Maskal* in 1888, exactly one hundred years earlier, the rains had long since ended and the skies were clear. It had been unusually hot and already there were murmurs of concern about the December harvest. Added to this, travellers were talking of a new disease in the north that was killing off all the cattle, and spreading south.

Like most human calamities, the Great Famine of 1888–92 was the result of a cruel coincidence of factors. A poor harvest was followed in early 1889 by the culmination of the rinderpest epidemic. Nine out of every ten cattle were to die, leaving no beasts to plough the fields. Then locusts swarmed and stripped the parched land of vegetation; what they left behind was consumed by a plague of caterpillars.

Ragged groups of people wandered the country begging for scraps in the name of the Virgin Mary. Too weak to carry on, many of them fell to be picked at by hyenas. Around churches and the houses of the rich, the number of bodies increased with the last attempts at finding food. There was a haunting silence to the country, with the usual noises of dogs and hens absent. Many popular verses record this time:

> When I try to flee from poverty
> It follows me;
> It perches on my head and sings and dances.
> O this useless world!

Some farmers killed themselves (rare in devout Ethiopia) when their cattle died, and there were reports of children being eaten. Another 'wax and gold' couplet from the time goes:

> Rather than go down to Metemma to trade in civet
> Incense is better for the daily supper.

But in Amharic it also means:

> The little child is better for the daily supper.

In Harar hyenas crawled through the drains beneath the wall and gathered around corpses in the dusty alleys. The French missionary Taurin built a house for children who might otherwise be attacked by the roaming beasts. Outside the walls, jackals, leopards and lions picked off the Galla if they strayed from their villages. At night the cry *'wasadanni! wasadanni!'* ('it is taking me away!') could be heard from among the huts as the hyenas lost their fear of the weakened people.

As many as one in three Ethiopians died during the Great Famine, and large areas of the country were deserted. One report suggested that of the Galla around Harar, only a half survived.

Father Emile was sifting through a pile of postcards. Each one brought a grunt of recognition. 'Paris . . . Paris . . . Ah, London . . . *ça* . . . *voilà* Stonehenge, you see . . . Rome – St Peter's . . . Rimbaud . . . Harar – here, look.'

He picked out an old black-and-white print entitled *Vue de Harrar*.

'You see here the minaret and the church. Now, some of the people say that Rimbaud built a house around here, that he bought land from Garad Mohammed Nagaya, a big landowner at that time. I have been wanting to find out about it.'

We traced the house to a low L-shaped building near Ras Makonnen's palace, now the provincial headquarters of the Ministry of Culture.

In the courtyard was a tethered goat. A mongrel growled at our approach and raised its head, but didn't get up. A family occupied a couple of the rooms, windowless chambers under a stone roof which leaked. Yes, they had heard of the Frenchman – this road used to be called Arthur Rimbaud Street in the time of the Emperor – but the actual house, they didn't know.

In Addis Ababa, at the Institute of Ethiopian Studies, I checked the proceedings of the Sharia court which included all land transactions. They had been microfilmed by UNESCO, and the viewing machine sat beneath a chintz dais shaped like a coronet, in the place once occupied by the bed of Empress Menen, wife of Haile Selassie. The years 1303–1306, in the Hegira calendar, were disrupted by Menelik's occupation, and probably by the famine too, and I could find no trace of a purchase by Rimbaud.

Wherever he lived during his later years in the town, it was not at the so-called Rimbaud house. That was built after his death, by merchants from Gujarat.

Rimbaud spent the last three active years of his life in Harar. He returned there in May 1888, having passed a fruitless year travelling up and down the Red Sea chasing plans: to go to Zanzibar, to run more arms to Menelik, to be a war correspondent, to explore the Ethiopian interior. He hated Aden and complained of rheumatism. Round his waist he wore his savings in a belt, but it weighed nearly eighteen pounds and gave him dysentery. So in the end he returned to what he knew best, being a trader in Harar.

The glimpses of him during the final years are sketchy, but cannot hide his misery. His pride and single-mindedness had hardened; the very qualities that inspired his exile destined his failure there. He was scrupulous to a fault and isolated himself from the other traders, avoiding the bars and cafés where they drank. He despised their drinking and vacuous camaraderie, so missed out on the information they exchanged, and antagonized them with his haughtiness. There was a lot of money to be made at this time, with Menelik modernizing Ethiopia, but others, not Rimbaud, were making it.

In Paris, Rimbaud had become the glamorous prodigy who had run off to Africa. Verlaine had published some of Rimbaud's work and he was the toast of a new group of symbolist poets.

But he knew nothing of this, and his occasional letters from this time tell only of his trading, and his dejection. 'What do you expect me to write about in a place like this? That I'm bored, that I have problems, that I'm worn out, that I've had enough, but that I can't get myself out of here etc. etc.!'

His letters are the only record of the last years; their rarity suggest he may have saved up his grumbles, and aired them on his family, a vent for his accumulated bitterness, perhaps even blame. But there must have been moments when he let his stoical guard drop. He had a deep feeling for the people. He learnt to speak Aderri and Gallinya and Amharic, and spoke Arabic already – he gave Koranic lessons to the town's children. Ras Makonnen was among his friends (they were probably neighbours), and one can only guess at the conversations between the Frenchman and the great Amhara warrior.

And perhaps too he found some deeper thread of solace in the walled city. He would go down past the Jami mosque to the Catholic mission and talk with Father Jerome, who reported to Evelyn Waugh forty years later that Rimbaud was 'not a good Catholic'. Father Emile imagines he had some eccentric affinity with the Church. A leaning towards Islam was more likely – a creed less given to sentiment than Christianity, closer to Rimbaud's own harsh view of the world.

But most of his time was taken up in a cathartic frenzy of work, travelling through the hills around the town, up to 40 kilometres every day – often on foot.

It was the restless walking – he had been walking ever since he left France – that he blamed for the first signs of stiffness in his right knee. It got worse and he was forced to bed. Still he maintained his feverish pace. He checked through ledgers, adding and re-adding columns of figures. Trading had been handed to a deputy, but, if he propped himself up, Rimbaud could see the scales from his window.

After three weeks the pain forced him to arrange a litter and head for the coast. He left Harar at the end of 1891, a little more than ten years after he first saw it. It was an ignominious retreat, not the glorious return proposed in 'Une Saison en Enfer':

> Je reviendrai, avec des membres de fer, la peau
> sombre, l'oeil furieux . . . J'aurai de l'or

In Marseilles his right leg was amputated high up the thigh. But the cancer was now rampant. In his delirium he spoke only of Harar, planning imaginary caravans and mistaking his sister for Djami, his Harari servant-boy.

Ras Makonnen wrote to him as a friend, reporting the horrors of the famine. He urged him to return and help him.

But on 10 November 1891 Rimbaud died, trying in vain to get a ship to take him back to Harar. An estate of about 30,000 francs remained. Of this he asked for 3000 to be sent to Djami in Harar. But the money came too late; Djami had already died, probably in the famine.

7

Father Emile had tried to track down Abdul Mahayman for me. 'He is Aderri, a great expert on Islam and on Harar. You would like to talk to him I think. But,' he added, 'he is . . . er . . . very elusive.'

I asked in the town. Everyone seemed to know him, had seen him earlier, or yesterday, but shrugged when I asked where to find him. 'Try the main mosque . . . ask his cousin in the market . . . go to Erer Gate at four o'clock.'

After thirty-six hours I found him, behind a pair of red gates just outside the walls. It was a more opulent yard than most. A Japanese car sat in the sun next to railings heavy with purple-flowering bougainvillaea. Out of the house rushed a man bent at the waist and clutching a bowl of teff-bread.

'Ah! Yes, yes. I have been expecting you. Come on.' Abdul turned and scurried into one of the rooms off the yard. He kicked off his shoes and sat cross-legged on the divan.

'We must talk. How long have you been in Harar? Why did you not come to see me before – yes, yes, I know. You could not find Abdul's house! I am like Al Khizr – everywhere and nowhere. All Harar is my home. This is my cousin's house.'

He paused and pushed another piece of bread into his mouth.

'You know that before Richard Burton came to Harar, no one outside the Muslim world was sure where it was! It is a secret place – hidden from Christians like you,' and he laughed.

I warmed to him at once, to his knavish charm and energy. There was something unlikely about him. His face was weathered and ageless. His hair was thin on a high forehead, but above erupted in a mass of tight black curls, like broken springs. Later he confessed he was forty-six and I was surprised.

'After twenty-seven days,' he announced, 'I will have been here for a year without travelling – the furthest I have gone is to

Alemaya, seven kilometres away. I have been to many places in Africa, but always I come back to Harar, to speak with the walls. Harar is my mirror! You know why I have kept so still this year? It is because I have learnt Sufism. I am collecting all my thoughts, meditating, reading, and then next year I go to Khartoum to study classical Arabic. I have a scholarship. I want to read all the ancient Persian poets.'

Later we went to the market. At this end of the town it was the Christian market, in every other respect no different from the half dozen Muslim markets. On the way I spotted a distinctive figure in a long white robe. He was walking in the middle of the road, and the ends of his hair glowed carrot-red with henna. Abdul saw him and sprang forward. He ran up and kissed his hand, then came back and said, 'Oh, oh, I love that man! For six months I lived in his house at Dire Dawa. He was my Koranic teacher. He knows all the texts by heart!'

The morning had ended with heavy rain, and in the market had left the narrow paths between stalls as boggy canals. Galla women squatted on islands of clean calico, grinning toothlessly, maintaining a slow banter with neighbours, plaiting their daughters' hair and coating it with ghee, or rearranging the tiny cairns of root vegetables, maize or green chillies that were their livelihood.

Abdul leaned towards me and whispered, 'A fool makes money and a wise man spends it. That is Harari saying!'

The more I saw of Abdul, his mischief and ebullience, his Arab guile, and particularly his eclectic responses and aphorisms, the more I thought of Abdi Abokr, the End of Time.

That Richard Burton should have been the man to 'discover' Harar seems one of the happier matches in the history of exploration. There is a degree to which all explorers become their quest, but for Burton the success of the Harar expedition seems, when placed against the frustrations of his later years, to be a high spot, the fulfilment of his first love – the Arab world.

While an account of his earlier expedition to Mecca was being published in London, Burton went to Aden to plan the trip to Harar. He outlined the city's appeal: 'The ancient metropolis of a once mighty race, the only permanent settlement in Eastern

Africa, the reported seat of Muslim learning, a walled city of stone houses, possessing its own independent chief, its peculiar language, its own coinage . . . amply, it appeared, deserved the trouble of exploration.'

But its greatest attraction for Burton was that unlike Mecca, Harar had never been reached by a European.

The journey started at Aden on 29 October 1854, nine days after the birth of Rimbaud. Burton crossed the Red Sea to Zayla and there spent a month in preparation, bartering for supplies among the coralline buildings, perfecting his Arab disguise, scribbling notes on a low divan and reacquainting himself with the face of Al-Islam which so intrigued him.

When Burton left Zayla for the desert he had four mules and four camels – and a number of curious retainers. Two of them were women with nicknames from his cherished *Arabian Nights* – Schehrazade and Deenarzade. They were attended by a one-eyed boy from Zayla whom they hated; he was called Calender after the mendicant order of dervishes.

Then there was Abdi Abokr, the son of a rich shipowner. Abdi had frittered away a fortune on a lifetime's travels, and now at forty lived off the chief of Zayla's charity.

Abdi had a stock of proverbs to suit every occasion. When asked to hurry he would warn, 'Patience is of Heaven, Haste of Hell.' Burton lodged a grain of rice in his beard while eating one evening. Abdi leaned towards him and said, 'The gazelle is in the garden.' To which Burton should have replied, 'I will hunt her with the five,' and searched for the rice with his fingers.

Abdi was known as the End of Time, after the Muslim belief that in the last era of the world the priesthood would become corrupt.

'The British – they are like snake under the carpet. That is what people say around here.' Abdul pointed a finger at me.

'And why's that?'

'Because they did not want to put Haile Selassie back on the throne after the Italian war. But don't worry – I tease!'

We were sitting on boulders of buff sandstone by the Umar river. A narrow track crossed the water, breaking into a series of stepping-stones. Galla women in shades of saffron and indigo paused here and watered their mules, beside banks flushed a rich green from the rains.

Abdul started to sing.

He sang in Gallinya, of his strange foreign friend who had come to Harar with an empty book to try and steal her heart, but she is like a young beauty who keeps her features veiled. The women laughed, glancing coyly at his foreign friend. Then they reloaded the mules and beat them across the stream, and up the hill to Harar.

For Burton's party this place was the last stop before entering the forbidden city. He climbed the bank and made a sketch while his companions bathed and wrapped themselves in fresh robes. By this time he had decided to declare himself an Englishman to the emir. He had no walnut juice to tan his skin and did not want to be mistaken for a Turk. But if he felt apprehensive about entering the city his account shows little sign of it – just dry records of passing warnings *en route*: 'They will spoil that white skin of thine at Harar' and 'the human head once struck off does not regrow like a rose', and on leaving the last village, his party was told simply 'you are dead men'.

He entered by the Erer Gate, and in the end his audacity probably saved him. He strode into the court of the young emir, refusing to forfeit his weapons, and greeted him in perfect Arabic. He then stayed ten days within the walls, unsure whether he would be released.

But two things protected him: his extraordinary erudition in Arabic language and custom, and the fear the emir had that the British might stop his caravans if anything happened to their subject.

Leaving the city, Burton passed through Erer Gate at dawn. He saw the guards still huddled round their fire. '*Selam! Selam!*' he cried from his mule, and felt the anxiety of the previous days drop from him 'like a cloak of lead'. But at the same time he was struck too with a sudden sobering thought. 'How melancholy a thing,' he reflected, 'is success.'

Abdul and I walked back to the city. He was talking about his daily routine. 'At dawn I get up and say my prayers and practise Sufi meditation, then a bit later I go to the mosque and talk with the elders. In the afternoon I do my business in the town and then as it gets dark, I start to read and study – that is Abdul's time! Sometimes with *cha'at* I stay up all night reading.'

'What do you read?'

'Oh, Koranic texts, poetry, English literature. Thomas Hardy I like. Every spring I read *Tess of the D'Urbervilles* – I love that book. I know so many men in Harar like old Mr Durbeyfield – Sir John!' He laughed and shook his head.

Our walk ended with the sun low against the walls beneath the Catholic mission. We found Father Emile in the compound, waving goodbye to a nun.

'Good, good,' he said. 'So you found each other.' Then he turned to Abdul. 'I heard about your sister-in-law. I am so sorry.'

Abdul raised his hands. 'May her soul rest in peace. But, no matter. We are all born to die.' Then he turned to me and said quietly, 'She was killed last week – in an air crash . . .'

'At Bahar Dar?'

He nodded.

Ali walked me to the bus station. Above it was a crowd of people standing beside some waste ground. Mostly they were young people, couples or small groups looking bored.

'What are they waiting for?' I asked.

'Public hanging.'

Two men had been convicted of murder the week before. One had already been hanged by the Erer Gate. His accomplice was due to hang up here by the Duke's Gate.

But Ali shrugged. 'I don't think they'll do it today. It's only a rumour.'

I said goodbye to Ali, and got on the bus. At Alemaya I went to the agricultural college and was introduced to the 'public relations officer', a man named Negussie. He took me to a nearby village in a Land Cruiser to look at the local co-operative scheme.

We drove along a pitted, fox-coloured track. Beside it stooped bulbs of ripe sorghum. Negussie said suddenly, 'The Ethiopians – they are the African English!'

'Why do you say that?'

But he just laughed and recalled the time he taught physical education in Glasgow. 'I was there for three years. Once I went round Scotland on a 50cc Vespa. I put all my luggage on the back and just took off! But I was a young man then.'

The track ended beside an altar of rural communism: timbers painted in bright blues and reds beneath a picture of Mengistu and a yellow star. Beside it was a notice-board covered in figures.

'The incentive scheme,' said Negussie. All the co-operative's five hundred-odd families were listed, and next to them was an eradicable number. On the basis of this, he explained, their individual performance, the community's resources were handed out.

On the hillside were neat rows of huts – not the traditional round ones, but rows of rectangular boxes with tin roofs. The secretary was found and started his spiel: set up ten years ago with five families on 3 hectares, two pairs of oxen and a donkey, now 603 hectares with 520 families, sixty pairs of oxen, three loading trucks, three tractors and fifty-six donkeys. The government had only provided credit and technical assistance.

'Production,' he added, 'has risen from twenty quintals per hectare to sixty-five. Now let us look round.' For the first time he raised his eyes from the ground.

I spotted a stout Korean in a doorway, his hands clasped magisterially behind his back. When he saw me he slipped back into the shadows. Negussie gripped my elbow whispering, 'Technical assistance' and grinned.

We walked on down to the fields, which were irrigated and neatly tended. In the far corner was a party of people bent over the furrows with mattocks. Negussie said, 'They used to come over and talk, but now with the incentive scheme, they don't even look up at us!'

Beyond them were reed beds and the lake. On one of the lakes at Alemaya, in 1907, the young Haile Selassie was out rowing with his elder brother Yilma. The boat overturned and the boys were left struggling in the water, unable to swim. A Greek came to rescue them but Yilma had already drowned. This was an early step on the Emperor's path to succession. His main contender to the throne was Lij Yasu, and the story goes that it was Yasu who had sabotaged the boat, hoping they would both die.

The secretary had not finished his tour. 'Surpluses have earned the co-operative two million birr. It is in the bank.'

'You have become bourgeois,' I said, trying to tease a smile from him. 'Soon you'll be buying capitalist goods.'

But he didn't rise. 'Everyone has televisions already, and we can buy Japanese imports.'

I kept looking for the catch. I asked about education and health: there was provision for each member. He even showed me a small mosque they had built. 'Mostly for old people and certain families. Many young don't want to go.'

We left with the low sun spilling through the eucalyptus. A troop of children chased the truck as we pulled away, and I felt that there probably was no catch, save that this was a show village, and that the land was very good. But I couldn't help thinking all that cash would eventually split up the community.

I got a lift back down to Dire Dawa in a diocesan Land Cruiser with a priest, Abba Dawit. He had to pick up a bishop from Kulubi Gabriel, a shrine on the crest of the Chercher Hills. So we took the high road, along the edge of the scarp where the mountains tumble north into the desert, and the Rift Valley ends and fans out into the Afar Triangle. It was early afternoon, and a blue-grey haze hovered over the horizon.

Dawit pointed into the hills. On a spur I could make out the walls of a modern church. 'Kulubi,' he said, smiling, his teeth spreading across his mouth like a broken fence.

I was pleased to make this stop – Kulubi Gabriel is the most important pilgrimage site in Ethiopia. In 1896 Ras Makonnen, still Governor of Harar, took this route on his way up to Emperor Menelik's new court at Addis Ababa. The empire was under threat from the Italians, who were planning to push south from Eritrea, and the emperor had mustered his generals for the campaign. At Kulubi, Makonnen stopped to pray in a small church by the wayside, vowing to the Archangel Gabriel that if he returned victorious, the saint would have a shrine there.

The campaign ended at Adwa, shortly after noon on 1 March, 1896. Ethiopia was assured her independence from Italy and from Europe; the empire was intact. Makonnen returned to Kulubi and had it consecrated. He died there ten years later, on his way to Addis Ababa.

We pulled up outside the gates of the church. Abba Dawit showed me into the compound and said, 'At pilgrimage time you cannot stand here, there are so many people . . . every people –

Catholic, Protestant, Muslim . . . even' – and he leaned to whisper in my ear – 'Party!'

I followed him into the church and took off my shoes. Here the concrete-coloured stone and high ceiling reminded me of Debra Libanos, the same poor proportions. But it was more lavish, trimmed – chandeliers and red velvet, garish icons, a carpeted floor all testified to the benevolent triumph of a journey's end.

Pilgrimage, and bi-weekly fasts, are the most profound penances for Ethiopian Christians, and for many are more important rites than the Eucharist. A ritual visit to a shrine like Kulubi is used to petition saints – Gabriel is found to help barren marriages.

Twice a year Ethiopians from all over the country make their way to Kulubi (some even come from Mecca). The December pilgrimage attracts more than 100,000 people, some carrying rocks or crawling along the road as added expiation.

Paul Henze, an American diplomat in Addis Ababa before the revolution, described the occasion in 1971. The Emperor, then eighty years old, attended and followed the patriarch and the *tabot* around the church. That year 120,000 went to Kulubi, and in the evening nobles danced at an imperial ball in Dire Dawa.

I stayed the night at one of the aid agencies in Dire Dawa, neat pre-fab buildings behind a high wall, and a compound shaded by jacaranda. There was a Frenchman working there, a seasoned field officer. We sat up late in his room which betrayed a life of rootless independence, a hybrid of France and Africa.

'You know, I have worked in six different countries in Africa, mostly West Africa, but I have been also to others – nineteen in total.' He was drinking pastis from a tall glass, and paused to top it up. 'And Ethiopia is totally different.'

'Why's that?'

He seemed surprised to have to qualify his claim, as if it was obvious. 'Well . . . many reasons. For example, I have a transport manager – an Amhara, from Wollo. He looks after the garage, thirty-eight trucks and eighty people under him. He does the job well – and he is only twenty-three. There are many people like him – with ability.' He lit a cigarette, then waved it towards me.

'Look, in other parts of Africa nothing works because of general incompetence. Here nothing works because of the system. I have many friends here in good positions, heads of the railway and others. Some are party members, some not. But they all complain of the system. They have no power to go with their position, and you know why? Because there are too many *petits chefs.*'

I picked up the theme with Billy, a couple of days later back in Addis. We were sitting in the back-room of his restaurant, among boxes of old unused china.

'I tell you, this country is at breaking point. I went down to the banana plantations earlier this week, and they were like a tropical rain forest – no one bothers to work. Why should they for a few dollars a day? And then there is the Italian mission in Sidamo – they have a school and a farm down there. They wanted to import some books and machinery – all to help these people – and were forced to pay full import duty at 249 per cent! It's really getting hard – the ports are blocked. Nothing's getting through. But you know, this place could work.' He chopped the air with his hand. 'It could work!'

The phone rang and Billy won an Amharic argument about supplying meat on a fast day. He shook his head and continued.

'Listen, a few years ago we could buy Ethiopian batteries for our cars – from a factory in Asmara. Good batteries – I still have one in my car, and cheap too. Then they asked to import the points and the government said no. So now all batteries come from abroad, while there's a factory here with a huge stock of nearly finished ones. It's crazy.'

One of Billy's waitresses – Almaz was her name – came through with some coffee. I'd met her here before, and stood to greet her in Amharic.

'It is well with you?'

'It is well, thanks be to God. It is well with you?'

'It is well, thanks be to God, and with you?'

'It is well.'

If I'd known her better we would have carried on, but instead she asked me about my journey to Harar.

'I thought you may have been on that bus,' she said, in the tone of so many Ethiopian women – at once soft and strong, like the white cotton shawls they wear, the *gabbis.* 'There were two people from my area who were killed on the bus, a woman and her child – terrible, terrible.' And she shook her head and frowned.

I had a message one Saturday evening to ring some friends in the UN. They were going down to Awash for the day. 'There's not much you can do on a Sunday. Why not come with us?'

Addis Ababa was always frustrating. On Sundays it was doubly so – unless you had a car with aid plates, or diplomatic plates. (Ethiopians stoically accepted the 'no driving' restrictions, and spent the day with their families.)

So, just before seven we met at a UN flat near the Hilton. The door had a sticker saying: THIS AREA IS PROTECTED BY DIPLOMATIC IMMUNITY. Inside there was breakfast – bacon sandwiches and Moët et Chandon. Afterwards we loaded a Land Cruiser with cold boxes and headed south.

The UN officers had just been to Jijiga.

'What news of the refugees?' I asked.

'Well, there are three hundred thousand Somalis just sitting in the desert. They need everything – tents, food, water, medical care. But the odd thing is that they're very well-organized. There's always a Somali spokesman at the camps. Very different from the refugees in Jimma.'

The road followed the railway, down into the dry scrubland of the Rift. In places the valley was narrow enough to see the ridges on either side, their elephant-hide slopes wrinkled with flood gullies. Yet in the Rift Valley there was always the distortion of space, so that sixty miles across seemed narrow.

Awash National Park pushes the Shoan border round its far edge, so no permits are needed. After three and a half hours a dirt track opened out into a corral of high euphorbia.

'What animals do you have in the park?' I asked the guard who had joined us at the main road.

'Beisa oryx, dik-dik, bushbuck.'

'Anything else?'

He fiddled with the stock of his rifle.

'Any lion, or leopard?'

'Asleep.'

He sat on the bank while we bathed in the hot springs. The sulphurous water was as hot as a bath, and left an oily film on the skin. Through the trees came a group of three Afar. They stood and watched us. Each held a rifle, and had a long dagger, a *jile*, around his waist.

The reputation of the Afar is well-known: perhaps the world's wildest people, they kill and castrate other men, displaying the testicles around their necks as symbols of status. Wilfred Thesiger had a sneaking admiration for them, but I felt we were a little vulnerable, naked in this steaming swamp with only one rifle between us.

But these ones were friendly enough. They followed us back to the Land Cruiser and refused offers of food. We had lunch beside the swollen Awash river, and monkeys swung down and stole the bread. Then later we drove back up the Rift Valley, and the low sun ignited the slopes with the colours of fire.

8

The Entoto Hills are now more or less deserted. Menelik's capital has slid down the hill into the modern world, settling on the lower slopes to sprout tower-blocks and cranes, and spreading on to the plain in the broad apron of Bole International Airport.

From Shiromeda at the top end of the bus route, I took a right fork into the hills where shanties gave way to large groves of eucalyptus, and the forest. In places the trees had been coppiced and from the stumps sprang shoots of green topaz and waxy blue.

I was heading for the church of Kidane Mehret. With me on the road were two priests and a young couple from Addis, he in a pork-pie hat and she hiding behind a *gabbi*.

Kidane Mehret – in Ge'ez, Covenant of Mercy – is a healing church built above a spring, the source of Addis Ababa's holiest water. In the trees around it a religious community has grown up to cope with the flow of patients who come for cures and ritual cleansing, even exorcism.

'We are going to visit a friend,' said the pork-pie hat.

'He's ill?'

'Yes, he had mental trouble last week.'

'I'm sorry.'

'Don't be sorry. Why don't you join us?'

'I'm sure he won't want to see a stranger.'

But when we arrived at the church, his friend insisted and I was shown into a dark hut. A single light bulb hung from a lintel between the two rooms. In the far room I could see a simple mud platform, and a pile of plastic plates, a couple of saucepans and a kettle. In the main room, two women squatted on a goatskin in one corner. Opposite them, on a crude wooden bed, lay Efrem. When I came in he propped himself up on one elbow.

'I haven't been well,' he muttered, gesturing to me to sit on the bed. Behind him, against the mud wall someone had pasted the pages of an Italian newspaper.

'I am glad you came,' he continued. 'Today I am a little better. When I arrived two days ago I was confused. Clouds hung over me.' He looked away, and stroked his shaven scalp; he was so thin I could see the cracks of the cranium beneath it. We drank tea and chatted for a while, then a distant peal of bells sounded and he said, 'I must go to evening prayers. Will you come?'

He put on a green coat and pulled the hood up like a cowl. In its shadow his features appeared even more skeletal. But when we got outside his eyes brightened, missing nothing.

'Today,' he announced, 'I shaved my head.'

'Why?'

'I don't know,' he shrugged.

Children generally have their heads shaved to prevent lice. In the remoter north a cross-shaped tuft is kept on the crown as protection against evil spirits. I wondered whether for Efrem his shaved head was a regressive impulse, a yearning for the uncluttered days of his childhood.

He pointed to a clump of brush. 'Behind there is the Holy Well. Every morning we go down and shower in the water. Everyone goes down – some have the devil in them, and in the water are beaten with crosses until they speak in tongues. Then we pray.'

We went into the church. A *debtara* was leading a chant.

'Everyone here is sick,' whispered Efrem, and pointed out a small boy who sat on the chancel steps. 'He was crippled when he came here a year ago – now he can walk.'

I looked down at the boy. He must have been about five. He was a spastic, with twitching limbs and a face flickering between confusion and a smile.

The prayers over, we walked out into the bright evening sun. One thing intrigued me: had Efrem himself chosen to come here for treatment? During the service he had seemed more intent on whispering to me – explaining the frescoes, pointing out the ailments of his fellows – than on prayer. He had said that the treatment had done him some good, yet he seemed sceptical, as though such superstition was for other people, not for the educated like himself.

'My family arranged it for me. I had been to many doctors, but still I was sick, not sleeping or eating. Then last week . . . well, I became very confused, so my family sent me here for two weeks.'

There was a juniper near the church gates. A collection of objects had been nailed into it, like fetishes. Most of them were small jars of coloured liquids, some with unidentifiable things in suspension. These, Efrem explained, were the bile of patients retching the holy water – to try and rid their stomachs of parasites.

'And what's that?' I pointed to a plastic bag of pharmaceutical packets and smoked-plastic pill jars.

Efrem smiled. 'They were left by a man a couple of weeks ago. He had had an illness for many years – then he took the water here and was better. So he brought all his modern medicines and left them here.'

We went back to his hut. He was getting tired, his speech slurred and his legs were wobbly. When I walked back down to Addis it was dark, and the eucalyptus smoke hung in a sweet-smelling mist over the town.

'You are from England? What is your church – you must be Anglican? Ah, yes sir, come quickly. I have a picture of your pastor.' I had come to the Church Office for a letter of introduction. I explained that I had a bus to catch.

Abba Mesfin gave a chuckle and ran into his office. He was an elderly priest, with a round face framed by a tangle of whiskers.

Tadessa, who I had seen about the Patriarch's service, was in a meeting. Mesfin gave the impression that I was better off with him; clearly there was some sort of rift between them. In Ethiopia institutions like the Church are as baffling as electrical circuits, fed by a confusion of power sources – family, region, class – and backed up by two thousand years of history. Add intrigues of byzantine complexity, personal feuds, religious dogma, politics (but rarely money) and occasionally there is a flash and the whole thing is exposed. But to outsiders, most of the time there is just rumour and the sense of a remote, persistent pulse.

Mesfin dug around in a drawer of his desk and produced a photograph. 'Your pastor!'

I looked at the picture. It showed an ecumenical meeting of some kind. One of the delegates was an Anglican with a balding head – but who it was, I had no idea.

'So, you are going to Zikwala,' said Mesfin. 'How are you getting there?'

'By bus and on foot.'

'Alone?'

'Yes.'

'But you cannot . . . the peasants will attack you! Some – they are very bad, you know.'

But in the end he gave me the letter, and we walked out into the sun.

'Have you ever been to Zikwala?' I asked.

He gripped my arm, whispering, 'No – I am very lazy man!' And he rocked with such helpless laughter that I couldn't help but join him.

The mountain of Zikwala, an extinct volcano, is one of those lone features that haunts its surroundings. In Addis – thirty miles north – it was a far, gruff figure at the end of open streets, framed between high buildings, peeping above tin roofs; it was no surprise that it had been deified and is the object of an annual pilgrimage.

I took a bus to Debra Zeit, and there found an old minibus full of pilgrims. I sat next to the driver, cramped on to a home-made engine cover. Behind me, as we rattled along the track, two rows of grinning faces bobbed up and down and a young girl gripped my arm against the violent lunges.

'This bus is twenty-nine years old – the finest from Italy,' explained the driver, adding, 'I don't know this route – it's only used once a year for the festival.'

We drove through avenues of sisal and yellow-flowering cassia, and Zikwala slipped in and out of sight.

The mountain was a perfect cone, the peak sliced off to leave a saddled crater. Its slopes were a soft blue shadow, and on the summit sat a single puffy cloud, white as an egret on the jaws of a crocodile. Soon the mountain filled the whole windscreen. Behind me pilgrim spirits broke out into song, with a chant and chorus and clapping. It became more vigorous, until we took a wrong turn and ended up in a village. The bus turned around and the song started again. Then we plunged into a dry riverbed and the bumper locked fast. Everyone climbed out and started shouting, pointing at bits of the vehicle with advice.

An elderly man with almond eyes ran up to me and cursed the

driver. He had blue gums and fewer than half-a-dozen teeth. When he ran back to the party I saw that his legs were bowed and stunted – and one was so twisted that his shoe pointed backwards; he too was going to climb the mountain.

I waited a while and then took my bag and walked towards the footslopes. Down here in the Rift Valley it was hot and dry, and small puffs of dust burst like gunshots at my heels. After a couple of miles I stopped in a churchyard, where parties of pilgrims were nibbling at *injera*, the rubbery teff-bread. I resumed the walk with a family from Addis Ababa, and the path wound beneath head-high heather, then lofty juniper as the slope steepened, and finally towards the top, plots of sorghum, and teff which cascaded down the hill in a bright green waterfall.

Stretching north, the plain behind me was a map. I could make out the Entoto Hills, darkened by storm clouds which smudged the roofs of Addis with heavy rain. Elsewhere, the fields spread in gentle folds over the topography, stained in places by the shadow of a cloud, torn by a gully or cattle track, or broken by a barren hillock too steep to plough, stripped of trees and left to scrub. The dark lines of lava-flows ran as mullions between fields of ripe crops.

I reached the top after four hours. The stumped peak of the mountain, the crater and its rim, turned out to be thickly forested. At just under 10,000 feet a chill mist had gathered, and seeped through the firs like a gas.

The church was built on an elevated section of the rim. Carved steps led the final few feet up to its entrance, and here I watched a stream of pilgrims file up to kiss the door. For some this was the end of a week's walk, maybe more, and afterwards they squatted in chattering groups in the grass or against the compound wall, stick-legged peasants, and tacit mendicants too exhausted to beg.

I walked down alone into the caldera. The trees formed a circle around the lake. Towards the crater floor the forest thinned and I found a landscape at once strange and familiar. Beside the lake grew sedges, and short grass dotted with clover; underfoot the moss padded the soil. As it grew dark, a tongue of fog crept over the edge of the crater, falling through the trees, licking their boughs, then swallowing them altogether. A damp breeze went before the cloud, and when it reached me, within minutes I was dripping wet.

Mount Zikwala is dedicated to St Gabre Manfus, patron saint of the animals. He is one of Ethiopia's best-loved saints. I had seen his picture in Giorgis Cathedral in Addis Ababa, a modern painting in bright colours. He is wearing an animal skin, and at his feet sit the beasts of the forest, a lion and leopard. From his right eye, as he prays, a thirsty raven is drinking.

In the synaxaria of medieval Ethiopia, Gabre Manfus is an ascetic, originally from Lower Egypt. He lived for 363 years, around the time of Amda Seyon I, the great fourteenth-century emperor. He never drank water and did not think about food. His later years were spent on Zikwala, among wild animals, having tamed the mountain's demons.

In the forest, I had been told, there now live several hundred *bahtawi,* anchorites living off berries and grubs, and sleeping in the shelter of rocks. But on 'Abbo Days' – the feasts of Gabre Manfus – they appear in the yellow robes of hermits, matted hair falling around their leathery faces.

Abbo Days also draw young lovers from Addis. They go into the forest, to a clefted rock above the trees. The rock is renowned for its punishment of falsehood. If you go between its spires, they say, bearing a false love, the rock will close and crush you.

I spent a short cold night in a hut with the family from Addis. The son, Girma, told me he wanted to study in East Germany after school, his sister flirted and their mother, Bizunesh, prepared *injera* over a fire. The hut, a large wattle structure, was the home of two priests and appeared to be owned by a fierce woman who crouched beside the fire. Through the evening it filled with woodsmoke and the shrill tones of Amharic. People came and went – eager faces emerging briefly from the night, sharing tales of their journey, bringing food and local beer, tickled by the sight of a foreigner.

Later a tall monk appeared and asked if he could sleep in the hut.

'No room,' said the fierce woman.

But he shrugged and sat beside the priests. The women ignored him and carried on with their chatter. Soon the monk stood up, pursed his lips and started a series of prayers in Ge'ez. From under his cloak he pulled out a horn cup and tipped it up. I watched his adam's apple bob up and down as he drank. Then he resumed the prayers, this time louder. The women had to stop talking and answer the refrains. The priests stared obliviously at the floor and there was a sudden tension in the room.

The monk became wilder, but soon the prayers lapsed into a sort of gibberish. The fierce woman stood and ordered him to leave. An argument followed, but the monk cowed before her attack, muttering that he had nowhere else to go.

In the end he picked up his prayer stick and horn, and shuffled out into the darkness.

When the fire had died we huddled on the mud floor to sleep. An hour or so passed, and I heard the drunken monk slip back into the hut. Later on I woke from a cold semi-slumber to the sound of retching: the monk's beer had disagreed with Girma. His mother lit a taper and sat with him. She read from her *Book of the Miracles of Mary*, her face a bright moon of dedication.

Just before dawn the thatch stopped rustling with rain and I went with Bizunesh to the church. In the forest thick fog muffled our voices and hid the path, but we followed the sound of the *debtara*'s drum. She bowed and left me by the west door to go round to the women's entrance.

Towards the middle of the morning, two priests appeared in the doorway of the inner sanctum with the *tabot* balanced on their heads. Beneath the gold-embroidered drapes I could make out something square; already the shadowy faces of the priests looked uncomfortable under the weight, and the procession had not yet begun.

Outside the sun was bright in the thin air. The path down to the crater was a gauntlet of beggars and amputees, preaching monks, penitents, pious performers spaced between the boulders. One man sat cross-legged, bare from the waist up. A large rock lay in front of him. He pointed from the rock to his shoulders and then placed it behind his neck where previous performances had gouged a bloody niche in his skin; the cloth beside him was spattered with coins and small notes.

The party emerged from the trees and started a slow march

around the lake. From time to time a *debtara* would take up the drum and begin a dance. Others stopped to draw holy water, handing tins to boys who waded through the reeds, or shinnied up a tree to collect holy moss from its boughs. Some pilgrims dug clods of black volcanic mud to eat as a purgative. Billy's maid had asked me for holy water – I added some mud for good measure.

Half-way round the lake I spotted Bizunesh in the procession. She had changed into costume, a long robe of loose-weave white cotton. She was padding through the marshy ground, from tuft to tuft, the hem of her dress raised to keep it from the mud. But she was alone.

'Have you seen Girma, or his sister? I think they must have stayed in the hut.' Her sad resignation exposed the gulf between her faith and her family. (Her husband drove one of Addis's perilous blue taxis, and would not come up the mountain.) Yet towards each she showed the same devotion, a quiet madonna-like virtue, typical of Ethiopian women.

'Wait,' I said. I felt I had to find them, and ran back to look. They weren't in the hut – they were at the back of the procession, dancing with the *debtara*, and a troupe of girls in blue and gold dresses.

There is a popular Ethiopian novel based on the Zikwala pilgrimage. It is written, in English, by Daniachew Worku, and called *The Thirteenth Sun*. The title is a play on the tourist slogan: THIRTEEN MONTHS OF SUNSHINE, from the Ethiopian calendar of twelve months of thirty days, and one of five – and the idea that the sun shines for all of them.

The book first came out in 1973, the year before the revolution. A sick old nobleman is taken up the mountain by his family. His son is cynical of the old Ethiopia, and wants women and change (now he'd probably be a taxi driver in Washington). The nobleman seeks a cure from the priest and from a white witch, the 'conjure-woman'. He is given holy water, and is treated with prayers and magic, and is scrubbed with the blood of a sacrificed sheep, but, in the end, he dies.

The story is set against the unchanging, medieval backdrop of rural Ethiopia: the tough peasant women and their herbal lore, the lascivious men, and the priesthood – part Christian, part mystical. One of the last scenes involves the Abbo Day procession. The *tabot*-bearer is rooted suddenly to the spot by some malignant force. A holy man in a leopard-skin climbs a tree and starts to preach about the eighth millennium and Judgement Day: sins against the Church and against the emperor have halted the *tabot*, the Ark, God's covenant with Ethiopia. Soon, he says, 'servants shall rise against their masters. Children against their parents. . . . Rising against their emperor. Against the emperor who feeds them with milk and honey.'

And as the holy man spits out these images of the coming apocalypse, the conjure-woman – the pagan – feels a creeping revelation, tinged with desire. Her ecstatic gaze focuses on him, and she sees Christ.

The sun was hot when the *tabot* reached the church. It was midday, and the mountain's slopes were flushed their bright, limpid greens. Dog-back branches of juniper spread shadows on the rocks, and beyond them the lake's surface reflected an amphitheatre of trees.

On the rocky ground below the church I said goodbye.

Bizunesh extended her hand. 'Yes, it is best you leave. Soon the monks will celebrate and drink. By the evening they become dangerous for you, as a foreigner. You see,' she added, 'many of those monks in the forest are criminals, from prison.'

9

At the top of Churchill Avenue in Addis Ababa there is a piece of muddy waste ground, used as a football pitch and a gathering point for shoeshine boys, waifs, and beggars. To one side a bronze horse rears beneath Menelik II, the city's father. Behind him is Giorgis Cathedral – which he built – a stone polygon that survived Italian efforts to burn it during the Yekatit 12 massacre. Turning round, beyond the concrete towers and cranes at the foot of the hill, you can see Mount Zikwala.

On the other side is the City Hall, where there had been running, twice a week for over a month, an Amharic production of Molière's 'Le Tartuffe'. It was raining hard and I arrived wet from a long walk through the car-less Sunday streets. The director met me and showed me to a seat in the upper tier.

The play was presented as a straightforward farce. Tartuffe, the hypocrite priest, indulged his furtive pleasures – drinking wine, smoking a pipe, seducing his host's wife – to a packed auditorium which cheered and clapped like a pantomime audience.

Each player bowed to something on the right of the stage as they entered. From where I sat I couldn't quite see it, but at the interval I walked round. It was a picture of one of the obelisks at Axum, symbol of Ethiopia's pre-Christian culture. I asked the director why he had not used a cross, and he looked sheepish and said simply, 'It is difficult.'

I marvelled at the double standards – outside the theatre was Giorgis Cathedral. When I had passed it earlier there were crowds wandering in and out, undeterred by the rain, and without a thought of harassment.

When the play ended there was an uproar. Everyone stood and the cast came back for three curtain calls. They carried on playing their parts, improvising mannered entrances, still chiding their stage rivals.

That evening I spoke to a teacher from England who had seen the play and derided its naïvety. The nuances, he said, had been lost, unnoticed and sacrificed for gut humour. Yet Molière's seventeenth-century France was closer to Ethiopia than to modern Europe. Both are chained by strict systems of behaviour and by sacerdotal dogma. In Ethiopia such constraints are pandemic, a noble tradition in themselves; there is an inherent fear among Ethiopians that is much older than the present régime. It is so much a part of national life that visitors often find themselves suffering from an unspecified anxiety, picked up like a parasite.

In some ways farce is simply a release from it. Laughing at a ridiculous priest is a way to assuage a fear of God, or fear of any authority.

But on the surface the play's appeal is that Tartuffe is an Ethiopian: the drunken monk at Zikwala, plunged into a grand Addis household.

The following day I had lunch with the translator, Tsegaye Gabre-Medhin, in the first-floor restaurant of a hotel near Abiot. He had flu, he explained, and wore a scarf wrapped around his neck the whole time. He was an impressive man, tall, elegant, with a high forehead and hooded, serious eyes.

'So, you enjoyed the play. Was the theatre full?'

'Oh, yes,' I said.

'You see, even when it rains they come to see it. And it was Sunday too – no cars. Some of them would have walked miles. The Ethiopians are a very dramatic people – they love the theatre.'

'But why Molière?' I asked. 'Why Tartuffe?'

Tsegaye rose above his illness. 'You see, he's a modern figure – people here are very confused in their faith now. The traditional authority of the Church has been undermined – this has allowed some charlatans to come in. There are many different things to believe in now – God, Marxism, the West – and some cannot decide, they want a little piece of this and a little piece of that. It is very confusing, particularly for Ethiopians who are so devout. They need to know.'

Then he said, 'You know, the Ethiopians are like the Irish. Of course, we are both Christians and have priests like Tartuffe, but also because of war. Here we have been fighting for hundreds of years – but we don't know what for, like the Irish. It's part of the condition of this country that war is never far off. I've known three wars. My father lived through four – he fought at Adwa. If it all ended – we'd fight over the peace! Ethiopia cannot accept anyone else – we have got used to our independence. Fighting for it has just become like a habit – but we don't really know why.'

I listened intently, reluctant to dispute points in case he should shrink back behind his scarf and end the show. He sipped a cup of coffee and carried on. 'You, for instance – a *ferenj*. You get asked by a beggar for ten cents. You might decide to give it to him, or maybe you don't. But the beggar is really saying, "What's he doing here?" He keeps his pride, never feels patronized. The beggar thinks you are his child. For here is where it all began.'

With little pause, he carried on to trace the development of civilization from Ethiopia to Egypt and Greece (Aesop, he said, was in fact an Aethiop, and added to classical thinking the more ancient Ethiopian traditions), and thence to Europe and the New World.

I remained rapt by his ideas, their deftness and ease, as he played with the basis of history, turned speculation into conviction and, for a moment, made it seem that it didn't matter.

On the corner of Taitu Street, named after Menelik's empress who was so suspicious of the foreigners' magic, is one of Addis Ababa's seven cinemas. It has a large auditorium with a capacity for at least five hundred. But when I went, on a warm Saturday evening, there cannot have been more than twenty people there. Above the dado on one wall was painted: THE TRIUMPH OF SOCIALISM IS INEVITABLE!

'Spartacus' was showing. The English soundtrack hissed and crackled, and the print glowed with a strange yellow hue and was speckled with scratches. There were subtitles in French and Arabic.

Kirk Douglas, training as a gladiator, is forced into combat with one of his comrades, an 'Ethiopian', who defeats him. At the kill, the Ethiopian hurls his spear instead at the Roman box. He is executed and Kirk Douglas, as Spartacus, goes on to lead the doomed slaves' revolt. In the box is the fawning slave dealer. He is played by Peter Ustinov, who won an Oscar.

Like Spartacus, the Ethiopian Emperor Theodore, in the nineteenth century, took on the world's great power, and was martyred for it.

Theodore too rose from humble origins: his mother was a street vendor. But he re-established much of the dissipated power of the Ethiopian Crown. A tireless Christian zealot, he was by turns savage and mad, and a statesman of great intelligence. But in his later years the madness prevailed and he drank too much mead and tortured indiscriminately. In 1868 at Magdala, his mountaintop fortress, Theodore was defeated by the British expeditionary force and committed suicide.

Tsegaye Gabre-Medhin wrote a popular epic drama which lionizes Theodore. I had seen it in London, and asked him why one of the few Ethiopian emperors to have been defeated by a foreign power should be a national hero.

'Because,' explained Tsegaye, 'he died to unite Ethiopia. Before he came, the country was a mass of warring principalities, and the Galla and the Turks were everywhere. Menelik would never have beaten the Italians at Adwa, and formed the empire, if it hadn't been for Theodore. His reign was the beginning of modern Ethiopia.'

Menelik II, the fifth husband of Taitu, had been imprisoned on Magdala by Theodore at the age of eleven. But during one of Theodore's mead orgies he escaped. In recrimination the emperor amputated the hands and feet of twenty-five prisoners and tossed the bleeding bodies over the cliff.

At the same time on Magdala, but more often in favour than in irons, was a Swiss missionary who helped build a seven-ton mortar for Theodore. During the battle of Magdala his wife gave birth to a girl named Magdelena; she was Peter Ustinov's grandmother. The mortar failed after its first shot.

One evening that week, I went to a party in the part of Addis Ababa on the plain, beyond the old airport. It was an embassy party, with an opulent buffet and specially imported beer. There was the usual gallimaufry of aid workers, diplomats and select Ethiopians, and a touring dance troupe from New York.

I was introduced to a small well-dressed man, a librarian I was told.

I said I'd been working at the Institute of Ethiopian Studies. 'I'm impressed with their collection,' I said. 'Which library do you work in?'

But the man just looked at me, a little sternly, and walked away.

I told my hostess what had happened. She put her hand over her mouth and broke into peals of muffled laughter. 'No, no. He's not a librarian, he's a Liberian – he's the Liberian ambassador!'

10

Flying north from Addis Ababa, in a small Twin Otter, I watched the afternoon sun play on a lime-green mosaic of crops. Soon the plateau collapsed into the gorge of the Jema river and the Blue Nile, and survived only as thin peninsulas and islands where mud-brown huts clung to the cliffs. The most remote spots, a sliver of flat land on a knife-edge ridge, the crutch of a scarp, seemed to be sacred groves, and from their midst, staring upwards, were the shiny circles of church roofs.

From here the plateau stretches north into the heartland of Ethiopia, broken by deep canyons, like a wooden floor half-eaten by termites. Nine out of every ten Ethiopians, I had heard, have more than half a day's walk to the nearest road. Many spend two or three days each week getting to market.

Around Lake Tana the land was friendlier. Sycamore figs cast shadows over fields stippled with niger seed. The lake itself was a cloudy blue, its northern shore, fifty miles away, too distant to see. But at this end, the shores tapered down to where the Blue Nile flowed out over a cataract, beside the treetops and roofs of Bahar Dar.

The plane banked towards the new airstrip. Out of the port windows the sun had rinsed the scene of its colour. But everyone leaned across to look. I had a clear view and saw the red mud scar before them. It ran across a field and into a small gully. Bushes lay flattened but still green. Behind me a girl bent forward in her seat, and was sick. We were level with the tops of the trees when there was a brief flash from the gully, and the sun caught the tailplane of the crashed Boeing.

Bahar Dar is a disappointing place. The Emperor nurtured it as one of his country's great cities, and harnassed part of the Blue Nile for hydro-electricity. He laid a wide avenue to follow the dog-leg line of the shore, and attracted institutions: a teacher-training college, a Russian technical school, a hospital now staffed by East Germans, and a textile mill. The town grew from a fishing village to a place of about 20,000 people by 1970. At one time – in the footloose tradition of emperors before him – he even considered making it his capital.

There is still a somnolent sense that development is happening, that the town is approaching a period of exciting transition. Perhaps it is – but it's now been forty years.

I avoided the two government hotels and found a private place towards the Blue Nile bridge. The manager took my permit and copied details on to a form. Then he said, 'Please hand in your pistol.'

'But I have no pistol.'

'No pistol?' He shook his head, and put a dash in the appropriate column.

I took my rucksack out into the yard. The rooms backed on to stone verandas that stretched the length of two low buildings. The garden was swollen with a wealth of shrubs, grown fat on the lake's fertile air.

'Mr Philip.' I turned to see someone I couldn't quite place. 'It's Abraham,' he said, not smiling.

I greeted him and then remembered. I'd met him on my last trip, at a service in Addis Ababa – he had helped me with some research I was doing for the BBC.

Later we walked down to the bridge in the last half-hour of daylight. The road ran above a marsh, on a grassy embankment, and bustled with marching crowds – barefoot farmers herding laden mules and cattle, lone fishermen, schoolchildren, bicyclists, occasionally a belching lorry or a bus hurrying into town before dark. This is one of only two roadbridges over the Blue Nile on its 400-mile journey through Ethiopia. There are also two footbridges, built by the Portuguese in the seventeenth century, and both within forty miles of Lake Tana.

The river was unusually full, and had half-swallowed its green banks. The spate tugged at a slack electric cable that struggled to cross it, and Abraham put one foot up on the parapet and leaned on his knee.

There was something odd about him. He seemed unsurprised

to see me, as though I was expected. I couldn't help thinking he was a government stooge. He asked about my permit and my work and altogether appeared very different from how I remembered him. He worked, he told me, as a development manager at the textile mill.

I kept thinking of bizarre, intricate connections, ways he could have known I was coming here. But none of them made any sense.

That evening was strikingly beautiful. The sun fell through burning strata of red and gold; on the embankment a ground mist wrapped itself around the feet of pedestrians; egret and tree-duck flew in silhouette against the cold northern sky, and in the rushes a thousand frogs croaked into chorus.

Of the world's great rivers, none has more consistently excited man's imagination than the Nile: rising from the tears of Isis, it brought fertile soil and moisture from the Land of the Sun, the Ethiopian interior, an elixir that spawned the earliest great civilization, and inspired Alexander and Napoleon to quest for its source.

The Nile was mapped finally in the late nineteenth century. Shrewd new Freudians liked to point out the graphic female image of the river's two lakes, Tana and Victoria: twin founts of fertility winding down to the great Nile Basin.

From Lake Tana the Blue Nile pays brief respect to the plateau before cutting through it, fifteen miles to the south. I drove there with Efrem who taught literature to teacher trainees at the college – mostly holy literature, he told me, the Bible, the Koran, but also European authors. He asked me about Hardy's Wessex and where the famous Lakes were.

'I have a friend at Leeds University,' he said. 'Where is that?'

'In Yorkshire,' I explained. 'Near Brontë Country.'

'Ah! Wuthering Heights. Tell me, the moors – are they really that craggy?'

'If anything, craggier,' I said.

Efrem smiled. He turned to look out of the Land Rover window, towards hills wrapped in green fur-like scrub, the course of the young Nile mirrored in a blue mist against it – and thought of Leeds and envied his friend.

The Tisissat Falls are ubiquitous. They appear, like the President, in framed pictures in hotel bars, on airline and tourist posters and on the back of the green, 1 birr banknotes.

In reality, they are impressive. But they pale beside the rhapsodies of James Bruce, who went there in 1770:

> it struck me with a kind of stupor, and a total oblivion of where I was, and of every other sublunary concern. It was one of the most magnificent, stupendous sights in the creation. . . .

He too saw the waterfall in flood and described a single sheet of water. Now the span is broken by rocks and small islands. Ferns erupt from every crevice, dampened by a perpetual mist, an oasis of tropical Africa in the mountains.

Efrem was standing beside an incense tree; he pointed out the small globules of resin bulging from its bole. Then he nodded towards the falls. 'You know,' he said, above the roar of the water, 'I think this year it is the most water I have seen. The rains were very big.' He shrugged and added, 'I don't understand it. Usually the rains are over before *Maskal*.'

Walking back to the village, we paused on the Portuguese bridge, the border between Gojjam and Gondar. A sentry had rested his rifle beside a massive rounded boulder, and sat to talk to a party of goatherds. The bridge is rough built, of stone, a single high arch. All the water that flows over Tisissat half a mile upstream is squeezed here through the narrow fissure. At its widest no more than 10 yards wide, there is a place where during the dry season a man can jump across, but the torrent is reputedly 150 feet deep.

From this point the Blue Nile is lost to Ethiopia. It enters a gorge which reaches a depth of over a mile. Ethiopians never enter its malarial abyss, and only in the late sixties was it explored.

On the Sudanese border it comes out again into the sunlight, and winds across the desert towards Khartoum.

'Now,' said Efrem, 'we must have some *tej!*'

Back in the village we found a *tej* house and sat inside against an uneven clay wall. A group of women half stood and nodded greetings. A barefoot girl shuffled across the mud floor and placed chemists' beakers on the table. She filled them with mead the colour of orange juice.

Efrem nodded. 'Good *tej.*'

Gojjam is renowned for its *mar,* wild honey sweetened by local flowers, and fermented into *tej.* Now the province's landscape, blossoming in the late rains, was a paradise for bees: vast bushes of poinsettia, flowering mimosa, jacaranda, and the Nandi flame tree's burning orange blooms.

Efrem emptied his beaker, and ordered some more. 'You know,' he said, 'whenever I go to Tisissat, I always think of the poem "Kubla Khan".'

He then recalled the lines:

> 'Where Alph, the sacred river, ran
> Through caverns measureless to man
> Down to a sunless sea.

'I think Coleridge must have come like you to Ethiopia!'

Coleridge had done the next best thing. At Cambridge in the early 1790s, he had read the five volumes of James Bruce's *Travels to Discover the Source of the Nile.*

James Bruce – Abyssinian Bruce – was a Romantic, but an active one. His journey was a medieval quest: twelve years of lonely privation through exotic lands, towards a patch of boggy ground seventy miles to the south of Lake Tana.

For Coleridge it struck a deep chord. Each time he read it, he was with Bruce in the mountains, following him through the barbaric splendour of the Ethiopian court, on constant campaigns, relishing the eccentric rulers, the fairy-tale landscape and gushing prose. He would recommend the book to anyone who hadn't read it, and is remembered in Bristol during the hot summer of 1795, running with Southey from Redcliff towards the river, one of Bruce's volumes tucked under his arm.

The thought of exotic places was a repeated prop for Coleridge. For a long time he fostered plans for a commune in the New World. One site was the West Indian island of Nevis, where Wordsworth's friends, the Pinney family, had estates. Here, he hoped, the combined work of himself, Southey and Wordsworth would make the place 'more illustrious than Cos or Lesbos!'

But Coleridge's travels were never much more than imaginary, and he relied on the accounts of others.

In *The Road to Xanadu,* John Livingston Lowes charts the geography of Coleridge's imagination. He cites Bruce's Nile as a possible source for Kubla Khan's sacred river. Yet there are others – the Nile is not the world's only sacred river. But in volume IV of his *Travels,* Bruce tells a story with more specific imagery. One day he and King Tekla Haimanot were riding to inspect a horse. Tekla Haimanot wore an imperial cloak. Only his eyes were visible and locks of uncut hair leaked through its folds. Crossing a brook, the king's cloak was caught by a sprig of *kantuffa,* a thorny shrub. Tekla Haimanot's face and shoulders were exposed. The king called for the local chief.

When he arrived, one of the king's officers drew two thongs from his belt. He threw them around the heads of the chief and his son. Then he hoisted them from a tree. The party reassembled and set off, leaving the bodies dangling by the neck:

> And all should cry, Beware! Beware!
> His flashing eyes, his floating hair!

Before Bruce had written his epic, Horace Walpole heard him tell this story at a dinner-party in London – he dismissed it as fantasy. Dr Johnson was able to pour his own informed dissent on Bruce: he had translated the account of the Portuguese Lobo, and from that it seems the Jesuits beat Bruce to the source of the Blue Nile by more than 150 years. (Bruce knew of the claim but 'hated the Jesuits as others hate rats', and was unwilling to accept it.)

If Lowes is right, Coleridge used Bruce's image as a spectre, a dark figure to haunt the shadows of Paradise. All through the poem, visions of an earthly paradise appear among green hills, gorges, dashing rivers, to be tainted with a sense of unease – like modern Ethiopia itself.

Efrem called for some more *tej*. It was almost midday and the sun threw spears of light between the thatch. The *tej* had dissolved the morning, and through the door I watched a child come into the shade, prop herself against the jamb, and stare at us.

Efrem was enjoying himself. 'Oh, "Kubla Khan" – the pictures! There is another place near here where the river goes underground. The people have many legends about it. They say it goes down to hell!

'But the poem reminds me too of other places,' his voice became suddenly earnest, and I could hear him explaining it to his Ethiopian students. 'The caves at Sof Omar, and the prisons where emperors used to send young royal children. Sometimes they were sent to the islands of Lake Tana, or to remote mountains – to teach good habits.'

Other than Xanadu the only specific places mentioned by name in 'Kubla Khan' are in these lines:

> A damsel with a dulcimer
> In a vision once I saw
> It was an Abyssinian maid
> And on her dulcimer she played
> Singing of Mount Abora.

Mount Abora is a fictitious place. Perhaps Coleridge confused it with the river Atbara of the Ancient World – Astaboras. In his third volume, James Bruce describes a torrid stream, the Tacazze, which rises in the Ethiopian highlands and joins the Nile near Berber in the Sudan. To the Ancients, the Tacazze was a tributary of the Atbara.

Or he may have been thinking of Mount Amara, close in spelling to Abora and to Amhara, Ethiopia's ruling people. I called up Coleridge's manuscript in the British Museum and saw that, originally, he *did* write Amara.

Mount Amara features in a good deal of that body of post-medieval literature that was part mythology, part travelogue. Coleridge's famously wide reading included a number of references to Amara. It crops up in Milton, in the fourth book of *Paradise Lost*. And in *Purchas His Pilgrimage* – the book on the poet's knee when he slept and 'dreamt' 'Kubla Khan' – there is a whole chapter entitled 'Of the Hill Amara: and the rarities therein'.

The rarities described have a Prester John-like opulence: turquoise, emeralds and coral (rarer in the mountains than gold), and a library – here the bibliophilic Coleridge must have gloated – of three great halls 200 paces long, with books on the sciences, cosmography, philosophy, the apocryphal writings of Enoch, Abraham and Job (when he was rich again), Aquinas and Augustine and many other authors that no one knew. In short, says Purchas, Amara had the greatest library in the world.

There is no doubting that from Purchas's other details of the hill, it is based on accounts of a specific place. It is clearly Ethiopia, Homer's Ethiopia: Purchas has the gods feasting there as they do in the *Iliad* – and biblical Ethiopia: Queen Candace is baptized on the hill by Philip, a eunuch (a confusion of the story of the Apostle Philip who converts the Ethiopian eunuch in Acts 8).

Within Ethiopia, Purchas narrows it down by having the library attached to the Monastery of the Holy Cross. But what confirms the site of Amara is that here, on the 'impenetrable' hill, were kept the princes of the royal line.

This means Amara has to be Gishen Mariam, the mountain-top monastery 150 miles west of Tisissat, site of the True Cross, and until the seventeenth century the place emperors sent their sons.

Coleridge's Abyssinia is Ethiopia. For centuries, the names have followed each other around the world's maps and literature, as baffling to strangers as a pair of identical twins.

Abyssinia derives from *Habashat,* the name given by Arabs to the people on the southern coast of the Red Sea (in Arabic, *Habashat* also means 'mixed' and the Ethiopians find it pejorative). The name trickled through the Arab world to Europe, but, strangely, not until the eighteenth century did Abyssinia become widely used: the Portuguese left Ethiopia in 1634, James Bruce went to Abyssinia in 1769.

In the years in between, something shifted the balance to 'Abyssinia'. Another favourite of Coleridge, Thomas Burnet, offers a clue as to why. In 1690 he published *The Sacred Theory of the Earth,* in which he cites a treatise from an ancient Abyssinian library (presumably Gishen): '. . . they say the first earth was much greater than the present . . . that it was smooth and regular in its surface, without mountains or valleys'. Then, when man became wicked, a great abyss was opened up and the waters spouted from it and the earth was flooded. The present earth, with its hills and jagged coastlines, serves as a constant reminder of the sins of the flood: for how could God have created anything so irregular?

The theory became known in certain quarters as 'The Abyssinian Philosophy'. In the early days of the Enlightenment its critics saw it as heretical as the ideas of Descartes. But Descartes and his colleagues won out and Burnet's theory – now unscientific – was remembered only for its dazzling imagery.

One possible reason for Bruce's preference for 'Abyssinia' was that, since the Portuguese had been expelled, Ethiopia had cut herself off from Western Europe. News of the country came indirectly, through the Arabic-speaking world.

But the phonetic link between the Arabic *Habashat* and 'Abyssinia' seems to me a weak one. Other spellings were around: Dr Johnson's Abissinia; the French used Abissinie, the Germans Abessinia. I like to think that, for dreamers like Bruce and Coleridge, something of the 'abyss' crept into the spelling, establishing it as Abyssinia, and colouring ideas of the country with the primeval images of Burnet's cosmogony.

11

Abraham was sitting outside his room, dozing beneath the dome of an outsize jacaranda. His arms were folded pompously across his chest, and at his feet lay a fat novel by James Clavell, unopened. I had tempered my suspicions of him, and decided he wasn't a spy. But I still found him odd.

He woke and offered me tea. Afterwards I slipped away to read in the garden. The afternoon was still and warm. A few cirrus had seeped high into the western sky above the lake, and the shrubs behind my chair hummed with bees. I watched a small blue waxbill wriggle down into the cooler dust, and sit there unmoving. Everything seemed suspended in that timeless moment of mid-afternoon.

A young woman came through the trees with an armful of dripping clothes. I had seen her before – she lived with her husband in the hotel, a few rooms along the veranda from me. She had high delicate bones and a powerful expression, dark eyes that were both shy and assured; hers was the refined beauty of so many Ethiopians.

Later, after dark, I went with her and her husband, Teklu, to the *kebelle* store. These government stores were the first to receive things in scarce supply, which included beer. It was a dingy hut, its rafters full of cobwebs. There were three wooden tables and some benches.

Teklu had a lazy eye and an ebullient wit. A few weeks earlier he had been due to fly to Asmara on the Boeing that crashed. When he went to the airstrip, they'd told him it was full.

'God smiled on me that day!' he grinned. 'Only eleven survived – four of them children.' He paused. 'You see, if we had the technology, fewer people would have died. When the plane caught fire, the peasants had to bring water up from the little river in buckets.'

Back in his room Teklu showed me pictures of his son. He was about to be two, and stared wide-eyed and pudding-faced at the camera. Teklu's wife turned on a small radio. All evening she had not said a word, silenced by the stifling conventions of her sex – even my praise for her child had brought only smiles.

A little later a friend of hers came round. She wore a canary yellow dress and had the more negroid features of southern Ethiopia: darker skin, fuller lips and hair more tightly curled than the highland Ethiopians. She was even more taciturn and offered no more than bashful mumbles to my questions.

'Why do you want to talk to her?' said Teklu, with more surprise than rancour when she had left. 'She's black.'

One day I walked over the Blue Nile to a new orphanage site. A team of barelegged workers was breaking the black soil with mattocks, in front of a row of dormitory huts.

'We will grow our own vegetables and fruit.' The director pointed to a grove of freshly-planted papaya. 'And the children will be able to learn about basic farming, as well as subjects in the classroom. Next month the first one hundred and fifty are arriving.'

The project had been set up by the Church of England, to deal with some of the orphans of the last famine, from Gondar and Wollo. Alemayu had been put in charge. He was a serious young man, and a committed member of his own Church.

'In Ethiopia our Church is linked very closely to the heart of the people – and also to politics. At the time of the revolution, the young intellectuals denied the existence of God. Other Christians wanted a more modern religion, and the pentecostal movement grew at that time. But in the last few years there has been a return to the traditions.'

'So young people go to church?'

'Oh yes, many young people.' He bent to pick some stones out of a new vegetable bed. 'There's a young singer – Ethiopia's most popular singer. He is rich, has good clothes and all the women want to love him. One of his girls took him to church – he had never been before. But now he goes often, and fasts each week and makes vows. And last year for the first time – there was great talk about it – he made the pilgrimage up to Mount Zikwala.'

We walked to the high point of his land. Across the stream, a huge new barn was going up. Three or four hammers pecked at its frame. In the distance was Lake Tana. The hinterland in this corner was a wide marsh, flooded by the escaping waters of the Blue Nile which dashed over the cataract at the start of the long journey to Egypt and the Mediterranean.

'What's that?' I pointed to the shell of a concrete building.

'Oh that,' he smiled. 'That belonged to the project that was here before. They had to abandon it.'

It seems some of the old superstitions about the Nile remain. The Ethiopians had plans for an irrigation scheme using a dam just below the cataract. But it had to be called off when the Egyptian government smelt an imperialist conspiracy to ransom their water.

Lake Tana's freight company had a pre-fab office above the concrete quay. I told them I wanted to visit the islands, and took my papers from one office to another until, after half an hour or so, I reached the manager. Behind his desk the flukes of an admiralty anchor had been painted with the legend MARINE COMPANY.

'Yes. I have a boat you can take. It is eighty US dollars per hour.'

'But I need to spend a number of days on the lake. Could I go on the freight boat?'

'The problem,' he said, 'is hospitality and entertainment. Also there is a risk for you.' The risk wasn't specified, and I told him that I did not want entertainment.

Finally he gave in. 'You may have a ticket. That is one US dollar. But you will need a permit.'

At Security, I was shown into the chief's office. He was away in Addis, and a deputy was enjoying his chair. On his desk, a book entitled simply *Marxist Philosophy* lay beneath two plastic flags – the Red flag and the Ethiopian tricolour. The man's face seemed set in a permanent scowl, and his lower lip hung towards his chin like a tumour. On entering the room I felt a sudden anxiety, a schoolboy's anxiety standing in the headmaster's study.

He read my papers slowly, and I knew then he was going to say no. I studied a fold of skin above the lid of his right eye which rippled and twitched; I marvelled at the symmetry of his belly, looking for flaws in the perfect semi-sphere it formed beneath his shirt. Were there, I wondered, any moments of joy for this man – did he beat his wife? Did his children hate him?

'From Gondar,' he grunted cryptically.

He handed back my papers. My route would take me into Gondar province. I would need, therefore, a permit from their local Security, and there was no chance of getting that before the boat left the following morning. I realized he knew that.

I took my papers and walked out into the sun, and noticed, almost immediately, a hardening in my attitude.

In the afternoon, I walked off my frustration down the far bank of the Blue Nile. Some miles to the south the Emperor had built a palace on a spur above the river. From here I surveyed the forbidden lake.

Twelve miles above Bahar Dar, the shores widened and stretched open-armed towards the mountains around Gondar. The hump-backed islands of Kibran and Daga Istifanos – both monasteries – broke the polished surface like stepping stones. Above them the sky was blue and cloudless – except for a tiny anvil of cumulus swelling above the far peaks.

A group of boys came up the slope. One of them spoke a precocious English. 'What is the main output of your country, sir?' he asked. 'Is it car, or camera?'

I told him I wasn't sure. Then I pointed to a pair of yellow weavers who were squabbling for the sanctuary of a stalk of maize. 'Look!'

But he turned away, saying, 'Ethiopia has six hundred and fifty-five species of birds.'

So I talked to his friends, and amused them by writing out their names in a hesitant Amharic script.

Half-a-dozen cattle grazed towards us; their cowherd stood against a dead acacia. He played a pipe, and its haunting notes hung on the breeze. Behind him, the sky dimmed to a dark blue in the dusk, and the new moon rose between the rotten boughs.

When I got back to Bahar Dar it was dark, but the surface of the lake pulsed with the reflection of distant lightning.

Beneath the neo-byzantine church of Bahar Dar Giorgis, the lake's fishermen land their catches for the town's co-operative. I found there a small fibreglass skiff with an outboard, its bilges writhing with Nile perch and a three-pound catfish. The boat belonged, I was told, to the monastery a few miles along the western shore. They agreed to take me there to ask the abbot's permission to use it – I planned to go to those of the islands under local administration.

We pushed through the reeds and out into the lake. A crane rose and dragged its long legs out of the water.

At the monastery I went to see the abbot, and gave him a letter from the patriarchate in Addis. He wore fish-bowl glasses and explained that he must ask his bishop about the boat. His bishop had gone to Addis – but he was going to speak to him that evening on the telephone.

Outside, a Land Cruiser pulled up and a large Dutchman got out. I had heard about this man in the town. He was acting as a consultant for the lake's fishery project. He had a high, bald head and a complexion hardened from years in the tropics. In his hut a local woman was squatting beside a stove, cooking fish.

I asked him about the boat.

'I give them the boat and then it is their responsibility if they want you to use it.' He picked up a packet of Rothmans, and flicked one into his mouth. 'The bishop will say no.'

On the wall was a pencil map of the lake speckled with soundings, an anatomical drawing of a fish and one or two spreads from colour magazines; a plaster-cast madonna stood in the corner. The Dutchman rose and filled two glasses with brandy and ice.

'My father started by fishing from a rowing boat in the Zuider Zee,' he said, handing me a glass. 'That's where I was born. Sometimes my mother used to beg – like these people.'

He emptied his glass and held it up for the woman to refill. 'Look, when I was young I was in England. I had an uncle and I listened to all his stories. You know, he told me that in England people used to walk in rags – just a little piece of cotton . . . like this.' He pointed at the woman behind him.

'At that time I used to fish on the Humber, and lived at Scunthorpe. Ah! We caught so many eels then!' He sighed and looked into his drink, dreaming of the tight lines of his youth. Then he leaned forward, and waved his finger. 'But I tell you, I have been all over the world – Africa, the Far East, America – but never have I seen so many fish in one place as at Arba Minch, in the south of this country.'

The next morning I walked the few miles back to the monastery. I arrived at eight, as I'd agreed with the abbot. The Dutchman was writing a letter in front of his hut, shaded from the morning sun by an acacia.

'They've been up all night yelling and screaming in the church.' He pointed through the trees. 'I saw the dean slip back to his hut a short time ago. He will know about the boat.'

The dean's maid told me he was asleep. But I heard him call, and pushed back a cloth that hung over his doorway. His room was a gallery of saints: Tekla Haimanot, Archangels Gabriel and Mikhael, Giorgis, the Apostles and Christ (but no Maryam). They were propped on shelves against the clay wall.

The dean sat up in his bed. 'Good morning, you are well?'

'I am well, thank you. Do you know about the boat?'

'The abbot tried, but the line was cut.'

So I went back to the Dutchman, and his twin passions of fish and poverty.

He commiserated with my problems. 'Of all the countries in Africa, Ethiopia is the most difficult. And I have been to all of them. Here it is permission for everything. No good – papers, always papers! Come, let me show you the fishery.'

We walked a little way around the shore. He pointed to a group of tatty huts. 'Those are for the begging monks. They sleep six to a shelter.'

One of the mendicants was reading a leather-bound Ge'ez text. The Dutchman swayed his huge frame as if to hit him, and the man ducked and dropped the book. The other monks grinned with pleasure.

'Is this your food?' The Dutchman pointed to a sheet of tin. On it were scattered corners of teff-bread, begged from local huts; they were crawling with flies.

'Soon,' he said, 'I think you die!' And they all laughed. As we left, a group of blind monks filed into the clearing, each one gripping the robe of the one in front. The Dutchman greeted them.

The fishery stood beside a beach of grey sand, a low wooden shed full of spares for the engines, and bobbins of white nylon. He had been teaching the women to make nets, wrapping twine around batons of a specific width. 'Soon they will be able to sell nets from here to the other lakes. Already they tie quicker than me!'

A fibreglass dinghy had just come in with a catch, and we took some perch for the begging monks, and walked back.

We met the dean on the path. He said to me, 'Did you come earlier? I think we have a boat.' He turned to the Dutchman and asked about fuel. I didn't find out what had changed his mind, and we walked down to the store.

'Do you have a permit?'

'Yes.' I showed him my papers.

'But you will need a visa from local Security.'

So a little later we drove into Bahar Dar. The deputy Security Chief was standing on the balcony of his first-floor office. He was wiping his hands with a cloth. When I went in to see him, his eye-lid twitched as he re-examined my permit.

He said no. There was nothing on the permit to say I could travel by boat – only by plane. He thrust the paper back at me, and told me to get out.

Outside the dean shrugged when I told him. 'You see, if we take you,' he sounded relieved, 'tomorrow Security will say – who was that? And they will put us in prison. They have authority to kill us.'

I said I understood, then walked through the trees to the lakeside. I sat beneath the huge, lion limbs of a fig tree, its roots swamped by the high water, its foliage full of the squawks of a hornbill. The day was warm and clear, and the sun played on the water like a glittering slick. From the north a light breeze chased tiny waves on to the tufa, and I thought of my first visit to Lake Tana, of the places I hadn't seen then, the monasteries near the eastern shore, the island where the Holy Family stayed during their flight from Herod, and the ruined Portuguese palace at Gorgora. I squinted at the islands, grey-blue shadows twenty miles through the haze, and cursed Security.

There was no defensible reason for denying me permission – no military installations, no guerilla activity for fifty miles at the very least, nothing unsightly or dangerous. But I placed it in the now familiar context of 'authority', that numbing yoke which is spread over the whole country, part petty, part terrible.

Sooner or later every revolution seems to reach a point when its advocates stop trying to gain power and become nervous about losing it, the point where ideology ends and dictatorship begins. In Ethiopia the conspicuous brutality of the Red Terror had been followed by a bewildered equilibrium: the Dergue's survival seemed now more dependant on confusing people than frightening them.

Since the early 1980s the authority had become a little calmer and was now simply irascible – and that made it unpredictable. The law was a whim, not a rule: an amorphous, unknowable force. At no time did I ever have a clear idea what I could, or could not do. Permission was denied by making it conditional, rather than by saying no. Security had said that I could have the papers, if I got them from Gondar, or, the second time, from Addis Ababa. So time could be wasted on endless battles, and the war forgotten. For Ethiopians, most chance of initiative – the seed of subversion – is swallowed by the tedious complexities of everyday living.

Some people are astonished that such a proud and ancient race, and one whose culture rests on the Covenant, could bow to this tyranny. But the truth is that the revolution did not change all that much. (Earlier travelogues are full of permit problems: Powell-Cotton was given a hunting pass by Menelik II for the area from Addis to a point on the road some distance north. But when he tried to use the permit he was told he couldn't leave the road.) Some power has been secularised, a few Maoist placards erected, and the statues of lions stripped of their sceptres and crowns, but not removed. For the majority of Ethiopians, life is still much the same: an esoteric bureaucracy has replaced the court and the nobility, the priesthood still deliver prayers in Ge'ez, and hide the mysteries behind clouds of incense, and behind the iconostasis, bright with benign images of the Trinity, and bloody ones of martyrdom. The Church, the legacy of the Crown, centuries of civil wars and thwarted invasions – these things make Ethiopia more conservative than the newer countries on the African continent. The Ethiopians are a people deeply aware of their past, which gives them, on occasions, an air of weary fatalism.

12

Dr Merid had arranged permits for me the first time I went to Lake Tana. He had a philosophy doctorate from some college in the southern United States, and useful influence in the party.

'Beware of the storms on the lake,' he had warned, 'and the *shifta!*'

'*Shifta*?'

'They are bandits, very dangerous.' Then he had given me a life-jacket, and one for Yared.

Yared was a Tigrean. At fourteen he had left his family, and gone into the mountains to fight for the Tigrean Peoples Liberation Front. At that time, just after the revolution, the country was in chaos and the Tigreans took the chance to escalate their resistance to Addis Ababa's rule. Some years later, Yared was captured. But he escaped and walked to Addis to be with his brother. There he lived in anonymity, the authorities unaware of his rebellious past. He had the happy-go-lucky manner of those who have lived with danger, and always wore the same ill-cut sports jacket and zip-up ankle boots.

He shared his name with the sixth-century father of Ethiopian church music. In Giorgis Cathedral in Addis Ababa, there is a painting of a young St Yared. He is sitting under a tree looking despondent. The myth tells of problems with his musical studies: he went out and sat by the tree and decided to give up. Beside him, a caterpillar was struggling up the tree to pupate. Three times it fell down, but finally reached a bough and wove its cocoon. St Yared resolved then to continue and, so the story goes, went on to compose all of Ethiopia's religious music.

Yared and I spent two days in a bus, then took the freight boat at Bahar Dar across the lake to Dek island. The boat was called *Yetana Nesh* and was dangerously overloaded. It smelt of diesel and was loaded with sacks of grain and wild honey. We bought a gourd's-worth of the honey, and lived off it for days, scraping away the crust of dead bees and wax and twigs, until that was all that was left.

Yetana Nesh pulled into a small jetty crammed with islanders. Sacks were loaded and unloaded, and a sick child carried on board. She gave two blasts on her steam whistle and chugged out of the lagoon. Yared and I watched her go, then walked the few miles to Dek's far shore, and pitched a tent.

'Swim?' said Yared.

'Yes! Any bilharzia – or crocodiles?'

But he just yelled, '*Aysore*!' (a Tigrean battle cry), and dived into the lake.

I joined him.

Through the trees came villagers in small groups. They washed themselves and collected water but did not swim. Afterwards a young boy pulled back the reeds and showed us why. A huge python lay rotting in the swamp. Yared shook his head and grinned.

One morning before dawn there was a rainstorm. For two hours it beat the trees and hissed in the grass. I woke to water rising in the tent. Already it had swamped my clothes and was creeping towards my notebook.

Outside it was still raining hard. We ferried our belongings to the schoolroom, running through marshy grass and unbroken rain. My bare feet slipped in some mud and I tore my shin on a tufa boulder. Inside the school hut, a woman lit a fire on the mud floor, and bathed my leg, stemming the blood with a dressing of fresh leaves.

Yared returned with some wood and said, 'Ah, what a beautiful adventure!'

All morning I sat beside the fire and felt my temperature rising. The rain tapped on the schoolroom roof, and the children's faces filled the doorway. But that afternoon the skies cleared, and the sun drew clouds of mist from the coffee groves. Yared found a *tankwa*, a papyrus canoe, and we paddled across to the island of Daga. A young monk watched us from the forest as we pulled the boat on to a black shingle beach.

From the lake, Daga appears as a green woolly mass, so densely wooded that no features appear. The island rises 300 feet but is no more than half a mile long. It is home to about eighty monks, but no women – not even hens – are allowed upon the island. Christianity was brought here in the thirteenth century, by a bishop who crossed the lake on a stone.

'What's that?' I pointed to a cairn beside the path.

Yared asked the monk. There, he said, the Emperor Zara Yaqob appeared sitting beneath a tree, seven years after his death. He had been wandering his kingdom in limbo. But among the placid shadows of the island's forest, he was able to finally relinquish his stubborn mortality.

On the summit is the church of Daga Istifanos. It seemed in poor repair – inside Yared pointed to talons of damp that had crept through the thatch, threatening the frescoes. He persuaded the monks to uncover a painting of the madonna that I had heard about. At her breast is Christ, and she is flanked by angels, a matronly figure in blues and earthy yellows. It is early – commissioned by Zara Yaqob in the fifteenth century – a relic of medieval Ethiopia, on this island too remote for the sixteenth-century purges of Ahmed Gran.

Beside the church is a stone-built feretory, the *Ika'bet*. 'This,' said the monk, 'is a very special place!'

The monk took down three crowns from a shelf inside. They were made of rosewood, and filigreed with silver.

'Who's were they?' I asked.

The monk put a finger on top of each one in turn. 'Tekla Haimanot . . . Tewodros . . . Yohannis IV.'

At the entrance to another, darker chamber the monk dithered, but Yared urged him to go in.

Two steps led down to a crypt. The candle threw a dim light on to more wooden shelves. The untreated slats glowed a pale ochre between dark timber boxes. Yared took the candle and held it above one of the boxes: they were glass-topped coffins.

In the flickering light he pointed at the skeleton of Emperor Zara Yaqob. Major Cheesman, who first explored the lake in the 1930s was told that this corpse was 'too holy to see'; but Yared would not accept this. The emperor's skull had broken away from his spine with age, as had fragments of the ribs and limbs. But his right foot showed a curious deformity.

Zara Yaqob's reign was the greatest of the Ethiopian renaissance in the fourteenth and fifteenth centuries. He merited the new power conferred on the Crown by the *Kebra Nagast*, and did much to establish the mystical bond between Church and State. In the monasteries, monks traced the Ge'ez characters of hagiographies on to parchment, and there was much proselytizing and church-building. Most of this work was later destroyed by Ahmed Gran.

'Look,' said Yared. 'You see his foot is bent.' He held the flame over the emperor's legs, and I could see the phalanges seemed to arch.

'Why's that?'

'He used to pray on one leg – all the time, says the monk!'

Other monarchs lay there: Dawit I (1382–1413), Za Dengel (1603–4), and on the floor a large box of assorted bones. 'More kings,' said the monk.

One other coffin contained the embalmed body of Emperor Fasilades. Tattered skin hung like vellum from his bones, and clung in places to his face. With him was his seven-year-old son Isur who had briefly succeeded him. His coronation was a hot, frantic day, and nobles bustled around preparing for the celebratory evening banquet. Musicians assembled and cattle were brought; later raw steaks would be cut from their living haunches. But when attendants went to collect the young king they found he was dead; his reign had lasted just six hours.

His father's reign had had more impact. In 1634 he banished the Jesuits from Ethiopia and stirred the xenophobia that lies so close to the surface among the highlanders. He isolated the kingdom from Western Europe for two hundred years. So vehement was his hatred of Europeans that Fasilades even courted relations with the Muslims.

For his father, Emperor Susenyos, had betrayed the Ethiopian Christians: he had become a Roman Catholic.

The Portuguese first came to Ethiopia in the 1520s, looking for Prester John. What they found was a kingdom cowering in the mountains, clinging to its faith in the face of repeated Muslim attacks. Near Lake Tana they helped the Ethiopians defeat the hordes of Ahmed Gran and by the beginning of the seventeenth century, they had been followed by a number of plucky Jesuit missionaries. The myth of the great Christian potentate faded and they became convinced that here was a people who needed the civilizing influence of Rome. The Jesuit author, Philip Caraman, has given a recent account of this bizarre mission in his book *The Lost Empire.*

Ten miles from the Tisissat Falls, in 1607, Susenyos won the battle that earned him the throne. The following year he was crowned emperor at Axum. Son of a prince and a slave, Susenyos inherited a country fragmented by squabbling princes. Not least of his problems was a corrupt and decadent clergy, but these foreign Christians impressed him with their temperance and learning, and their firearms: his letters to them are full of requests for guns. He gave them land at Gorgora on the northern shore of Lake Tana, and had its boundaries marked by burying goats' heads. A fine palace was built and monks from the islands would paddle ashore to dispute the dual nature of Christ.

Around *Timkat*, the Ethiopian Christmas, in 1626 there arrived at Gorgora the rather pompous figure of Alfonso Mendes. He had been awarded the Catholic Patriarchate of Ethiopia by his King, Philip IV of Spain. Soon after his arrival he was summoned to the court of Susenyos.

Mendes was met by a show of 15,000 armed horsemen, dancing *debtara,* and bowing gentry. He rode to the church on a piebald horse tacked in white damask. He dismounted and walked up to the chancel; as he approached the emperor, a sung Benedictus filled the church.

Susenyos had already announced his allegiance to Rome, explaining that the Monophysite tenet was a mistake. He cited the sins of the Ethiopian clergy, their abuse of young virgins, and the profligacy of Bishop Abuna Petros who had to be imprisoned on Dek island and was later killed in battle. On that day, 11 February 1626, the emperor and a host of the nobility were received by Mendes into the Catholic Church.

The rest of the country was not so receptive. The account by Mendes's missionary Jeronimo Lobo was translated into English by Dr Johnson and published in England in 1735. It describes the horrified flight of Ethiopian villagers as the Jesuits approached with the Roman Mass, and a terrible famine blamed on their heretical mission.

The country collapsed into religious fratricide. On 27 June 1632, Susenyos's brother led a force against him and 8000 people died. The Ethiopians, who were well used to fighting Muslims or pagans could not bear to kill their kin.

'How long,' they demanded the emperor, 'shall we thrust our swords into our own bowels?'

Susenyos abdicated in favour of his son Fasilades, who pronounced a return to tradition with a mass baptism and circumcision. There was great celebration and the people danced and broke their rosaries, chanting:

> At length the sheep of Ethiopia freed
> From the bad lions of the West
> And safely in their pastures feed.
> St Mark and Cyril's doctrines have overcome
> The follies of the Church of Rome!

Back on Dek I walked with Yared around the northern shore of the island to the remote church of Debra Kota Mariam. It stands alone in thick woods beside the lake. Through the leaves I watched the unruffled water stretch twenty miles into the haze, towards the dim outline of the land around Gorgora.

The only other building in the area was the hut of the priest. He wore the church key around his neck, and appeared through the trees rubbing a midday sleep from his eyes. The priest told us the church had been built in the fourth or fifth century, after the reign of the twins Abraha and Atsbaha. Records on Daga put it more plausibly in the thirteenth century. Its round outer walls were crumbling wattle and daub, and the thatched roof was supported by a series of columns carved from a single bole of sycamore. Inside, the floor was spread with dried grass.

The church's only embellishments were the frescoed walls of the *maqdas*, the inner sanctum. Here, among others we had found the story of Balaya Sab, a graphic reassurance of the power of forgiveness, the supremacy of good over evil.

Balaya Sab was a cannibal. In the first picture he squats ogre-like surrounded by severed limbs, his eyes bulging gluttonously. One day in the forest, out hunting for human flesh, he comes across a leper. Rather than eat him, Balaya Sab gives him some water and goes on his way. In due course Balaya Sab dies and is sent to Purgatory. St George places the sixty-nine victims of the cannibal in one of the scales of divine justice. So heavy are the cannibal's sins that the devil prepares to take him away. But the Virgin Mary steps up with the wasted figure of the thirsty leper and puts him in the other scale. The leper outweighs the others, and Balaya Sab is released into Paradise.

In the west of Dek, Yared and I found a group of villagers spearing catfish in the flooded grass. We bought some fillets and made a fire. Then I dozed for an hour, feeling wool-headed with fever.

Here the shore breaks up into small wooded islands and peninsulas. To reach Narga Selassie in the rains, you must take a boat around the shore and enter the church by the old water gate. But Yared took me through the papyrus swamp. '*Aysore!*' he cried, as we slashed at the reeds with sticks.

We reached a causeway of tufa blocks. A lone priest watched us from the shade of a fig bough. Fifty miles south of Gondar, the old monastery of Narga Selassie survives as a rogue example of Gondarene architecture. Empress Mentuab built it in the mid-eighteenth century. She put a dungeon beneath the compound wall and topped the two-tiered gatehouse with the plain cupola of Gondarene buildings. It was a haunting place. Always in church compounds I felt a timelessness, the secret calm of walled gardens, but nowhere more than on this remote island.

Mentuab was the wife of the Emperor Bakaffa, one of the more powerful rulers of the Gondarene dynasty of emperors. She was very beautiful – distinctive for her fair skin and traces of Portuguese ancestry. Inside the church, if this is so, there was a bad picture of her. But she reclined at the feet of the most striking madonna I was to see in Ethiopia.

It was based on that of *Our Lady of St Luke* at Santa Maria Maggiore in Rome. A copy of the Italian painting was made by St Francesco Borgia and taken to Goa in about 1580. From there copies fanned out to the far Jesuit missions, to Japan, China, Mogul India – and the mountains of Ethiopia. In the picture Christ is seated on his mother's left arm. This was hard for the Ethiopian monks to accept: the left was unclean, the cack hand, and the sword hand of Ahmed Gran (*gran* means 'left-handed' in Amharic).

But Ethiopian images of Mary now bear the crudely-copied iconography of this picture – her fringed mantle and *mappula fim-*

briata, the child's right hand raised in blessing, his left clutching a book. Although stylized, the figures at Narga Selassie have a curious poignancy, the faces less slavishly European, the pigments rich and unusual, the details fine. And the dim ambulatory of the church seemed filled with their presence, and the stare of two pairs of wide, doe eyes.

The last evening on Dek we ran through the rain to the island's main store, and stayed the night there among grain sacks and bags of nails. A teacher joined us for the evening and sifted through my books. In a collection of Yeats he found the poem 'Solomon to Sheba'.

'Ah, that a *ferenj* should write about the mother and father of Ethiopia!' He shook his head in disbelief.

When he asked me why I wanted to visit such a poor country as his, I pointed him to 'Song of the Happy Shepherd', and ended up by giving him the book. Later I slept on a goatskin pelt, and all through the night the sound of the rain rose and fell from the trees.

It was still raining hard in the morning when we pushed out from the shore in a *tankwa*. We strapped the life jackets to the boat where the rafts of sodden papyrus tapered to a bow.

'If we go in the rain,' explained Yared, 'there will be no storm. Last week they say three people died in a storm.'

Three hours of paddling took us to Lake Tana's little-known western shore. '*Aysore!*' laughed Yared as we rowed, the rain running down our necks.

We found a village close to the shore. That evening was clear and the moon threw long shadows across the maize fields. We shared a hut with three muttering hens, insects that buzzed around my face and crawled up my leg, and the chairman of the local Farmers' Association.

He wasn't convinced about his post. 'My duties keep me from the fields. I have a big family. I am elected, but they don't pay me.' He turned to me. 'Will you tell them the problem in Bahar Dar?' I said I would do what I could, and left a letter, for what it was worth, at Bahar Dar's government office.

Next morning we loaded a mule and set off for the Zeghie peninsula.

The woods had been cleared for the plough and a heavy, saturated loam clung to our shoes. We hurried through the morning and midday. The mule's legs buckled in a swamp; we lifted it by the saddle and chased it out.

Yared talked of the Battle of Adwa, how the Ethiopians had tricked the Italians, and of the sorties of the Patriots during the Occupation; and of his own days with the TPLF, living in caves with small raiding parties, cleaning the Soviet weapons they had stolen from the army. One night when he was sixteen he was captured, but escaped a few days later. Two years later, he was taken again. This time they imprisoned him in a camp. They beat the soles of his feet, the bastinado torture, so that he couldn't walk properly for six months. But one night his comrades broke into the camp and freed him. When he had recovered he walked down to Addis.

He told me of his plans to escape from the country, and gestured into the bushes to our right: from here the Sudanese border was no more than three nights' walk. And in all this, amid his matter-of-fact humour and enthusiasm, I could detect no trace of bitterness.

Some days later we went back to Addis Ababa, by bus through the Gojjam mountains. Yared told me later that Dr Merid was surprised that we had had no trouble with the *shifta,* notoriously savage in that area.

'He didn't expect us back!' Yared joked, with a hint of disappointment.

When I got back to England I exchanged a number of letters with Yared. In one he told me of a trip he took down the River Omo. His boat was overturned by a hippo, and he had to scramble for the bank. 'It was a beautiful adventure!' he wrote. But my reply brought no response, and there were no more letters.

Three years later I was back in Addis Ababa and went to Dr Merid's office. I peered through the painted-up windows and saw a dusty room cleared of furniture. I asked a teacher what had happened, and he explained that one day Dr Merid had disappeared. Soon afterwards he had been heard of in prison, but since then, nothing. No one could tell me what became of Yared.

13

I abandoned my hopes of getting back to Lake Tana, and thanked the Dutchman and the monks for their help. I left Bahar Dar to its acting Security Chief, and his twitching eyelid, and took a bus to Gondar. At the checkpoint on the Blue Nile bridge, the soldiers asked for my papers. I remembered the quibble about only travelling by plane. But here they didn't mind, and we drove on between low, treeless hills and the lush fields of the plain.

At Worreta the bus was stopped again and searched. The day before – on the same bus – they had opened a bag on the roof. In it were two hundred rounds of ammunition for a Kalashnikov. The owner had swallowed his baggage slip and they never found him. Today there was a bag of contraband clothes and perfumes from Dire Dawa. The smuggler was wearing a Michael Jackson T-shirt under a satin jacket, and gold chains hung around his neck and wrist; the officer took him into a shed and we drove off.

Gondar is in the foothills of the High Semien, Ethiopia's highest mountain range. Clearing the north shore of Lake Tana we faced a horizon of dark peaks, worn volcanic molars against a clear blue sky. Sixty miles to the north-west was the summit of Ethiopia's greatest peak, Ras Dashan – out of sight and well out of bounds. Away from the towns this was lawless country, untenable by any except *shifta* and the anti-government guerrillas.

We stopped two or three times more, and then started to climb. The first hills were long and smooth, like the first swells blown before a storm. In places high columns of reddish rock rose from their slopes, the remains of ancient magma intrusions. The bus laboured through the contours, past parties of road men clearing rockfalls, and slow military trucks in clouds of grimy exhaust. But for the approach to Gondar, we dropped down again to the plain and came up through familiar groves of eucalyptus.

Until the middle of the nineteenth century Gondar was, nominally, still the country's capital – the grubby streets seem to echo a grumbling resentment towards Addis Ababa, its young pretender. Gondar and Harar are the only large settlements of any antiquity in present-day Ethiopia. Until Gondar's foundation in 1636, Ethiopian emperors roamed the country with their court, trailing a retinue of as many as 50,000, a mobile city on a ceaseless round of banqueting and fighting.

It was Emperor Fasilades who stopped all this, when he had got rid of the Catholics. God chose to reward his virtue in restoring the monophysite faith by revealing the sacred site of Gondar. It had been prophesied by Archangel Raguel to Fasilades's forebear, Emperor Lebna Dengel. But only the letter G had been given. Subsequent monarchs all found places beginning with G, but none of their buildings lasted.

One day Fasilades was hunting a buffalo on horseback. After a long chase he lost the animal in a brake above two rivers. He pushed through the thorns into a glade and saw that the buffalo had disappeared into a pond. Dismounting, he knelt to drink, whereupon a holy man rose from the water.

He was old, with a long white beard that reached his feet, and was majestic like a lion and radiant as the sun. When he spoke it was with the voice of an angel: 'This is the paradise of Ezra and Enoch. Here where I stand – until now uncontaminated by a human foot – build your castle. All those who dwell here will enjoy the Kingdom of Heaven – even if they are not baptized.'

The bus stopped outside the walls of Fasilades's Castle, in a square terminus filled with other rusty buses, and shiny United Nations trucks and Save the Children trucks, and traps yoked to bony horses.

I walked up to the town's summit and found a garden full of poinsettia shrubs. An old Italian villa passed as the government hotel. It was an ugly building, rendered in sand-coloured plaster, yet clipped with the cold neatness of its fascist designers. The Italians reached Gondar on 1 April 1936, and occupied it for five years. They laid out the main street and lined it with 1930s buildings, and built municipal offices above. All these are still used, protracting the importance of those few unhappy years.

In the late afternoon I went down to the castle walls and into the imperial compound, the heart of the old city. The walls enclose an area of perhaps five acres, in plan similar to Harar. Like Harar, the perimeter follows the spine of a low hill, safe from attack, a prominent reminder of imperial power. The walls themselves though are very different from Harar's, higher and made from coarser, yellower stone. There are twelve gates, with names like Gate of the Judges, the Enigma Gate, Gate of the Pigeons and Gate of the Flute Players.

Within the walls the imperial buildings rise at random from long, uncropped grass. The main Chancellery is now an office of the Ministry of Culture, the Dining hall was being restored, the old Library is used as a new library, and the House of Lions still housed two dozing lions. But many of the original buildings had fallen into disrepair, or been destroyed by the Mahdists in the 1880s, and one by British bombs during the Second World War. I couldn't find the House of Nuptials, or the House of the Chief of Cavalry, or the bull arena where the court loosed the lions to slaughter bulls for sport. And the Castle of Songs, whose hall from the early eighteenth century rang with ballads and *kene* poetry, is a ruin.

The original palace – Fasilades's Castle – is in good shape. Its floors have been retimbered and the thick walls and roof are intact. The plan is square, with round turrets and a high watchtower. From here lookouts could scan the far plains above Lake Tana, eager for the first sight of returning armies, back from campaigns to quell the Galla or some rogue Amhara chief. Under Fasilades, their news was usually good. But the later Gondarene rulers faced a mounting chaos of civil unrest, and during the eighteenth century the country slipped towards the *mesafint*, the era of the Judges, named after the Book of Judges when, in Israel, there was no king.

In the main courtroom of Fasilades's Castle, the late sun fell through swirling clouds of dust. The room was bare, but a family of doves had nested in the rafters, and mottled the stone floor with its droppings.

Through one of the unglazed windows, I could see a minaret rising out of the market.

One hundred years after Fasilades's reign, James Bruce was

shown the place where three Catholics had been stoned, on a corner of the city's waste ground; it was still scattered with the executionary rocks.

The short-lived Gondarene civilization saw traditional allegiancies reversed. Muslims were allowed into the new city to trade and Catholics became the bugbears (it was less than a hundred years since the Portuguese won favour by helping to rid the highlands of the Muslim Ahmed Gran).

The twin legacies of the period are art and architecture. The Catholics left behind an iconography, the greatest single influence on Ethiopian religious painting. But their hurried departure left no time for proper training.

With the architecture there was a choice, but it was a simple one for Fasilades. No details survive of the original plans for Gondar's first palace. The only clue is the reference to an Indian architect at the court of Fasilades in the account of a Yemeni envoy.

Fasilades did not want the elaborate baroque that the Catholics had brought from Goa; he had seen the dainty stonework of Pedro Paez's palace at Gorgora. Gondarene architecture is sturdy and unembellished, and, in the shadow of the failed Catholicism, reaffirmed the austerity of life in the Ethiopian mountains.

By the middle of the nineteenth century Ethiopia was no more than a group of feuding provinces. Gondar had become a provincial town. In the 1880s the Sudanese sacked it and burned the town's churches. But two were spared: Medhane Alem in the palace compound which refused to catch fire, and Debra Berhan Selassie where the Muslim invaders were repelled by a swarm of bees.

Through the gatehouse of Debra Berhan Selassie, I found a low rectangular church murmuring with the chants of the morning service. A *bahtawi*, a wandering hermit, sat in yellow robes and a yellow hat against a sycamore, knitting a purple blanket. He grunted into his needles and said he was from Eritrea. He had spent years – how many, he didn't know – in the mountains of the north, wandering from monastery to monastery. But his eyes, when he looked up, were distant and his manner was slow and confused.

Around the compound was a high wall spaced with turrets. A

monk was reading a text at the foot of one of the turrets. When I approached, his long biblical face broke into a smile, and he said, 'Please, go inside.'

I stepped into the tower. Its hollow space was about seven feet wide.

'It is where I live,' said the monk, and swung a fly-whisk across his face. He pointed to a roll of matting, blankets, a couple of water bottles, and a half-empty sack of grain; on the wall was a print of the madonna. That was all.

Then he waved the fly-whisk at a ladder. The tower tapered towards the cupola, and when I poked my head above a wooden platform, I found a much narrower space. Through a high slit in the wall the sun fell on to a pile of neatly-folded blankets – the home of a novice.

I thought of all the other monks' cells around the mountains, away from imperial Gondar, the caves and huts and remote summits, the dwellings surrounded by vegetable plots and the *bahtawi* sleeping in the juniper forests. Then I thought of the glee of the feast days and the dancing behind the *tabot*, and I was struck, not for the first time, by the integrity of Ethiopian monks, how their practical lives were not much different from the peasants. Monks here were not so much an alternative to normal life, as a devoted extension of it.

Debra Berhan Selassie means 'The Trinity of the Mountain of Light'. In the church the walls are covered in frescoes, and the ceiling and crossbeams painted with countless winged angels. But the thatch has thinned and allowed damp to seep through the timbers, and pigeons nesting in the rafters have streaked the paintings.

Recently the head of UNESCO stood on the steps of Fasilades's Castle and announced that Ethiopia's antiquities, including Debra Berhan, formed part of 'the heritage of humanity', and proposed a fund to protect them. The Ethiopian government has put up half, but the rest is still to be found.

Above the door into the bema is a picture of the Trinity, whose iconography was left behind by the Catholics. But the idea goes back to the time of the Axumite Empire.

In the centuries just before the birth of Mohammed, Axum and the port of Adulis controlled the Red Sea. They formed a nexus between East and West: traders from India settled there (and may have introduced the yellow vestments worn by *bahtawi*); Nestorian and monophysite Christians fled there from the Mediterranean; and Jews and Arabs crossed from Arabia. Axum became a melting pot of faiths, all of which (except Buddhism) centred on the new idea of a single omnipotent deity. The new god subordinated the old ones, including the trine cults: sun, moon and Venus; Zeus, Ares and Poseidon; and the native Mahrem, Beher and Medr.

The Trinity in Ethiopia now rivals the Virgin and St George in popularity. The Emperor chose, when he was crowned, to be called Haile Selassie, 'Strength of the Trinity', and now that he has gone, public places are watched over by placards of the new triumvirate: Marx, Engels and Lenin.

One morning in the hotel I met Teklu, a young commercial pilot. We sat beside a mimosa drinking coffee. The sun had just risen above the hills but in the shadows lingered a night-time chill.

Teklu had the quiet voice of big men. 'I heard yesterday's bus from Metemma hit a landmine on its way up here. I think there were many killed and injured.' He said it matter-of-factly, with his forearms resting on the table between us.

Teklu came from a village on the edge of Addis. Three-quarters of his friends had 'gone north', a euphemism for the war. They weren't allowed to write home, and since the state of emergency had been declared some months before, all leave had been cancelled. He claimed that, as a rough average, only about half came back – the rest were killed or captured, or they deserted. But Teklu was lucky; he had a skilled job.

A couple of years earlier, when he was a trainee, his *kebelle* selected him to join a troupe for the Revolution Day parade. Rehearsal was a strict duty, and truancy would have meant the loss of his traineeship. Teklu missed a day and was given a warning.

One weekend he flew down to Dire Dawa on his staff ticket to visit his brother. One or two flights had been cancelled and his last chance to get back in time for the rehearsal was the Monday morning flight. But the flight was full, and his staff ticket did not allow stand-by. 'Then I thought – I will lose my job and have to go to the war.'

Desperate, he walked up to the barrier with his finger covering his concessionary number. In the confusion he got through and filled a spare seat on the plane. By luck he knew one of the stewardesses and managed to explain the problem; he reached his home as the rehearsal was starting.

We turned back to talking about the war, in the discreet tones that one got used to – until it seemed as though it were simply local custom, a question of good manners.

Teklu said that morale was low, and that many of the government's losses that year had been bungles. 'Every time there is a big offensive, the guerrillas are waiting. There are many spies among the officers. The generals have to give their plans to Party members for approval – and somehow they get out and then the enemy know the plans. But once or twice, they have not told the Party, and then it is OK – the government troops win the battles. Then two days later the general is taken away – for bad discipline.' Teklu ran his finger across his throat.

The sun had climbed a little, and lit the battlements on the castle wall below us. I could hear the rattle of carts and an occasional grunt from a truck as it changed down a gear to climb the hill. Fan-tailed kites drifted over the town letting out a shrill cry, the commonest voice of the highlands.

Teklu rose to leave. 'I have to go down to the airport now. Why not go and see my friend Teshome? You would be interested to talk to him.'

With Teshome I went to Fasilades's bathing house, the oddest of the Gondarene buildings.

It is possible that it is later than Fasilades, perhaps early eighteenth century, but in the popular lore that passes for history it has been attributed to the greatest of the period's emperors. So the label has stuck.

Walking down from Gondar we found the Keha river lined with women washing clothes, the banks laid out in squares of white cotton. In the early days of the new capital water was carried up to the castles in gourds and sewn-up skins. But bathing was a problem, so teams of peasants diverted part of the river, and dug a large pit – about 60 yards by 30 – and lined it with stones. They built a low wall around the pool with six stunted turrets in it; behind it sycamore and juniper were planted. Boughs still stretch over the parapet and frame the place with their billowing, unkempt foliage. The trees' roots had grown through the stone wall in places, creeping towards the pool like parched tongues. But now they will find water only at Epiphany when the priests enact a ritual baptism.

In the middle of the pool – attached by a short bridge – is a castle, a miniature of those on the hill, with its wooden balconies and bald, semi-spherical cupolas. Teshome had shown me the main room, which used to be a private chapel. Before their ablutions the emperors would pray here in front of the tabot; even bathing was made a liturgical rite.

I was reluctant to leave this haven, with the midday sun warming the stone and the light playing on the plump sycamore leaves. So we sat against the crumbling wall and talked.

Teshome was one of the damaged generation, like Ali in Harar. But he had not been to prison, nor to war. He had managed to keep ahead of recruitment with odd jobs, university in Addis Ababa, and more recently occasional work at the Gondar tourist office. But there wasn't much to do.

There was something of Yared in him, the same bright expression, and the hope in a hopeless position. I told him about my earlier expedition to Lake Tana, and of Yared's disappearance.

'Yes, I knew Yared,' he said. 'He brought tours up to Gondar – sometimes I helped him.'

'What happened to him?' I demanded, dreading what he might say.

'He walked to Kenya. He took a tour down the Omo river, and then walked on over the border. I think he's in Mombasa now.'

I was struck with a sudden, remote admiration. I marvelled at his courage and enterprise, and pictured him walking at night across the wide savannah, filled with the fear and elation of escape.

But I felt too a pang of remorse: defection is the deepest criticism of your own country – and those like Yared who have the qualities needed to escape, are precisely those most needed to stay.

Teshome had one more of the Gondarene palaces to show me. Remote from the whirl of court intrigue in Gondar, Empress Mentuab built her palace on the far side of the Keha Valley, at Kuskwam.

The church had been restored, and its round tin roof shone like a paste jewel. In its heyday the thatch was covered with a crimson cloth and, reputedly, 380 pieces of mirror. The Royal Chronicles report that people thought it was on fire, and strange fevers were contracted because of its brightness. Inside the church, Mentuab used to watch the service from behind an arras: like many of the Gondarene royalty she affected Ottoman court habits.

In the church were the same latticed windows as at Narga Selassie, and a lectern standing alone before the chancel. On it a monk showed us the half-completed pages of an illuminated Bible – between services the delicate Ge'ez lettering and illustration was continued. I asked the monk what had happened to the original.

He paused, and turned a couple of the vellum pages before answering. 'You have it.'

Teshome explained, when the monk had gone. The Bible had been plundered by Napier's officers during the return from Magdala in 1868. It was now in the British Museum.

He showed me down some steps into a vault with whitewashed walls. It was empty, except for a glass-topped coffin, raised on a plinth: inside was the skeleton of the Empress Mentuab.

We went out into the sun. Below the church was the ruin of her palace, a confusion of walls, half-standing or wholly collapsed, bound with ivy and decorated with quiffs of grass and *maskal* daisies.

James Bruce arrived here in 1770, after his long journey from Massawa. At once he won over the powerful matriarchy – Mentuab and her daughter Princess Esther – by ridding Kuskwam of smallpox (the Chronicles do not tally with his own account). For this he was given a house in the palace walls, and set up – true to the spirit of his age – a barometer and quadrant, and a telescope to record the stars of this distant place.

But to begin with, most of his attention seemed taken up by Princess Esther, who was so beautiful that it was hard to be with her, he said, 'without being attached to her for ever'. So beguiling is the princess in Bruce's work that there may be something of her in Coleridge's 'Abyssinian maid'.

After all his adventuring Bruce left Kuskwam for the Sudan on 26 December 1771. A week later he pitched his tent in a dusty town on the edge of the scarp. A messenger came to the camp and urged Bruce to follow him into the town, through a courtyard to a dark inner room. There, miles from her home, he found Esther on a divan. And she announced she'd like to go with him: in order to pray at the Holy Sepulchre in Jerusalem.

But it was not to be. Bruce had to cross the desert without her: he had left Margaret Murray in Britain eleven years before. It was she, he had once claimed, who had been the inspiration for his voyage and they'd agreed to marry.

Before Bruce reached England they met by chance at the theatre in Florence. Margaret fainted, since she'd been told he was dead: she was now the Marchesa Accoromboni.

Having threatened her husband, Bruce returned to England where his tales were met at best by scepticism, at worst ridicule. He was never able fully to share with anyone his days in the mountain kingdom, the rhino hunts and campaigning, the bizarre theatre and intrigue of the Gondarene court, or his love of the wild and beautiful Abyssinians.

Towards the end of April in 1794, Bruce had guests at Kinnaird, his ancestral home. The house had a museum room for his African relics, and the park was full of grazing fallow deer. He helped an old lady into her carriage, and fell down some steps. His huge frame made the fall a heavy one and the next morning he was dead.

14

Princess Esther's mother, Mentuab, shared her daughter's yearning for Jerusalem, as did many of the nobility. At his first audience, in her chamber at Kuskwam, Bruce says the empress talked of the Holy Sepulchre, Calvary and the Mount of Olives, and knew all their positions.

Later she pointed out the irony: he had left Jerusalem (as she supposed) in order to risk a lonely death in his quest for the Nile's source, to her a worthless marsh. She on the other hand, the mother of kings, wanted nothing more than to go to the Holy City, and would beg there if she could just be buried within sight of the Temple. 'This was said,' Bruce observed, 'in the most melancholy tone possible; an unusual gloom hanging upon her countenance.'

When I came to the village of Wolleka, some miles to the north of Gondar, I found an unusual gloom, and Jerusalem too was its cause.

I drove there with the guide from NTO, the National Tour Operation. The village was established as a showpiece before the revolution. Even now, unless recent fighting prevented it, the occasional tourists were taken to Wolleka as part of the Gondar tour. Day permits were issued to NTO on request. For many, particularly those from America, the village was the sole reason for visiting Ethiopia.

For Wolleka is one of the villages of remaining Ethiopian Jews. It is situated on Ethiopia's main north–south road, now closed, beside a river lined with poplars.

On the edge of the village women sat behind rows of pottery. All the figurines were earthenware, finished in a distinctive matt-black glaze. There were animals: flat-nosed frogs, crocodiles and goats, and lions with their heads crested with the Star of David. There were bearded priests clutching the twin scrolls of the

Torah, and a curious pod which, when opened revealed a couple in a stilted embrace, enacting the mythical union of Solomon and Sheba, the conception of Ethiopian monarchy.

I wandered through the dusty paths of the village. There was little to distinguish it from any other mountain village. Wattle fences bordered the homesteads, there were hens and screaming children, women winnowing grain and carrying water in the bulbous earthenware jugs.

But there was also the 'House of the Curse', where women were confined during menstruation, and the finial of the synagogue was a Star of David, rather than the usual cross studded with ostrich eggs (otherwise from the outside the building could have been a church).

And there was also something missing. I thought perhaps it may have to do with the false economy, the trickle of tourists, and the money that filtered through from international Jewry. Then I realized the population was skewed. It was like a village emptied by war. I had seen only women, the very old, and young children.

In the synagogue, schoolroom chairs were arranged in rows in one half of the room. The walls had been daubed in white a long time ago, and the brown chaff had worn through. Pasted on the wall behind some shelves was a colour poster: Beth Hatefutsoth, the museum of the Diaspora, Tel Aviv. An elderly *kes*, more a priest than a rabbi, showed me the Torah, and a Hebrew Pentateuchal text. I asked him about the origin of his people.

He sighed and tugged at the frosted curls of his beard. Then he played with the pages of the Book and said, 'Three thousand, three hundred and thirty-three years ago a man arrived from Greece. He was a Jew called Gadadiya.'

And that was all. Others in the village traced their arrival from Egypt, following the Blue Nile and eventually settling here, to the north of its source, and in the High Semien mountains where they hid from the persecutions of the Christians.

We went out again into the sunlight. An elderly woman was there who had been hovering behind as we walked around the village. She wore her *gabbi* like a whimple, tight against the face and neck, and pulled over one eye. She shuffled up to me and said, 'I have problem with my eye. Do you have medicine?'

'No,' I said, but gave her some money for treatment. 'Where are your family?'

She looked down, and pressed her toe into the dust. When she spoke, it was so quietly I had to ask her to repeat it. She said simply, 'In Jerusalem.'

Years of religious ostracism sharpened the Falashas' image of Zion: 'fountains flowing all year', 'quiet living, no work . . . no disease', 'very green country and, right at the centre, the Temple on a hill.'

In the years after the revolution, the Israeli authorities began to respond to the pleas, and in 1980, MOSSAD was put in charge of their 'escape'. By the end of 1982, 2500 had reached Israel.

Then came the famine and thousands of Ethiopians – Jews and Christians – flooded down from the highlands to the Sudanese border. It was from here that Operation Moses, and later Operation Sheba, transported about 13,000 Ethiopian Jews to Israel.

When they arrived at Ben Gurion Airport, barefoot, emaciated and in rags, many knelt to kiss the tarmac. The Israeli airport staff who saw it were reported to have wept at the sight: this was the Zionist ideal enacted.

But there were murmurs from conservative camps: could these primitive black starvelings really be Jews?

There are various views on how Judaism reached the mountains of Ethiopia. Some have the Ethiopian Jews as part of the Lost Tribe of Dan, descended from Jacob and his concubine Bilhah. Others bring the Queen of Sheba into it: Jews followed her home from the court of Solomon.

The folk tradition of the Nile route has been endorsed by some scholars. They trace the faith through Elephantine in Upper Egypt, where there were many Jews, and up into the mountains via Meroë in present-day Sudan.

But the version that is most widely accepted is that which has the Word crossing the Red Sea from Southern Arabia. Whether the Ethiopian Jews are converts, or descendants of the Arabian Jews is not clear; their appearance – indistinguishable from Ethiopian Christians – suggests that they are ethnically no different from the Amhara and Tigreans.

These two groups, which make up the core of Ethiopians, are a blend of Arab and indigenous Cushitic stock. It was they, largely, who formed the Axumite Empire, the ancestor of modern Ethiopia. From the fourth century AD, after the conversion of Emperor Ezana, Christianity became the official religion of the empire and filtered, quite slowly, through to its fringes.

Monotheism had reached Ethiopia before that, and pre-Talmudic Judaism was practised in small communities, as it was across the Red Sea. Christianity attracted some of these communities, and they converted. Others questioned Christ as the true Messiah and stuck to their original faith. Christian and Judaic influences mingled for some centuries, before being cut off from the parent communities by the teaching of the new prophet, Mohammed.

Ethiopia's insularity has made its Jews and Christians close in custom and descent, but it has not meant accord.

From the fourteenth century, the Royal Chronicles report periodic wars with the Jews. Part of this was tribal. The Agaw people, some of whom were Judaic, were constantly warring with their Christian neighbours. It was the Agaw, under the Amazon Queen Judit, who routed Axum in the tenth century, burning churches and monasteries and destroying the last traces of the Empire Axumite.

Doctrinal differences would have been highlighted from the thirteenth century, by the Ethiopian renaissance. At this time there was a great resurgence of Christian teaching, hagiography, evangelism – the work of St Tekla Haimanot and the writing of the *Kebra Nagast*. As Christianity grew stronger and better defined, those who practised Judaism became more and more isolated.

In the fifteenth century, the Emperor Yeshaq defeated the Jews and declared:

> He who is baptised in the Christian religion may inherit the land of his father, otherwise let him be a *falasi*.

This is the probable root of the name Falasha, by which the Jews are known to other Ethiopians: it means an exile or wanderer, one without land.

The inherent mistrust of the landless in peasant society is one cause of the persecution of Falashas. They shoulder the grumbling suspicion of *buda,* the evil eye. A popular proverb hints at the attitude: 'The sky has no pillar, and the Falasha has no land.' For how can they feed themselves honestly without land?

They have been forced into non-agricultural pursuits, smithying and pottery, things that only Muslims would do. For the Christian highlanders, this confirms their guilt: smiths had put the cross together and fashioned the nails that pinned Him to it.

I met Mesfin in the New City of Jerusalem. He was tall and wore a faded denim jacket, and his forehead was scored with worry lines.

He looked down as we talked, pushing a matchbox backwards and forwards along a desk. 'When I came here,' he said, 'I had to be baptized again.'

Arriving in a modern state was shock enough – many of the refugees had never even been to Gondar. But then they were told they were not proper Jews. Bewildered mothers forbade their children to go on school swimming trips, knowing that it was a plot to get them in the water to baptize them.

Mesfin was more open-minded. 'It is a bit easier for me now – I have an American wife.' He looked up at me and smiled. Yet when he came to talking about his early life in Ethiopia, and his journey, the nervousness returned, and he could not meet my eye.

Mesfin came to Israel from the village of Wolleka, and asked me for news. He had been born in the mountains behind Addis Zemen. When he was nine his father died, and with his mother and sister he went down to Wolleka. They learned to make pottery for the tourists and for a few years eked out a living. At school in Gondar, Mesfin also learned to keep quiet that he was a Falasha.

When Mesfin was fifteen, there was a famine. He scoured the hills for food and was constantly hungry. And that year just after the rains, news came from Addis Ababa that the army had taken control from the Emperor. Fighting rumbled from the mountains to the north, and the province soon suffered under the grip of a new governor, the brutal Major Melaku.

In the early 1980s, Mesfin left Wolleka with five friends. It took them less than six days to reach Sudan, walking by night and frequently changing directions to avoid being caught. At the border they asked for asylum, then worked for a week to earn passage to Gedaref, one of the main refugee camps.

At Gedaref they worked for six months, sometimes taking Arab names to get a job. Mesfin recalled the horrors of the camp: constant hunger, corruption among the Sudanese, and the disease – malaria, typhoid and hepatitis coursing through their cramped quarters, fouling the water and killing those already weakened by the journey. But with enough money saved, Mesfin managed to get from there to Khartoum, and then to Israel.

'All my people,' he said, 'are dreaming about Jerusalem – not Israel, Jerusalem.' He pointed out of the window to a tenement block, built in Jerusalem stone, parchment yellow, and sprouting with TV aerials. 'We get here, and find it is like any other country. It is not heaven!'

15

On a grey morning I took a shared taxi down from Gondar to the airstrip. We stopped on the edge of the town, just up from the Keha bridge, while the driver got some papers from the *kebelle*. A military truck pulled into the kerb in front of us. Two or three men in civilian clothes climbed down. They approached a young man leaning against a wall.

They grabbed him, and he started to shout. He writhed and kicked against his captors with such abandon that I realized he had nothing to lose. He was put in the open back of the truck and driven away, still shouting.

Beside me there was a woman teacher. I turned to her, wanting to ask what had happened. Was this a press-gang or an arrest – did it make any difference? But she had averted her gaze, and I knew she was too embarrassed to explain.

So I was left to guess. As we drove on over the river, and up between rust-coloured banks towards the hospital, I couldn't help thinking of Teshome and knowing that at any time the same thing could happen to him.

The taxi dropped me off in a heavy rainstorm. At midday it was dark enough to be dusk, and I ran along a sodden track, my head bowed beneath the rain, dodging puddles, and into the shed that is Gondar Airport.

Teklu was there, waiting to fly a month's supply of cigarettes down to Humera on the Sudanese border. The temperature, he said, would be more than 100 degrees – up here in the mountains it could not have been more than 60. He pointed beyond the dripping eaves at his tiny Cessna, dwarfed by an ancient DC3 on the grass beside it.

Dug in around the perimeter of the airstrip were four or five garrison posts, with machine guns and tents, and two with fierce-looking armoured cars. But it was not a military airport, and there was just a small company of soldiers posted here, sitting around the terminal, idle and slightly scruffy, looking bored in their bottle-green fatigues.

Back in Addis Ababa, the news was that the late rains had brought disease. On the plateau it was too high, but down in the Rift Valley there was malaria, and from Dire Dawa came rumours of yellow fever.

The dry season had started late – only in mid-September did the daily rains stop and the skies clear. But after two weeks it had started to rain again. Then every patch of swampy lowland had become a hotbed for malarial mosquitoes, and all manner of viruses and parasites.

I went to Billy's house for lunch. He looked tired, and straightaway started to talk about the epidemics. 'Look, I have a friend who works at Bole Airport. He said that the other day some spraying-planes arrived from Europe, and drums of DDT to spray the lakes. And then my cousin phoned yesterday from Geneva – he works for World Health Organization there. From what he had heard, he said we should all stay in addis.'

I no longer found it odd that someone in Geneva should tell us what was happening on our doorstep.

'I'm due to go south,' I said.

'Well, I think you'd be mad to go. I'm telling you, it's serious. The embassies are telling everyone to stay put. There's yellow fever, typhus, hepatitis and four different strains of malaria. And the worst is this cerebral malaria – some say it's now resistant to chloroquine. If you get that, you go into a coma very quickly, and it's fatal. There's only one hospital with the treatment. Even then, it doesn't always work.'

Billy stubbed out his cigarette. He shook his head. 'Shit, you know in Dire Dawa they're dying like flies. The French school has been closed and the teachers are being sent up here.'

Billy's maid brought in some pasta, and we went to sit at a veneer table. 'Thank you . . . er . . . Misrak,' he said, pulling out a chair. With his litany of horror interrupted, he seemed subdued, and for a while we ate in silence.

I remembered a night in Dire Dawa when I was kept awake by the persistent, ominous buzzing around my ear. The next day I found a rash of mosquito bites on my neck, and around my ankles. I thought of all the other places I'd been. On the plateau there is no malaria above about 6000 feet, and most people don't bother with prophylactics. In recent years poor rains had reduced the amount of malaria in the lower regions; this year everyone had been caught by surprise.

Billy said the cerebral malaria had a typical incubation of about twenty days, but it could be up to six months. And it was resilient – a mosquito brought up from the Rift Valley had remained infectious for a week in Addis.

'I don't know what's happened this year,' sighed Billy. 'The farmers don't know when to plant. You used to be able to say which day the rains would come, and when they'd end.' He shook his head again, and then pushed away his plate. 'I'm not hungry.'

He lit another cigarette, then looked at me with wide, tired eyes. 'I have to get out of Addis soon. I'm being driven crazy up here. I had planned to go to Lake Langano with the kids, but now the malaria.' He gave a chuckle. 'For years we have bad rain and then it comes – all at once! You'd be crazy not to stay in Addis for a while. You know, even up here an Italian woman died last week. Malaria fever gave her a heart attack. . . . But it's worst by the lakes – in Zway, they say, about four or five people are dying each day.'

Zway was the place I had planned to go next.

After lunch I went to Merkato, the largest open-air market in Africa. It was a bright Saturday afternoon and the sky over the market was filled with the whirling silhouettes of tawny eagles and kites.

Merkato is a huge sprawl of low buildings and muddy, open plots in the west of the city. It leaves a shadow over the rest of Addis Ababa, a corner of illicit commerce and hidden wealth, powerful cartels, and an anarchic exemption from the normal constraints. Foreigners are advised not to go there after dark, and I heard stories of violence and people disappearing in the vortex of its lanes.

But they may just have got lost. It is laid out in a grid of such baffling uniformity, that only the merchandise can be used as signposts. If you ask the way, you risk being directed up a blind alley, and then attacked. So you find your way by looking for the leather market with its flies, or for fruit, or the tiny pyramids of coloured spices, or the section of textiles with luminous vegetable-dye wools glowing from the stalls.

Somewhere in the middle is the bus station. I had directions from there and found the house I was looking for behind a high protective wall, its top lined with broken glass, like dragon's teeth.

I was shown into a darkened room. The shutters were closed and for a moment I could see nothing but the blue flashing glow of a television.

That morning I had received a confused message to come here. I didn't know what it was about. I thought I might recognize someone when I arrived, but as my eyes cleared I saw only strangers: a girl in denim sitting cross-legged in front of the TV, two or three others on chairs. And in the middle a huge woman lying on a divan.

On the wall were pinned some baskets from Harar, and further into the darkness I could see the occasional flash of teeth – someone chewing *cha'at*. So here was one of the famous Harari clans: Muslim, mercantile and curiously matriarchal. But I still wasn't sure what I was doing there.

The girl in denim swivelled round. Her jacket was studded with sequins. 'My grandma has this parcel for you,' she said in an untainted East-Coast drawl.

In front of her grandma, on a low table was a brown paper package, addressed to me in my brother's writing. In it was some transparency film and a book, and a newspaper cutting about a dog.

Someone brought me tea. 'It's my cousin's wedding,' said the girl, nodding towards the TV. 'In Washington. That's where Grandma came from – she was given the parcel by some girl on her way through Heathrow.'

The woman grunted at me and swept her hand across her broad chest. She said something in Aderri.

'What's she saying?'

The girl sniggered. 'She hid the parcel inside her bra on the journey.'

She had smuggled it. I couldn't help admiring this giantess, who would smuggle a package from a stranger, to give to another stranger – through the jaws of Bole Airport.

16

That night I packed my rucksack for Zway with a can of Mobil insect repellent and two cloves of garlic. In the morning I had second thoughts, thinking of Billy's warnings. But then I remembered his frustration, and recognized it. It seemed churlish to waste my precious permits by not going.

So I took a bus from near La Gare, from a sub-station which dealt with all routes south. We bumped over the railway and slalomed between potholes, cleared the checkpoint on the edge of town and headed down into the Rift Valley.

Mount Zikwala stayed with us nearly the whole way to Zway – its profile in the right-hand window hardly changed as we turned off the Dire Dawa road and on to the dusty road south.

But I kept thinking of malaria. And by the time we reached Meki for a stop I had willed the first signs of fever upon myself, and found the pages of my book slipping in and out of focus.

My interest in Lake Zway was based on the work done there by the American diplomat and writer Paul Henze. In the years just before the revolution, he had found on the lake's islands an enclave of medieval Christianity.

Until Menelik II pushed south at the end of the last century, this part of Ethiopia had been Galla country. Mainly Muslim, the Galla had spread along the Rift Valley, on the tide of Islamic expansion in the tenth century. Subsequent waves eventually swamped the traces of Axumite civilization, and its Christian faith.

But the islands of Lake Zway were spared; the Galla couldn't build boats. So, as their kin retreated into the mountains, the Zay islanders became virtual prisoners.

On the islands demand for the land increased. Terraces were carved higher and higher up the slopes and planted with millet and teff, and later with cotton. Grazing had to be restricted. But instead of meat they now had fish, a limitless supply of *tilapia* from the lake.

On certain days the Galla granted an amnesty. They were keen on the islanders' woven cotton, and allowed them to paddle ashore and trade it for salt and butter, hides and various goods brought through on the trade routes. Then they were given free passage back to the islands.

In the Christian highlands they were not forgotten. Rumours of their survival were fuelled by accounts of a dogged faith and stores of religious treasures.

On the high point of Tullu Guddo, the largest island, the Zay consecrated a church to St Mary of Zion, later elevated to the status of monastery. Other islands had brought in sacred *tabots* and built churches around them, to Tekla Haimanot and Mary, and the Four Creatures (from the Revelation of St John the Divine). On Tullu Guddo an impressive library of illuminated manuscripts was established.

Over the years, isolation earned the Zay a Prester John-like mythology. The Shoan king, Sahle Selassie, planned an expedition in the mid-nineteenth century to the lake of the lost Christians:

> In it be many islands which contain the treasure of my ancestors. There are jars filled with bracelets of solid gold. There are 40 drums of elephants' ears and many holy arks pertaining to ancient churches, beside 700 choice Ethiopic volumes.

He went on to describe the elephants there, and ferocious black leopards, and the lake itself full of monsters and brightly-coloured fish. The king had heard too of wondrous cures for diseases.

But he never made the crusade. It was his grandson, Menelik, who succeeded in liberating the Zay people. Since then, the lesser islands have been deserted, and on the mainland the small town of Zway has become the hub of the lake.

Modern Zway is torn between the lakeside and the main road. The main road seems to have won the tussle, and its dusty kerb is lined with the newer buildings, wooden shacks that pass for shops. Outside one of them there was a man banging nails into a wooden box. Behind him there were two boxes he had finished, and one smaller one, propped against the wall; each one had a cross on the lid.

The bus pulled off the road and came to rest beside a tree. Under it was a crowd of children who ran up with baskets of fruit and roasted maize. I waded through them and put my rucksack down in the sand.

At a couple of thousand feet below the plateau (but still well over 5000 feet), Zway dozed under a bright, heavy heat. The lake brings an enervating humidity, and now in the early afternoon there was no breeze to clear it. I bought some oranges and asked about a hotel.

Later on, the air lifted and it became cooler. I followed a wide track down to the lake. Sunday afternoon had brought some of the town's carters down to the swampy foreshore with their horses. The animals splashed about with the coltish high spirits of sudden freedom. Others stood still, while their ill-fed flanks were scrubbed clean of caked mud.

Nearby a wild dog squabbled with some vultures over the carcass of a horse, plunging into the bloody cavern of its ribs, tugging at a strand of flesh with bared teeth and front legs flexed like a fighter.

I walked a little way round the shore, turning over comparisons with Lake Tana. But Zway is a different country: it is Africa, with its savannah and thorn scrub, the huge horizons, the faded yellow of the grasses, and the hazy biscuit tones of the far hills. To the south I sensed the Rift Valley, the huge tectonic scar scratched down the side of the continent, playing about with the sense of scale, and the twenty-five mile lake seemed suddenly very small.

Then I noticed clouds of mosquitoes hovering over the stagnant pools, and hurried back towards the town.

A Land Rover was driving very slowly up towards the main road. On its tailgate lay one of the boxes I had seen earlier. Beside the track a woman was standing by her hut.

'A child,' she told me. 'Just nine years old. This week there have been three or four every day here. Up in Awash, they say maybe thirty.' And she followed the procession with dark expressionless eyes.

To get to Tullu Guddo, the lake's largest island, I needed a boat from the fishery. But the manager said, 'You will need papers from the Ministry of Agriculture.'

I sensed the familiar deflection tactics and walked back to town. Outside a compound of low buildings a team was filling tanks with DDT to spray the swamps; one or two were ready to go, wandering about, bemused in goggles and protective clothes, and tanks strapped to their backs; they looked like apprentice divers.

The local official was taciturn, but gave me the papers and I set off in a trap to find the captain.

The captain was a young Galla called Yohannis. He was planing a thwart for a new boat, but was happy to stop work. 'Yes, I need to pick up a net from Tullu Guddo.'

Towards the middle of the morning, having done a good six miles behind a bony mare, I realized that the little expedition might be feasible – after Lake Tana, I kept thinking something would go wrong. I bought oranges and cheese, and some bottled water, and went back to the fishery with Yohannis.

The fishery at Zway had been funded by the EEC, and now provides most of the fish for Addis Ababa. There are two or three cold stores, and a small boatyard. In the lock-up we found a toolbox and life-jackets, among endless warps and nets and rifles, and a boxed Volvo outboard for the new boat. Everywhere there were stencils saying: Donated by the European Economic Community. I paid for 30 litres of fuel, and we went down to the lakeside.

It had been some days since the boat was last used, and it had fried out in the hot sun. I could see daylight between the bottom-boards. So we plugged the biggest of the gaps with cord and bitumen, and poled out through the reeds.

Yohannis pointed out the dark shapes of hippos eyeing us, and a python wriggling round the shore. The lake's smooth surface was broken with the occasional white dots of pelicans, and on the foreshore waded egrets and sacred ibis. For the first hour we battled against the leaking hull, but gradually the boards took up and sealed.

I had put Yohannis at about thirty but he told me he was twenty-one. Eight years earlier he had left his family in Wollega, western Ethiopia, and come to Zway. For some years he lived with his sister. Then at sixteen his schooling finished and he went to learn to be a carpenter. He chiselled and sawed boles of hagenia into beds and chairs, and strung them with thongs of goatskin. Soon afterwards the EEC agreed to sponsor the proposed fishery project and a German came for a month to teach him to build boats. Since then a small number of fishing launches had been made from a simple plan, and Yohannis had been put in charge of the workshop.

At midday the island of Galila slid past the beam, now deserted but for a herd of wild cattle. Stands of papyrus lined its shore, up to 15 feet high, their slender stalks rising to a cascade of leaves, like frozen fireworks. A fish-eagle spread its wings as we passed, and flew around the island. Somewhere in the trees was an abandoned church, its new metal roof only a few years old when the last residents left in 1972.

Further away, to starboard, was Debra Sina, 'Mount Sinai' in Ge'ez. When Henze visited the lake just before the revolution, only a few families remained on the island. Now, Yohannis told me, an easier life on shore had drawn away all but one old woman ascetic.

We chugged for two hours across the empty centre of the lake. It was hot and the rippled surface flickered in the sun. Beyond the far shore the slopes of Mount Chilalo rose to 13,000 feet. The peak of the extinct volcano is twenty-five miles away, yet seems to tower over the lake. At its foot were the rutted scars of storms, which had torn away the soil and left only crumbling rock. Patches of thorn scrub stood out from it like the dark spots on the coat of a hyena.

To the north the flat horizon was broken only by a distant shape, no more than a grey pimple in the haze. But I recognized it as an old friend: the unmistakable profile of Mount Zikwala.

The eastern islands, further from the modernizing influence of the town of Zway, have remained occupied. Tullu Guddo still supports about a thousand people, though during the time of isolation it was three times that. The higher of its twin peaks is stepped with more than two hundred terraces, the upper ones now abandoned. Between the peaks a saddle fans out to an expanse of meadows and pasture beside the water.

After the rains these lush flats are a tempting treat for hippos. When it is dark they waddle out of the lake and graze on the terraces. The islanders keep 'hippo watches' through the night, burning fires and chasing the beasts with flaming torches.

Yohannis cut the motor and let the bow ride up the mud. The high sun drummed a harsh light on to the island, on to corrals made from euphorbia and cactus, on to grazing mules and a horse, and on to the faces of three girls in muddy dresses who had watched our approach. They pointed up towards the church: there was a funeral going on.

We walked around the shore, and up a steep rocky path to the high shoulder of a promontory. A group of about thirty women was squatting in the shade of rocks and scrub. The men stood clustered around the door of a makeshift church.

Soon the door swung open and a wooden bed was passed out over their heads, bobbing along on upstretched arms. On it a corpse was wrapped from head to toe in white cotton. With a good deal of shouting the bed was lowered on to the shoulders of two pallbearers, and the procession began. The women got up and joined the rear. We clambered down another rocky path, and along the side of the hill. After fifty yards the woods thinned to a clearing made in the undergrowth. A narrow grave ran beside a pile of newly-dug earth.

The forest was filled with wailing. The first to arrive at the grave clasped their hands behind their necks, and rocked slowly from side to side, muttering prayers. Others threw back their heads and cried out. From the back of the crowd came the distinctive trilling of the women.

In the highlands at funerals an *alqash* would be commissioned to compose a special dirge. Many were women, and a good *alqash* might travel three days on a mule to chant her lamentation, but down here it was too far.

I asked the man beside me who the funeral was for.

'Young man,' he said.

'Malaria?'

The man nodded and looked away. How did they feel about

these epidemics? I imagined that some sort of baffled grief burned beneath the Ethiopian reserve and the ritual wailing, but to me it was a masquerade, and I could feel little more than curiosity.

Half-hidden in the trees, a priest quietly chanted the rites. A deacon stood on either side of him, one holding a large cloth-bound book, the other a tall brass cross.

A *gabbi* was stretched over the hole, and the white bundle discreetly laid to rest beneath it. A boy jumped into the grave to ensure its safe entry, and the women slipped away to continue their vigil by the church.

His chants complete, the priest walked up to the grave and the *gabbi* was pulled away. The wailing stopped and he read a short prayer. Then he bent and scattered some earth on to the corpse, and walked back into the forest. A few of the mourners stepped up and did the same, and for a moment there was silence.

But then someone picked up a shovel and scooped a clod of earth into the grave. Another man snatched the shovel, and told him he was doing it wrong. The crowd started chattering, offering advice; others wrestled for the tool, shouting and arguing over the task like a road gang.

Two men struggled with a rough headstone, experimenting with various positions at the eastern end of the grave, before agreeing an angle and digging a small trench for it.

The ceremony had ended abruptly, but few seemed willing to leave.

Back at the church, I found the priest sitting on a rock. He was swishing a horsehair fly-whisk in front of his face.

I asked about the Church of St Mary of Zion, the most important of all the island's churches. There had been a church on the island's summit since the twelfth century.

But the priest said, 'It was too difficult to get to.'

So, eight years ago they had brought the *tabot* down, and consecrated this small shed to house it. Earlier in the year work had begun on a new church. The priest showed me progress, just across the knoll from where we were sitting.

Wooden scaffolding sketched the plan, and the breeze-block walls were rising to meet it. Part of the wall reached as high as the eaves; in other places it had barely left the ground. An apse was taking shape at one end, and the plan was basilical, rather than the traditional circle.

A large blue drum, half full of water, stood beside a thorn tree – around it the ground was covered with the off-white scars of concrete mixing. But today, there was no one working.

'We have run out of cement,' said the priest, 'and we need money. It stopped two weeks ago.' He shrugged, 'I don't know when we start again.'

He didn't seem concerned, and I thought of the great Gothic cathedrals of Western Europe, on-going medieval projects, built with no plan for completion and added to as patronage permitted. The work itself was a devotion, half-completed buildings a reminder of mortality, the striving towards, rather than the completion.

We walked back to the funeral group. The women still sat among the rocks, seeking shade, chatting and laughing as if waiting for a market to open.

From my bag, I pulled a copy of Paul Henze's book and showed the photographs of Zway to the clergy. One picture showed the Zay hereditary chief sitting with a rifle in his lap, in a dark jacket and a white shirt buttoned to the top. They smiled and shook their heads when they saw it: he had died some years before.

Beside it was one of the pages of Tullu Guddo's famous sinkesar, an illuminated hagiography. The book is one of the finest examples of the early period of Ethiopian painting, and was made in the fourteenth century. No one is sure whether it was written on the island or brought there afterwards.

But the priest could not authorize me to see it.

Most art historians dismiss Ethiopian art as crude and uninteresting, at best an ethnic curiosity. And in most cases they are right. There has been no consistent tradition of training for artists, and it is usually carried out by monks in isolation.

Religious painting is performed as a rite, as in the Orthodox Church. The monk goes into retreat for some days to seek guidance, and fasts as he paints.

From the fifteenth century, a trickle of Europeans brought tokens of the Renaissance to the Ethiopian court. 'Pictor Venetus', a half-educated monk called Nicolo Brancaleone, was among the first. He lived for about forty years in the country, and died there early in the sixteenth century, a rich and powerful man. But he was not a good painter at all, and displayed few of the sophistications of his native Venice.

Brancaleone is credited with elaborating the myth of Ethiopia's patron saint: he introduced the dragon to the story of St George, or Giorgis. In Italy it was also quite new, the whim of a Genoese in the thirteenth century. The dragon had gone almost full circle: in the Louvre is a fifth-century image, probably Coptic, of a saint plunging a lance into a Nile crocodile.

Then there was Lazaro de Andrade who arrived with Alvarez in the Portuguese embassy of 1520. He was a professional painter, and did an accomplished picture of Emperor Lebna Dengel, which was presented to Pope Clement IV. A copy of it now hangs in the Galleria degli Uffizi in Florence.

It was reputedly Andrade who painted the imperial icon, *Kwer-'ata re'eso,* Christ with the Crown of Thorns. During the Gondarene dynasty the painting surpassed its liturgical function and was taken into battle. Soldiers swore loyalty in its name, promising to die for their king, but in 1744, the Sudanese captured it. Emperor Iyasu II returned to Gondar in shame.

When the painting was recovered James Bruce recorded the celebrations: 'Priests made processions from church to church singing hallelujahs. . . . All Gondar was drunk with joy.'

In the nineteenth century Theodore had it hanging above his bed, but after his defeat at Magdala it was taken back to Britain by Sir Richard Holmes. In 1950 it came up for auction at Christie's in London. Haile Selassie's embassy was outbidded and the painting disappeared. It is thought to be somewhere in Portugal, where Andrade's journey began.

From these painters, Ethiopian art gained movement and dimension. But something was lost: too many of the later paintings are derivative and charmless.

Paul Henze's photograph of the earlier Tullu Guddo sinkesar shows something altogether more beautiful. The picture is of a priest and a king. They are in identical poses, in orant, the early gesture of prayer with upturned hand to reflect Christ on the Cross. Their long apostolic faces are indistinguishable. The image is completely flat, but achieves a powerful, abstract sense of proportion: broad robed body, a decorative stole, tiny feet and elongated fingers, and long thumbs curved like a calligraphic comma.

Somehow the figures managed to combine the nobility and the holiness, so like the physical presence of many Ethiopians.

As they looked at the book, I asked the priests if they remembered Henze. 'Paul Henze,' I said. 'An American, a large man with red hair and a beard.'

They looked at each other and frowned, then shook their heads.

'*Ato* Paul?' I tried the Amharic address.

More head-shaking.

'Wait,' I said. ' There is a photograph.' And I turned to the inside flap of the dust cover.

One of the older priests squinted at the small black-and-white picture. Then he leaned forward until his beard brushed the paper.

He raised his head. 'Ah, Paulos. It is Paulos. Look!' He passed the book around the group, and they all grinned at the photograph.

They said he was a good man, and asked when he was coming back, and if his health was good, and they chatted happily and thanked God for his memory. I said he was well (though the truth was that I didn't know him, further than a couple of words exchanged at a conference on Ethiopian art two years before).

Yohannis pointed towards the boat. The sun had dropped a little, and a light wind blew in from the lake. We would have to leave now to get back before dusk.

Two teachers walked down with us. They taught at the Swedish-built school, a large oblong building put up in 1972 beside the lake. I could see a green, yellow and red flag flapping against a pole in its compound. Children still paddled here to classes from the other islands in papyrus boats.

I asked them about malaria. They pretended not to understand and I could see they were embarrassed, so I dropped the subject. They pointed out their house, a two-storey villa standing alone on a raised portion of the foreshore. It used to be the bishop's island residence; to find a second storey was unusual anywhere in rural Ethiopia, to find one here was extraordinary.

One of them returned without warning to malaria. 'There is a bad problem this year,' he said, not looking at me. 'There has been much fever on the islands. Fifty have died in the last month, maybe more.'

The wind had chased away the midday haze, and brought out colours of a numbing intensity: the sky and lake a cobalt blue, sandwiching the island, which glowed bright green and bristled with euphorbia. The wind freshened as we motored back, hoping to reach shore before the sun fell behind the mountains, and the reed beds started to hum with mosquitoes.

17

On the hotel terrace, the morning sun had begun to seep through the vines. A bearded Galla was telling a story about his lorry breaking down. The punchline was a loud shout and a vicious, prolonged stabbing action with his right arm. Everyone laughed, but I was unsure of the details.

The Galla had agreed to give me a lift to Sheshamane. He had a Soviet petrol tanker with a trailer coupled behind it. Behind the two seats, a turbaned guard snored on a pile of clothes. We followed the road south, an arrow-straight route down the Rift Valley. Sometimes here it appeared for miles ahead, shimmering in the heat, giving the illusion of unlimited access, a mirage of travel without checkpoints or permits or rationed fuel.

On the edge of Sheshamane, just before the military checkpoint, there was a new Ministry of Transport checkpoint. A sign writer was painting the words 'WEIGHTS AND MEASURES' in English as we pulled up. The tanker driver dropped me off, and I walked into the town.

At the government hotel I had lunch and watched an Oxfam Land Cruiser park in the shade of a date palm. I knew the girl who got out: she was an American. She stretched, and tugged at the back of her T-shirt where the hot seat had stuck it to her back.

She walked over to my table with her driver, and peeled off a pair of Ray-bans. 'Hi, fancy meeting you here. Where have you come from?'

'Zway.'

'Yeah? I thought they had a malaria problem there. We drove through Zway with our windows tight closed.'

She peered into the empty dining room. 'God, I'm thirsty. There anyone here?'

She was on her way south to Sidamo for a donors' meeting. Three of the big guns – Oxfam, Save the Children and Band Aid –

had co-funded a rural development scheme. A few of the chiefs had flown out from London, and were going to see that the money was being spent properly.

We talked for a while, and promised to meet when I got back to Addis. Then I went to phone Brother Moody.

'Just ask for Jamaica if you get lost now,' Brother Moody spoke in the thick, singsong accent of his Caribbean island.

His directions took me a little way back out of Sheshamane on the road north. The sign writer had finished his lettering, and was now working on some white lines for the approach to the weighing bay.

'Where is Jamaica?' I asked him.

He pointed with his brush a few hundred yards up the road. To him, as to all the locals, Jamaica was the name of Ethiopia's small community of Rastafarians.

From the road, Brother Moody's house was an incongruous sight, a little piece of Kingston shanty in the African Rift. A solid fence surrounded his half-acre plot. Over the top of it, I could see a tin-roofed gable, among shrubs and high grasses, and fruit trees. But all around was open land, unfenced fields stretching towards the blue shadow of the hills.

The gate was locked, but when I knocked a young boy opened it. I found Brother Moody making bread.

'Welcome,' he looked up through clouds of flour. He was a small man with kind eyes and a straggly goatee beard. As he talked he kneaded a slab of dough on to the table. 'A little nutmeg here, like this,' he said, and went on to explain how he came to be in Ethiopia.

In 1967 his uncle had come out to the community, bringing with him a bag of tools and hard-earned building skills. It was he who had built the house, a simple structure, but put up with much more care than the Ethiopians' dwellings.

After eight years, 'family pressures' forced him back to Jamaica. He went to Prince's Street, Kingston, where Moody ran a shop. The shop was called Addis Ababa Bookshop & Artistic Mart, and catered for the demand for all writings on Africa, particularly anything on Ethiopia. Moody needed little persuading to go to Ethiopia, and live in his uncle's house. The Moody House now has the community's only telephone, and acts as something of a centre for the others.

Brother Tagessa appeared, his hair pulled back tight by a green, yellow and red hairband before tumbling to his waist in a jungle of matted curls. I had met him in Addis Ababa; he had come out from London earlier in the year.

'Ras Tafari,' he greeted Brother Moody.

'Ras Tafari,' said Brother Moody.

Tagessa's son ran around with a piece of broken cane, hitting the walls, and our legs, and anything else he could.

'You stop that now,' warned his father, and turned to me. 'Always he's like this when he's tired. Came down on the bus this morning, bunched up with the dust and all, and the drums.'

He pointed to a pair of tall bongos, painted in the colours of the Ethiopian flag: green, yellow and red. 'Got the drums now for tomorrow. For the celebrations you know, of His Imperial Majesty – Ras Tafari!'

'Ras Tafari,' echoed Brother Moody, and palmed the dough into a loaf.

The following day was 2 November. On that day fifty-eight years earlier Ras Tafari exchanged his title for something grander, and in doing so inspired the cult that now bears his name. Tafari, eldest son of Ras Makonnen, Duke of Harar, became Emperor Haile Selassie I, King of Kings, Elect of God, and Conquering Lion of the Tribe of Judah.

The coronation drew a good deal of attention from around the world, which surprised everyone. Royal Houses and governments sent important envoys with gifts: the Italians sent an aeroplane, the Germans sent wine, and the British sent the Duke of Gloucester with a pair of sceptres inscribed in Amharic. *The Times* sent Evelyn Waugh. Poles and Swedes, Japanese, Americans and Dutch joined them on the train up from Djibouti to Addis Ababa. Waugh recalls a week of chaotic official celebrations, and a protracted service at Menelik's Giorgis Cathedral for the actual crowning.

In Jamaica the event was heralded in Marcus Garvey's *Blackman* newspaper. The editorial of 8 November 1930 read:

> The Psalmist prophesied that Princes would come out of Egypt, and Ethiopia would stretch forth her arms unto God. We have no doubt that the time has now come. Ethiopia is now really stretching forth her hands. This great Kingdom of the East has been hidden for many centuries, but gradually she is rising to take a leading place in the world and it is for us of the Negro race to hold up the head of Emperor Ras Tafari.

The coronation brought a prophetic hope from the Old Country. Out of her obscurity, Ethiopia had unknowingly thrown up another mythical champion: Ras Tafari had become Prester John. Prester John's kingdom had remained intact from the spread of Islam, but modern Ethiopia's independence was more tenable: the Battle of Adwa in 1896 had kept her free from the clutches of colonial Europe.

And now the Europeans themselves had come with gifts to pay homage to the new king.

The Rastafarian cult has its roots in a much older, pre-colonial movement. Wherever Africans found themselves under White rule – in the West Indies, the Southern United States and in South Africa – the same mixture of charismatic Christianity and African myth emerged. It became known as Ethiopianism and found its first established advocate in George Liele who in 1784 set up the Ethiopian Baptist Church in Jamaica.

Marcus Garvey was the most powerful modern voice of the movement, and did much to revive its flagging spirits. He stated the beliefs:

> We Negroes believe in the God of Ethiopia, the everlasting God – God the Son, God the Holy Ghost, the one God of all ages. That is the God in whom we believe but we shall worship him through the spectacles of Ethiopia.

But that was as far as Garvey went. His ideas were taken on board by the Rastafarians, but he denied association with them. It is Leonard Howell who is most closely linked with the emergence of the cult.

Howell was a well-travelled Jamaican. He had been to West Africa and in 1896, the year the Ethiopians chased the Italians back into Eritrea, he had fought for the Ashanti against the British. Later he became a Baptist minister and, after the Emperor's coronation, started preaching the good news in the Jamaican slums: the coming of an African Messiah. During the early 1930s the first followers gathered in the Kingston shanty. The Book of Revelations became popular reading, and was found to be full of prophecies concerning the advent of Haile Selassie.

Howell produced pictures of the new ruler and advertised them as passports to Ethiopia. He sold them for a shilling apiece. At a rally in December 1933 he pronounced the six principles of Rastafarians: supremacy of the Black race, hatred of the Whites, revenge on the Whites for their evils, resistance to the Jamaican constitution, preparation for the return to Africa, and the recognition of Emperor Haile Selassie I as the supreme being and the only ruler of Black people.

After the rally Howell was arrested for sedition and sentenced to two years in prison. On his release he set up the Ethiopian Salvation Society and took to the hills. In the thick forest of the Jamaican interior he lived with his followers on a commune named Pinnacle. He was the self-styled African chief of the group and had thirteen wives. Fields of banana and ganja were planted and Pinnacle's members let their hair grow. To cut hair or shave was unnatural, sinful, a legacy of the White man's wilful quest for order. The hair thickened into matted rats tails, and became dreadlocks, the badge of Rastafarianism.

Pinnacle's location remained a closely-guarded secret. But neighbouring villages came to know of the group, since Howell ordered his men to collect taxes from them in the name of Haile Selassie. The villagers reported them to the police. In 1941 the Jamaican authorities raided Pinnacle. Howell slipped the net and disappeared for ten years.

In the early fifties rumours of a re-established Pinnacle reached Kingston, and another raid was organized. This time Howell was caught, but the courts judged him as no more than a nuisance, and acquitted him. He died in 1960 at Kingston Mental Hospital.

After dark we sat around talking, in the dim light of a low watt bulb. We had been joined by another pillar of the settlement, and he was telling me about sin.

'It's quite clear in the Bible. Ain't none of us not sinners. We's all sinners!' He laughed. 'You see I was a Baptist minister, in Georgia, the U-nited States. You know Georgia?'

He didn't wait for a reply, but stood and opened his arms. Then he started to sing:

'Rainy ni-ight in Geor-gia
Seems like it's raining
All over the wo-orld . . .'

He held the last low note for a long time, and afterwards began to preach. 'Look, a girl came to my house today. And – Lord, forgive me for saying this – but she was nice, I mean, *nice*,' and he ran his hands down the imaginary curves of her torso. 'And when she left I said to my wife, I said this: TEMP-TATION! Lord deliver me from temptation! Oh Lord!' Then he leapt up, and slipped as he landed, laughing.

No one seemed to take much notice, and soon it was Brother Moody's turn to hold the floor.

He was sitting cross-legged on a blanket in the corner of the room. 'Hear this,' he said. 'In this space age, man want to get up to the planets and the stars. And he builds the space programme with rockets and all of that. But,' and he placed his hand on the concrete floor, 'man is of the earth. And not even of the world – he is of the earth.'

'Truly,' said Tagessa.

'Rasta is of the earth, of Africa,' continued Moody. 'That's why he want to come back here. He don't need no space programme. He just want his African roots.'

At this point Tagessa turned to me and injected a favourite slogan. 'You see, you can take the people out of the country, but you can't take the country out of the people.'

The phone rang, and Moody went into the other room to answer it. I could hear the lilt of his thick patois, but could not make out a single word.

'That was London,' he explained, taking his place again in the corner. 'The EWF, but the phone got cut off.

'The EWF?' I asked.

'Ethiopian World Federation,' pronounced Tagessa. 'For a time

I worked for them in London.'

He went on to explain their origin, in the wooden tones of a tour guide who'd been through it too often before. 'In 1937, when His Imperial Majesty was residing in Bath, England, he was approached by a group of Blacks offering help in the war against the Italians. With them His Highness drew up the constitution for the Ethiopian World Federation. Some of them went out to Ethiopia in the end to fight in the resistance.'

Then, in 1948, the year Israel was created, the Emperor granted the Federation 500 acres of land for a settlement. For some years there were no takers. Then in the mid 1950s Helen and James Piper arrived from New York, and things started to go wrong.

Early plans to build a town on the land foundered when they realized no one had any money. Like settlers anywhere, the early arrivals tended to be misfits, single unskilled men with nothing to lose, and not much to offer. There was one woman in the community. She was approached by one of the settlers and rebuffed him, but not before he'd half-severed her right hand with a machete.

The Pipers refused to hand out the land as agreed. A community tractor had to be abandoned when jealous locals trampled their crops. And since the revolution, when land was nationalized, the community has been reduced to a holding of just 50 acres.

One morning in March 1958, before the sun had risen, three hundred Rastafarians gathered in Victoria Square, Kingston. They bore high banners of red, gold and black and announced they had captured the city.

The police moved in and the Rastas cried, 'Touch not the Lord's anointed!' But they were moved on before Kingston's citizens rose from their beds.

In the brief history of the cult, these isolated gestures of civil defiance belie a more patient thread of millenarian mysticism. In 1961 the Rastafarian Repatriation Association was set up to give classes in Amharic and Ethiopian history. But on 21 April, 1966 came the event that they'd all been expecting, the parousia, the arrival of Haile Selassie in a plane.

It was raining hard at Kingston Airport and the 100,000-strong crowd, about a tenth of them dreadlocked Rastafarians, were soaked to the skin. But the Rastas said, 'Don't you worry, as soon as He comes, rain will stop.' And they were right.

They rushed across the glittering tarmac to get a touch of the aircraft. The Emperor was overwhelmed. For thirty minutes he refused to get out. He had not expected this – his visit was simply part of a Caribbean tour.

No official record survives of the Emperor's attitude to his followers, but perhaps he felt like his forebear. In 1441 the Ethiopian mission to Rome brought a curt message from their emperor: 'My name is Zara Yaqob – "offspring of the prophet Jacob". My second name is Constantine. Why do Europeans call me Prester John?'

In 1969 the Ethiopian patriarchate accepted an invitation from Kingston, and sent some priests. Jamaicans flocked to become members of the ancient African Church. But many Rastafarians seemed disappointed. Where were the priests' dreadlocks? And, though the Emperor was titular head of their Church, why was he not a god?

L. E. Barrett, who studied the cult in the 1970s, was told by one woman member of the Church, 'We had an [Ethiopian] bishop but we drove him about. This man cut his hair, and his wife straightened hers. . . . One day the brethren asked if he believed in Jah Rastafari, and he could not give a definite answer. We can't have that.'

The next morning was crisp and clear. I sat on the step of Moody's house in the first warm rays of the sun. The gate was pushed open and a stocky Rasta appeared in a white T-shirt. I greeted him as he walked past me into the house, but got no response. He and Moody came out, arguing, a couple of minutes later.

'Movements, movements,' muttered the stocky Rasta. He was wild-eyed and belligerent. 'Sunshine day. Yer carder venue der tree now.'

The rest of the argument was lost on me.

Several times the stocky Rasta walked away towards the gate, only to turn back and say something else. Finally he reached the gate and disappeared, leaving it rattling against the jamb.

Once or twice I had felt a draught of dissent from the community. Now Moody said there was some dispute about where to have the celebrations. He shrugged and said it would clear up; there was no reason why the venue shouldn't be beneath the big tree up by Dyer's house.

Later I took a cart into the market with Tagessa and his boy. Waifs shouted 'Jamaica! Jamaica!' as we passed.

Tagessa grinned and said, 'Everyone loves Rasta in Ethiopia.'

In the maze of wattle stalls I bought rice and oranges, and at the bakery some cakes for the children. I found two bottles of Ethiopian champagne for the celebrations. Then we sat and had coffee in a small hotel by the main road.

Today Tagessa wore his locks heaped in a brand new woollen hat that one of the settlers had made: green, yellow and red in three broad stripes. He had kind, impressionable eyes and features that hinted at mulatto somewhere in his ancestry.

At the age of seven his family had moved from Birmingham, where he had been born, down to London. He had stayed at school until he was sixteen and then gone to technical college, deciding, as he put it, to 'get a little education under my belt, yer know'. He learned building skills and got a job with one of the big contractors, and did well: his manager began to put him in charge of small gangs on the site.

But then he became restless and sank his savings in a pilgrimage to Africa and Jamaica. He returned to London in the early 1980s with his hair in dreadlocks. In the meantime, riots in Brixton and Bristol, and the Scarman Report, had made people nervous; unemployment was high and there were no jobs for a Rasta.

So he set up his own business. He bought a van and drove around London doing refurbishment work. He was efficient and hard-working, and benefited from the great property boom of that time; in six years he had a tidy sum to show for it.

'But I wasn't happy,' he said. 'I didn't feel at home in England any more. It was never my culture. So I brought my wife and two children out here. There's much more I can do here with my skills – for the Ethiopians, and the community.'

Tagessa had started to learn Amharic, and had done the trail of government offices, offering his skills, applying for planning permission for a house at the community. So far, he had had no results and was beginning to feel frustration.

Before we left, Tagassa told me of one other plan he had for the community. He wanted to see if there was any truth in a story that was a recurrent part of the settlers' mythology: Emperor Menelik had sent a ship to Queen Victoria loaded with £120,000,000 worth of gold for the welfare of the freed slaves. Only £20,000,000 can be accounted for – sent to the slave owners themselves to compensate for the losses they incurred after Emancipation.

There are plenty of historical flaws in the claim, not least that Menelik had no money to spare for magnanimous gestures. But, like all myths, it says a lot about those who hold it: the persistent, bitter shadow of slavery and the equally persistent idea that money will make it tolerable.

Of the twenty or so households that remained at the settlement, Noel Dyer's was the oldest. He had been there for nearly twenty-five years, and was now in his early sixties. Last year his young Ethiopian wife had borne him his third child.

But that morning I found Dyer alone with his dog, sitting outside the shack that had been his home for all those years. He wore a woollen bobble-hat and a broad grin. He was reading the Bible. He pointed me to a wicker chair and put the book on the ground beside him.

In the 1950s he had left Jamaica, on one of the immigrant ships bound for England. At that time Rastafarians would go down to the docks and chant at the ships, 'Ethiopia – yes! England – no! Let my people go!'

Dyer was the only one to fulfil the cry. 'England,' he said, 'was my crossroads.'

One morning, in September 1964, he had woken up in Peckham and resolved to walk to Ethiopia. 'That day, Babylon left me. From then on, I was in Ethiopia. I had new Wrangler jeans and a mountain bag. And I took five pound, five shilling, and five pence,' he paused, adding, 'and a ha'penny.'

At Victoria Station there was a problem: since he couldn't read, Dyer was unable to find the Dover train. He stuck his hands deep into the pockets of his new jeans, and waited for something to happen.

'Young man, what's in your mind?' asked a Dutchwoman.

'I'm looking for Ethiopia. I'm the son of a slave and I'm going home.'

She pointed him to the right train.

His plan was to reach the Nile. If he found the Nile he knew he could follow it down to Ethiopia. So he went through France and Spain and into Morocco, and along the North African coast. He reached Egypt and walked down the banks of the river. He slept in houses deserted because of the Aswan Dam, and watched the new lake rise and lap at his feet.

In the Sudan he was arrested for being an alien. 'How can I be an alien in Africa?' he said to the judge. The Ethiopian Embassy in Khartoum agreed to give him a visa.

A year after he'd left London, Dyer climbed up into the Ethiopian highlands. He made his way to Addis Ababa.

'His Majesty asked me to come and paint a house in Sheshamane, 'cause I had done painting. So I came down here – that was when I found out about the land grant. Didn't know nothing about the land grant till then. And I been here ever since!'

He leaned back in his chair, and flashed his white teeth in a smile.

'Did you know I am an abstract painter? Taught myself – here, come see.'

Dyer took me inside and showed me a couple of his paintings. We carried a large hardboard work out into the sun, and propped it against a tree.

'See, this one I haven't finished yet, been doing it 'bout a year.'

It was a massive fantasy of images, naïve, brightly coloured. One of the bottom corners was a bright green field, surrounded by splashes of green, yellow and red, and a tractor and palm fronds, and a Rasta sitting against a tree. Everywhere else, the tones were pale, and showed buildings and barbed wire, big cars and cruel faces.

''s Babylon up here – and down here, Zion,' he explained, though it was hardly necessary.

Next he showed me a chicken run he had made years before. There were half-a-dozen birds inside, and Dyer bent to tap the wire and coo at them.

'They lay good, these chickens,' he said. 'But if I had more, I could sell the eggs in the town. Always get a good price for eggs in the town.'

'Why don't you get more?'

Dyer shrugged. 'No money for another run. I need money for the timber and all.' I had the same sense from him: that he felt he was owed the money.

In the early afternoon, I went with Dyer down to the sycamore on the other side of his plot. There were a few people there already: Tagessa was setting up his drums, a couple of others were dragging a big cedar log to the tree to sit on, and the stocky Rasta shifted from foot to foot, still looking aggrieved.

Presently Tagessa sat down on the log, shook his rat's-tail hair free from his hat and looked out into the afternoon sun, down the corn-coloured corridor of the Rift Valley, into Africa.

'Hmmmm . . .' he muttered, his chin raised. 'Ras Tafari!' Then he started to paddle the drum in front of him.

Others drifted up to the site in the next couple of hours, some taking up the drums, or singing, or chatting in small groups on the side. When the sun was low, some of the settlement's children came home from school and joined the party with their mothers.

Then I saw the Baptist preacher coming up the path. He was walking beside a field of ripe wheat, dressed in black clerical robes with a black umbrella over his shoulder. A huge white cross hung down his chest, and he wore dark glasses.

He dropped to one knee when he saw me, and waved his umbrella at the sky. 'Will you praise the Lord! Will you thank him for his mercy!' Then he came up, and put his hand on my forearm, confiding, 'These shoes, you know, had them for thirty years. Only wear them for special occasions. Ain't good shoes a holy thing?' Then he drew together the tails of his gown, and went off to find a drink.

Brother Dyer was sitting in his cane chair, grinning and smoking, looking very much the group's senior member. He showed me his Bible, an authorized version. 'Couldn't read when I was in Jamaica, when I was captive of Englishmen.' He looked at me darkly. 'Four hundred years we was in Babylon, slaves of the Englishmen.'

I shifted uncomfortably, and he could see he'd made his point.

He carried on. 'Got this Bible in Egypt, and taught myself to read from it. Psalm 87 was my psalm, used to know it by heart.' He closed his eyes and tried to remember it, but couldn't. So he read it to me:

'His foundation is in the holy mountains.
The Lord loveth the gates of Zion more than all the dwellings of Jacob.
Glorious things are spoken of thee, O city of God. Selah.
I will make mention of Rahab and Babylon to them that know me: behold Philistia, and Tyre, with Ethiopia; this man was born there . . .

'This man was born there,' he repeated. Then he smiled, and cocked an ear at the drums. I recognized the chorus of a Bob Marley song. 'The players on instruments, you see. These drums, we took 'em with us from Africa when we went. And now we brought 'em back!'

At dusk the drumming was hushed for a moment, and Brother Moody stood in the middle. 'On the occasion of the anniversary of the Coronation of His Imperial Majesty. . .'

'Ras Tafari,' mumbled the others.

'. . . Ras Tafari, Emperor Haile Selassie the First, I will read the verses of Psalm number 19.'

He read the text, to echoes of 'truly' and 'I-n-I'.

Then Brother Dyer rose to put a light to a pile of brushwood beneath the far branches of the tree. Tagessa started the drumming again with a song:

You must be ready when Ras Tafari comes . . .
– Soon come –
Make sure your heart is pure and bright!

The smoke rose through the sycamore's thick canopy and scattered the late sun into hazy shapes. About ten people had gathered in an arc around the drums, rocking backwards and forwards, repeating the refrains in an interminable, rhythmic litany.

A party of local Ethiopian boys had stopped on the path to watch the gathering. One of them clutched a football under his arm.

Brother Dyer had returned to his cane chair, and the Bible.

Tagessa's son was chasing a couple of the other children with a stick.

The Baptist minister stood waving his arms near the fire, partially obscured by smoke, like a genie, preaching on the evils of

Russia.

I stayed for a little longer, but was glad to leave. I walked back to Brother Moody's plot beneath a bright moon.

18

All morning the bus climbed through a catalogue of landscapes. At dawn we headed east from Sheshamane out of the Rift Valley on a sandy road, and into pine forests. The pines thinned to patchy hardwoods hung with creeper. Then we came to thick damp jungle where epiphytic ferns covered the boughs, and palm fronds leapt through the foliage.

I dozed off, and woke to open moorland. Its mattress of dark earth was cut by hidden valleys. We fell into one of these, and for a while seemed lost in its folds. Then the bus rattled over a brook and climbed out.

After that we came to a wide prairie. Across it marched a column of red combine harvesters. This was Ethiopia's wheat belt, a vast acreage of fertile land in the flood plain of the Webe Shebelle. But the land was given over to the grain factories, the collective farms run by the State.

For the other passengers, mostly poor farmers, it was an opulent fantasy. They craned their necks, or stood in the aisle pointing at the grain stacked in blue bags beside the road. At about midday a darker line rose from the horizon, the first ridge of the Bale Mountains.

Soon we were winding through a wooded valley. Its steep sides were thick with firs. We went higher, over high rock passes, above the tree line, before dropping into another, flat-bottomed valley.

We pulled up in the remote, dusty town of Dinsho, beside a flock of sheep and a man on a horse.

Back in the thin mountain air, I felt a sense of freedom and relief. Behind me was the hum of malarial mosquitoes, and the drums of the Rastafarians, so much more resonant than their ideology.

Bale is the least populated of Ethiopia's provinces. About the size of England, it has no more than half a million people. A part of the mountain massif has been put aside to form the Bale Mountains National Park, enclosing some of Ethiopia's wildest places. Just above Dinsho are the park's headquarters.

I found some low buildings in a clearing, and asked for the warden.

But the warden had gone to Addis Ababa, and had taken his assistant with him. The park's resident biologists were away, and the chief guide had been dismissed the previous week for some unstated mischief.

In the office there was a man in a pale green safari suit. I showed him my letter of introduction, and he looked at it for some time, his lips forming the words as he read. Then he handed it back to me, and said he was going to show me the nature trail, a short introduction to the park's exotic flora.

But it wasn't a great success – his was a new appointment and he seemed less sure of the species than I was. So I excused myself and went off alone into the forest.

When I returned, at dusk, there was a Land Cruiser in the clearing.

A young Amhara came and introduced himself as Mikhael, a biologist. 'I am sorry I wasn't here earlier,' he said. 'We've been in Goba sorting out papers.'

We walked up to his quarters, a room in a log cabin on the edge of the forest. The horned skull of a bushbuck hung outside. Inside, above his head, hung a reproduction of a Gondarene icon of St George.

Mikhael had studied biology at Addis Ababa University. 'But what I really want to do is to write,' he said.

'Scientific books?'

'No, no, novels. You know, sometimes I think I'd rather be an author than a biologist.' He looked at me with eyes full of enthusiasm. 'In my second year at university, I started to write a book. I wrote about half, and then, well, what with the exams and everything . . .' He pointed to a locker beside the bed. 'It's in there now.'

'What's the book about?'

'Facial expression.'

'Facial expression?'

'Yes, I discovered that one of the distinctive things about our species is our variety of expression – all with the facial muscles. What I have done,' he was using his hands now to colour the idea, leaving bright traces in the half-darkness with a cigarette, 'is to create a character with a completely blank face – no expression at all.'

'That's an interesting idea,' I said. 'You should carry on with it.'

'Yes, I know. I'd like to.' He stubbed out his cigarette and looked out through the open door. 'But the problem I have is that up here – in the mountains – my thoughts are different.'

The government tobacco company in Ethiopia has one standard brand of cigarette, packaged in a white carton with a large red circle on the front. They have called the brand 'Nyala', after Bale's rare antelope, the mountain nyala. The Ethiopian Post Office, meanwhile, has honoured another of the country's animals by featuring it on a series of stamps. Reproduced from a photograph, the stamp shows a Semien fox, the world's rarest canid, standing among everlastings in Bale's hardy alpine scrub.

Both these species are endemic in Ethiopia. They have become emblems of a whole group of flora and fauna unique to the country – species of rodent and primate, trees and shrubs, flowers like the Abyssinian rose, and at least twenty-three different kinds of bird.

The Ethiopian plateau is perfect for endemism. It is Africa's largest mountain region. It is temperate and fertile, and, like an island, is surrounded by habitats of a very different nature. Species in the Ethiopian mountains soon adapt and cannot survive at lower altitudes.

I couldn't help thinking that the reverence given to the endemic species by Ethiopians stems, at its core, from a feeling of identity with them.

For the Ethiopian plateau has also isolated its human inhabitants. Having pushed south into the mountains, the highlanders resisted the great changes that took place in the lowlands – Islam, and later, the Europeans. The scarp has formed a cultural filter and allowed separate development.

Like the fauna, many highland Ethiopians find it hard to survive lower down. There are the cultural differences, a different climate, different crops, diet and husbandry. All these make the environment a strange one, and there is the disease: centuries of living in the mountains, too high for tropical diseases, have destroyed their natural resistance. Malaria, yellow fever and a host of other horrors lurk at the foot of the mountains.

Mikhael agreed to show me the Harenna Forest in his Land Cruiser, provided I paid for petrol. We set off early, on a grey, damp morning, and drove round the edge of the high peaks to Goba, Bale's capital.

On the way, a stranded motor cyclist flagged us down. He cursed his machine, but said he'd stay with it, and gave us a letter for the Goba Security. Outside the office I found the usual forlorn group of people waiting while the clerks did nothing: the system idly flexing its muscles. I gave the letter to the manager and he grunted. I was glad not to have to ask him for anything. Behind his head was a hand-drawn diagram of 'management structure'. I had seen these in government offices all over the country. It showed a family tree of job titles, fanning out from a single large box, the boxes multiplying at each stage, getting smaller, each echelon harder to read, each job less intelligible.

Goba, itself little short of 10,000 feet high, rests in the shadow of a scarp. Up this scarp a road winds through thinning forest towards the Sanetti Plateau, and the highest all-weather route in Africa.

At the top there was a metal sign nudged by wisps of low cloud, announcing the boundary of the Bale Mountains National Park, and all the things that shouldn't be done there, like cutting wood, burning heather or grazing.

'Look out here for Semien fox,' said Mikhael. 'Sanetti is one of the best places.'

So I scanned the cold tracts of the moor. It was hard to imagine anything alive up here; the giant lobelia, now out of season, had forfeited its pagoda of bright leaves for a broken husk; and the white clumps of helichrysum looked like lifeless boulders. All that moved was the reflection of clouds in a few chrome-surfaced ponds.

But then I noticed a darker shape in the distance, then another, and another. Soon I could see half a dozen. Too big for Semien fox, and slow – they looked like cattle.

I pointed them out to Mikhael. He said nothing, but frowned and shook his head.

We stopped the vehicle and watched them through binoculars. I got out and felt the sudden stroke of air too thin and cold to turn its moisture to rain.

'Cattle,' confirmed Mikhael, 'from one of the villages down below.'

He leaned back inside the car and asked the driver to record the sighting. 'Sanetti,' he dictated, looking through the glasses again. 'Thirty, thirty-five head, heading north-west – and the time.'

We pulled back on to the dirt road. 'We spend so much time telling them not to graze,' he explained. 'Last week, I went down to talk to their chiefs. They all said: yes, yes, of course we will keep our animals out of the park, and now . . . But what can you do? They just don't understand.'

The idea of endemism has been grasped wholeheartedly by the authorities, but for the farmers, giving land to wild animals is hard to accept. Like most African peoples, Ethiopians cannot understand the passion for wildlife. Wild beasts are a source of fear or embarrassment, as though in civilized countries, almost by definition, nature is benign.

It was Dusty Golobitsch who brought to Bale the idea of a national park. He worked for the Peace Corps, and came from Colorado where wilderness is a way of life. In the late 1960s he rode and walked for hundreds of miles through the region, mapping it, working out possible boundaries, logging the area's wildlife and plants – and he made a special point of talking to the local people about the reasons for the project.

One night, shortly before the revolution, Golobitsch sat next to a fire at Dinsho with Paul Henze and a bottle of brandy. He explained to Henze that he was frustrated with the Emperor's government. They had not granted legal status to the park, so there was still no authority to curb the damage being done to the area by ploughing and burning heather. The number of nyala continued to fall.

When Henze returned to Dinsho the following year, Dusty Golobitsch had gone. But his work has continued, and now has official backing. Since the early 1980s the nyala population has risen to a stable level. According to Jonathan Kingdom, a biologist recently studying endemism in Bale, Ethiopia's Wildlife Conservation Organization is 'exemplary in Africa'.

The southern edge of the Sanetti Plateau is very steep. Looking down, all I could see were hairpins curling into the mist. Everything had faded in the grey light: the grey cloud and the grey of the land, an emulsion of earth and sky.

Ahead of us was an old Land Rover. As it descended, it kept passing in and out of sight, out of bends far below, into the cloud, under a spur, until I thought it must be an hallucination, a trick of the light. We sat in silence, staring through the windows.

The Harenna escarpment falls more than 5000 feet in four miles, though the road, endlessly traversing and doubling back, is many times that. For botanists the scarp face is a textbook model: at the top, above the tree line, is the thin Afro-alpine scrub, then heather, and giant heather woods, mixing with giant St John's wort, and the ubiquitous hagenia (though no juniper on these southern slopes). At the bottom are *podocarpus*, stretching into the distance as the flocculent treetops of the Harenna Forest.

Until 1983, few people had been into the Harenna Forest. In that year, the road from Goba to Dolo Mena was finished and now carries a little traffic, government officials, park staff, an occasional lorry laden with bottles of coke and lemonade.

In its wake came a team of scientists, a combined expedition of Ethiopians and the New York Zoological Society. They spent twenty days in the forest, and covered just a tiny fraction of it. But it was enough to justify their efforts: of the specimens collected, there were species of amphibia, rodents and plants previously unknown to science.

We drove straight through the forest, a forty-mile avenue down to Dolo Mena. Here the main street was hot and dusty. Lines of women squatted in the shade selling fruit and spices, and a pair of camels dawdled beneath a fig tree.

On the way back out of town, a man flagged us down. He had a khaki jacket over his shoulder, and wore sunglasses.

'Security,' whispered Mikhael.

I gave him my papers.

He said, 'You should have come to our office when you arrived. We have to check everyone going through the forest.'

'I didn't know.'

'It's just that in the last two days there's been trouble with a lion.'

We crossed the plateau again in a cold, haunting twilight. Cloud rose up from the gorges, and Tullu Deemtu, Ethiopia's second highest mountain caught the last of the sun.

It was late when we stopped in to Goba on our way back to the park headquarters. We found a hotel that would serve us food, but only if we sat outside on the terrace. They told me why but I still didn't understand. The terrace was cold and so was the food.

In the first light I walked round to the valley above my tent. I hoped to see nyala grazing, but all I could find was hyena spoor and a black bull which stared at me from the trees like some mythical creature.

Then Abdellah came over the brow of the hill with three horses, and a little later we left Dinsho, riding south. We climbed up through the forest and out on to a moor above the tree line. Abdellah, a Galla, was an ox of a man, with the easy manner to go with it. In the cool air, I coveted his riding boots and windproof coat, standard issue for the park's wardens.

At midday we dismounted and ate bread and cheese in the heather. The sky was a brilliant blue, broken by a few flecks of clouds. Behind us rose a steep scree-slope, topped by cliffs running as a frieze round the whole valley. Abdellah pointed out the caves where the hyenas lived.

Then he turned and nodded across the valley floor, grunting, his mouth full of cheese: a herd of about nine nyala was moving towards us.

An old bull turned his head and sniffed the air, sensing the horses. Then he changed direction, without nervousness or fear, avoiding us without appearing to do so, and the herd followed him.

The horizons of the Bale Mountains are unlike anywhere else. Paul Henze recalls a map of Tolkien's Middle Earth hanging in Golobitsch's house at Dinsho, and as he came to know Bale's strange landscape found the association more and more apt.

The mountains are fairly recent, formed by lava flows in the tertiary era (the Rift Valley has since split them from the rest of the Ethiopian highlands). But the lava is now scoured smooth – except in the old necks of the volcanoes themselves. Here the magma cooled more slowly, and survives as more resistant rocky outcrops, thrust up like fists into the mountain sky.

Towards dusk, thick cloud drifted across the plateau. We made camp on the edge of a gorge and built a fire. As soon as the sun dropped behind the mountains, all traces of warmth vanished and the cold wind dashed round the cliffs.

Abdellah crouched beside the flames. Our conversation had been limited. I spoke no Gallinya, and he had only a little English. So we pooled our Amharic and translated the names of plants and animals for each other.

'No Semien fox yet,' I said.

'No.'

'Tomorrow maybe we'll see one.' It was the reason for our expedition.

'Maybe.' Abdellah poked the fire.

Some hours later I heard one of the horses snort. Abdellah jumped up.

'What is it?' I asked.

'Hyena.'

Then the horses whinnied, and we took the torch down to the boulder where they were tied.

I walked out a little way into the darkness. I heard the far rush of a waterfall, but could see nothing. Then a pair of eyes flashed, mirrored retina in Abdellah's torchlight. And others too, all around me. There was no noise. Darting about, apparently unattached to anything, the flashes looked as innocent as fireflies. But I could smell the animals: in the crisp night air the musty hyena smell was unmistakable.

They cowed from the torch and our shouting, and one by one their flashing eyes disappeared.

I woke from a cold semi-conscious sleep and pulled back the flap of the tent. The brighter stars still shone in a milky-blue sky. But they were being engulfed, slipping into the no man's land between night and dawn.

Beneath the line of far mountains a stiletto of mist stretched down the valley. Nothing moved but a nyala trotting against it, its deliberate movement out of place in the intense stillness.

I walked up through the boulders to the foot of the cliff. Ladders of hoar frost crunched under my feet, and covered the rocks in tiny crystals. It was deathly cold – a numbing, primal cold.

Somewhere in this lunar place, Semien foxes were sleeping out. They don't burrow, but live out, shouldering diurnal temperature differences of as much as 40°C.

The sun caught the highest peak. Around the arena, others were lit up, transforming dull basalt columns into shining spires. The shadows slid back, to uncover flecked yellows and greens, down the steep slopes around the peaks, quicker across the moor, down towards the waterfall beneath our camp.

I went to the waterfall, and reached it with the sun. Here the young River Web tumbles over an overhanging lip and joins a smaller stream. I sat above it in the sun's first rays. The mole rats peered out of their holes, and they too sat in the sun, as yet untroubled by the threat of the Semien fox.

For a moment everything was still, basking in the surprise of sudden warmth. The frost melted on the white everlastings. Ravens, and a group of hyrax sat unmoving on an outcrop above the falls; the sky was still, empty of clouds and the spinning cruciforms of the eagles. Up here, the beginning of each day was like Spring accelerated.

Abdellah was boiling a pan of water when I got back, my hands full of heather stems for the fire. The camp was still in shadow.

'The hyenas returned,' he said. 'I stayed up until after two with the horses.'

'You should have woken me.'

But he shrugged and smiled, and poked the embers with a stick.

We drank tea and I said, 'I thought I'd walk up the valley. Maybe I will see a Semien fox.'

I went down again to the falls, took my shirt off and washed in a clear pool. The water was as cold as snow-melt. It fell into the pool with the continuous rushing sound of a millstream, echoing in the small basin. I walked up into the Wolla Gorge.

Low cliffs squeezed the banks into the stream, and I climbed beneath the long mouth of a cave. In there, I imagined, last night's hyenas were sleeping off their scavenging. Hurrying past it, I scrambled up on to the scrappy turf of the moor.

I saw a pair of Wattled Crane. The scarcity of these birds can be understood by watching their comic, long-legged gait. Their heads bobbed up and down as if operated by strings. They were a joke species, out of scale; I couldn't decide whether they looked more like old men, or gauche fumbling lovers.

Crossing a low saddle, I came across a hut, and after a while, a cluster of about six more. I couldn't believe that people lived here, but as I approached, scrawny figures appeared in the doorways and we stared at each other, each too surprised for any greeting.

At this height, the morning sun was so harsh that it seemed to allow no shadows. Instead, away from its beam there was just a cavernous darkness, so that I could not see the eyes of the villagers, and the cliffs looked like rows of broken teeth, white on black.

In Gallinya, *waqa*, means both sky and God. Now it was a deep upturned bowl, pale blue at the rim, almost violet at its height. But at night the sky turns dark and hardens the earth with frost. When it is clear, there are so many stars, they seem to be the ceiling of a larger hut, embracing the mountains, stretching beyond even Goba. And when the sun comes again, it blesses the morning with its warmth and transforms the frozen tundra into a dry semi-desert.

But still I had not seen a Semien fox and kept thinking of its image on the 15c stamp. I walked back down the valley, peeling off layers of clothing as the sun rose. I crossed and recrossed the Wolla. The cliffs screeched with the sound of hyrax.

At one point I looked up and saw three hardy baboons sitting on the cliff top, following my movements; when I looked again, they had gone.

Down at the waterfall, I watched a pair of buzzards spar in the gorge. Then something red bloomed into view, over the brow of the hill: a lone Semien fox, a male. I was surprised at first by its height. It was the colour of a European Red fox, but bigger, with much longer legs. Its chin and breast were tufted with white hair, and it moved towards me with a jaunty, untroubled stride.

Jonathan Kingdom calls the Semien fox the 'Ethiopian wolf'; its colour, he says, is the most fox-like thing about it. It is certainly a more powerful animal than a fox – its jaws have been known to break a lamb's back with a single bite. But, strictly, it is neither fox nor wolf. Its two remote niches, here in the Bale Mountains and in fewer numbers in the High Semien in northern Ethiopia, have allowed it to develop into its own genus (*canis simensis*), far from any of its closest cousins.

Some years ago, before the National Park, the Semien fox was classed by the International Union for the Conservation of Nature as 'critically endangered'. Now, despite my own slowness in spotting one, there are as many as four hundred in the park. In the Semien Mountains, there are fewer. No one is sure how few the war has cut off these mountains, but a total count of seven hundred is accepted as reasonable for Ethiopia's – and the world's – most obscure member of the canine family.

This one was getting closer to me. I crouched and kept still. I was downwind, but knew that he would soon sense my presence. I saw him stop dead, looking down at something quite close. He had seen a mole rat that hadn't seen him. For at least a minute he was still, chin pressed down on to his front legs, as if about to pounce. But instead he took two steps forward, and froze again. I froze too, watching the predator watching its prey, and the buzzards stopped fighting and sat on a ledge, and the hyrax were quiet. Everything froze with the Semien fox, waiting for the attack. Everything except the waterfall and the mole rat.

Then he did pounce, in a sudden flowing movement. But he was too slow. The mole rat was deep in its hole by the time he reached it, and he padded away, his long snout empty, his tongue darting out for a moment to lap up a drop of saliva.

He went up to the edge of the cliff, and let out a long squeal, a strange high-pitched noise for such an animal.

When he saw me, now no more than twenty yards away, he barked three or four times, very loudly – so loudly that the echo bounced off the rocks and rolled down the valley. Then he looked straight at me, and I could see his eyes, austere, pencilled black, lodge some terrible accusation before he turned away and ran back towards the river.

Abdellah was watering the horses in the small stream below the camp. He had heard the barking, but said nothing. We saddled up and rode down to Dinsho.

Some of the scattered forces of the park team had regathered at Dinsho. The park manager had come back from Addis Ababa with his assistant, and one of the resident biologists had arrived with his wife and parents.

But first I went with Abdellah to see his children. His wife was winnowing corn on the grass in front of their small house. Abdellah bent and scooped up a two- or three-year-old girl. She sat on his arm and leaned against his huge chest, staring at me. Abdellah beamed.

I said goodbye to Abdellah and went to see the manager. He lived in another clearing, in a rather bigger house with a Calor gas stove. His maid roasted some coffee for us. He was an Aderri, and we talked about Harar.

The park's hierarchy, in Addis Ababa and down here, bore out the unstated pecking order of Ethiopia's ethnic groups. Management is highland Ethiopia – Amhara, Tigrean, perhaps an Eritrean. In amongst them is an astute Aderri. Drivers and wardens tend to be Galla. A litle apart from all of this are the foreigners, ghosts in the machine. There aren't many, and over the years here they've played bit-parts, each inspired by the place itself to inject a little time or advice.

It is they, for instance, who know the importance of having the National Park governed by one central authority; they know the value of tourists, how to lure them to the honeypot, what they want, what they expect; they know about equipment, vehicles, radios, issues of warm clothing for the morale of the wardens. And they know also, with the slight embarrassment of the post-colonial white in Africa, that they mustn't interfere, that the park as a protected piece of Ethiopia should be, in the end, run by Ethiopians. Their role is always transitory. But there is the other wider motive, more enduring than the altruism of imparting expertise: that in Bale as in all Africa's reserves rests the delicate future of a great deal of wildlife.

After a silence, the manager said, 'The BBC came here last month. Just for a few days – they said they had ten or twenty minutes to film. Part of a series about the Rift Valley. But they were so impressed they're coming back next month. They want to make a whole film about Bale. They said they had no idea about the Bale park, and how much was here.'

He smiled. He realized that his job, in some small way, was significant outside Ethiopia. It was an exciting period. The following month a pair of new buildings was to be opened for visitors.

The Swedish ambassador was coming down for the official opening; they were going to kill an ox. The buildings had been a gift of the Swedish, and displayed all the softwood finish of Swedish design. There was an element of debt in the gesture: the original building had been destroyed in a fire in the early 1980s, a Swedish professor apparently its cause.

19

In my absence President Mengistu had made some surprising announcements in his annual address to the Central Committee. Addis Ababa, true to form, was buzzing with the news.

Until this speech there had been no sign that Mengistu and his ruling Dergue would pay any heed to the tide of change that was sweeping through the communist bloc. Word was that he had done the tour of his patrons earlier in the year and heard the same ultimatum in Moscow and Peking: liberalize or forfeit the arms handouts. But he made no concessions and I imagined Ethiopia, ever the stubborn independent, clinging to hardline Marxism–Leninism for years to come, an ideological museum, a place for the next generation of political students to peer in and see how governments used to behave in the bad old days.

But now Mengistu was talking about economic reforms, limited private ownership of capital and of opening up the agricultural markets, even foreign investment. And there was an admission that over half of the government spending was used up by the army and the war in the north.

Billy had the inside story. 'They don't trust him,' he said, as we drove up past the old palace to Arat Kilo. 'There are rumours that he's going to devalue the birr to attract foreign money. The black market rate for US dollars is about double the bank rate. If they float it, that's what it'll be. Suddenly, you've got half the money you thought. So everyone's desperate to get rid of their cash.'

He lit a cigarette and for a moment steered the pick-up with his knee. 'So, you see, business has gone crazy. My brother-in-law sells spare parts and he says everyone's buying up his stock – he's had to close up. I'm telling you, it's just crazy.'

'But just mentioning economic reform – surely that's a good sign?' I said.

'Maybe, maybe.'

We arrived at his restaurant, and went through to the back room. Almaz brought some coffee. It was a bright, cloudless day and the sun fell through a pair of skylights, dividing the room into fractured pools of light and shadow.

Billy went to the kitchens, and Almaz asked me, 'Do you have malaria medicine?'

'Yes, but . . .'

'Could you give me some?'

I knew she was not interested in a specific. To her, medicine was medicine and you could never have too much of it, whatever its properties. I thought of giving her some paracetamol as a placebo, but somehow couldn't bear the deceit.

So I said, 'Where do you live?'

'Shiromeda.'

'In Shiromeda, Almaz, there's no malaria.' It was too high.

'But, so many people die up there.'

'It must be something else. Is it fever?'

'I don't know,' she shrugged. The symptoms didn't seem important. 'My neighbour, she got ill and they said: you take fifteen shots. Fifteen – so many!' She held up her hands and started to count. After four, she dropped her eyes and said, 'And then she die. Terrible. So many people die – maybe four or five people I know. Terrible.'

Billy came back, and Almaz slipped away. He shook his head when I told him. 'I've told her not to worry. What else can I do? I have a good doctor if she gets ill. Of course she's frightened when her neighbours start dying. But shit, a few paludrine aren't going to do much good.'

That night I dreamt there was a coup. I was driving at speed through Addis, down Churchill Avenue, left at La Gare and into Abiot. It was very important I got somewhere fast. But where? The airport – Bole Airport! I had to leave the country.

But when I got there everything slowed down, the dead weight of procedure, and soldiers, and endless barriers. Next I was in a bare room and Mengistu was asking me questions. The brass buttons of his tunic were as bright as jewels. I realized then that the coup had been my idea.

I met an English friend for lunch next day, in the Hilton. We had sandwiches beside the swimming pool. He said, 'Yes, I have dreams about him too. I think it's inevitable. If you spend long enough here, all that anxiety eventually wraps itself around him.'

Hugo was the UN field officer for Wollo and Gondar, his job to monitor food supply. In 1940 his grandfather had been a brigadier in the force that helped liberate Ethiopia. Hugo, I could see, was exhausted. He had been here nearly two years, waging an unending campaign for information.

'I can't wait to leave,' he said. 'In the last couple of months I've felt ill – nothing in particular, but enough to give me a couple of days in bed. And I can't seem to concentrate. I think it must be a combination of high pressure and high altitude!'

He looked away at the pool, which was full of Ethiopian children and big-bellied men. Above them a new block of rooms had been added to the hotel, based apparently on the design of Lalibela's rock-hewn churches. To begin with I had hated coming to the Hilton. In a way I still did. But it was always the place people wanted to meet, and I found myself less strident in my objections, forfeiting them for an attraction I couldn't quite identify. The food perhaps – or worse, was it the same reason the rich Ethiopians liked it: that it wasn't Ethiopia?

Hugo carried on. 'At the back of all our minds I suppose – the fear *ferengi* are encouraged to feel – is expulsion. I'm always aware that with ten minutes warning they could throw my driver in gaol and tell me to leave. It's happened often enough before. You see, we're here on sufferance. You never feel really comfortable or safe – even with other aid workers.'

'But surely you're on the same side?'

'Well, yes, but the officials, wily as they are, play a very clever game of divide and rule. They give permits to one agency and not the other, or they'll air confidential suspicions about a friend in another agency. And before you know it you've been sucked into the intrigue and there's a barrier between you. You can't afford not to play the game, and risk your own position and your own permits.'

'Are you disillusioned?'

He thought for a moment, and then said, 'If I am, it's only professionally. I have a great respect for the Ethiopians, despite the problems that some – and it's only some – create for us. But it is disappointing that after all this time none of us really has any clearer idea about famine, or how to deal with it.'

We walked back up into the hotel and out to the car park. Hugo offered me a lift. 'A couple of days ago I went to see the head of Security in Gondar – a great big man, wears his uniform like an Italian fascist. For months he'd made things very difficult for me. I had come to apply for a permit I'd wanted for weeks, and to say goodbye. I told him my replacement would arrive in a week or two. I shook his hand and said, as a sort of jokey understatement, "It hasn't always been entirely satisfactory." And he just smiled broadly and said nothing, as if the whole thing had been a game which he'd won.'

We drove down towards Abiot. On the right is the palace, on the left the ECA, the United Nations' African headquarters; elsewhere are the main offices of the Organization of African Unity. The Emperor had a vision of Addis Ababa as the continent's capital and persuaded a number of pan-African organizations to have their headquarters there. But until the country is more stable, it is unlikely to be fulfilled.

'When are you going to Dessie?' asked Hugo.

'Tomorrow.'

'Well, there's a young painter there you should see. Ask any of the aid workers how to find him.'

'I'll do that.'

Just before the bridge that runs into Abiot, there is a thirty-foot bronze statue of Lenin. His left hand grips his lapel in a characteristic gesture, and he is striding forth, chin raised in hope, towards Abiot.

'You know the joke about that statue?' asked Hugo.

'No.'

'They say he's hurrying towards the airport – clutching his exit visa!'

Waiting for a taxi near Giorgis Cathedral, I watched an old Peugeot rattle to a halt beside me. An elderly man leaned across the passenger seat and offered me a lift. He wore a neat grey suit and had a patrician dignity that was almost precious, and I associated him at once with the *ancien régime*.

He said he used to know Sylvia Pankhurst when she lived in Addis Ababa, 'a great lady'. 'You know her son, I suppose,' he said.

'Oh, yes.'

'And her grandson?'

'Yes.' He was an anthropologist, doing an ethnographic study in western Ethiopia. I had been mistaken for him on a number of occasions. I added, 'Her granddaughter is also in Ethiopia, an anthropologist in northern Shoa.'

He smiled and shook his head. 'Ah, you see how much that family loves Ethiopia!'

We turned off the main street, and I asked him about his work.

'I am a priest,' he said. In fact he was the chief secretary of the priesthood. 'In our country priests are very important. We have very many priests.'

'How many?'

'Sixty thousand.'

I did a little mental arithmetic. Assuming a Christian population of twenty million, that meant there was about one priest per 350 people.

Then I remembered a theory about the Ethiopian priesthood, in J. S. Trimingham's book *Islam in Ethiopia*. Why is it, he asked, that the two great monotheistic faiths in Ethiopia are so clearly defined by geography: the mountain-dwelling Amhara and Tigreans remained Christian, while the surrounding peoples accepted the teachings of Mohammed? The answer, he said, lay in the sedentary nature of Ethiopian highland society, their fixed farms and fertile land.

Such a people can support a priesthood with tithes, while the pastoral lowlanders, with fewer permanent settlements, cannot. Islamic worship does not require the intercession of a priest, just somewhere to lay a prayer mat a few times a day. Ethiopian Christianity, on the other hand, is a sacerdotal faith, and heavily dependant on the fixed site of a church and its clerical community.

At the entrance to the Church Office we were stopped. Two guards armed with rifles peered through the windows and asked questions.

They let us through but I sensed a change from when I had been here a couple of months before. There were no groups of clergy beneath the juniper, no wizened elders tugging at their beards or sitting alone reading psalters in the sun. The compound was empty.

I asked my friend what it was, but he shook his head and

shrugged. I went to see my allies, Abbas Tadessa and Mesfin, but was told they were busy.

Later I heard what had happened. Power was realigning itself in the Church hierarchy. Since the inauguration of the new patriarch, the old supremacy of the Gojjam faction was being threatened by Gondar. Subtle manoeuvres were taking place, new pressures in new places, old loyalties tested and changed. And in one place, it seemed, the pressure had not yielded: the executive head of EOC DICAD, the Church's own aid agency, had been shot dead by his driver. The driver, I was told, had become 'suddenly deranged'.

I met Billy, by chance, one evening in a bar near Sidist Kilo. It wasn't long before curfew.

'Hey, Philip! Come and have a drink.'

Billy had been there most of the evening, and his face was puffy with drink. He ordered some more whisky. 'So where are you off to next?'

'North again. I'm trying to get to Gishen, the mountain monastery. Have you been there?'

He shook his head, and looked down into his drink. 'Things are hard at the moment. Some of the authorities are making problems, and still I haven't managed to get out of Addis. It's not fair on my family. Normally I go hunting when things get too much – but with the malaria and everything I haven't been for nearly two months. This country, I don't know. I just don't know.' And he shook his head again.

'Have you ever thought of moving away – maybe to Kenya?'

'Kenya! All the business there is run by the Indian mafia. They won't let you get started.' He threw back his drink. 'And their wildlife! You can walk up to those lions and kick them in the arse. Here you never see lions in the day. No, they'd have to drive me out. I love this country.'

It was still dark in Abiot when I walked across it, but dawn glowed above the far hills. A van full of Ethiopian Airlines staff stopped and they offered me a lift to the airport. My flight to

Dessie, I had been told, was at seven that morning. No, said the airline staff, the Dessie flight leaves at eleven.

So I sat in the departure lounge and gleaned a faint, vicarious pleasure from watching the board announce flights to Cairo, Rome, Paris, even Moscow.

A boisterous EAL official came up and said, 'Did you hear that Gorbachev has sealed up Lenin's Library?'

'Where did you hear that?'

'On the BBC this morning.' He turned to tell his colleagues the news, and they all laughed at the thought of the Great Man being delionized.

Ethiopian Airlines can afford such irreverence. The oldest airline in Africa, they have the reputation of ranking with the world's better outfits. In Ethiopia the company is also something of an anomaly. Perhaps because its standards and operations have to be internationally-based, the management insists on autonomy, and it is highly profitable. Despite the Bahar Dar air crash, my present delay, and the occasional defection of pilots, I felt a certain admiration for the company.

And I thought of the French aid worker in Dire Dawa who'd levelled blame at the 'system' for frustrating the natural, un-African efficiency of Ethiopians.

'Look! Oh-oh!' The small plane dipped over a canyon. The young adviser from the Ministry of Agriculture recovered himself. 'There is the problem!'

He leaned across me and pointed through the window. 'How do you introduce technology there? Not even a tractor can get into those gorges to plough – certainly not a harvester.'

Now nearly two months after the rains, the land was the colour of tanned hide. Even from up here the slopes looked vertiginous. The terraces broke the hills into hundreds of carefully-crafted steps, sharp light and shadow in the high sun.

'You see how many people live here,' continued the adviser. 'Everywhere there are farms. Once, it was all trees, but the farmers have cut them down. Now the soil is washed away when it rains. So many people, you see.' He sighed and looked out of the window, his work spread out below him.

'What about resettlement?' I asked. The policy of transferring people from here to the fertile lowlands is defended on the grounds of overpopulation. Fewer than one in seven of Ethiopia's usable acres is under the plough. But the scheme is fraught with problems. Lower altitudes mean different crops, different ways of farming. There is malaria, and the unseen problems: disorientation, split families, the same human costs that many of the Falashas have faced in their own flight from war and famine.

The adviser continued to stare past me, out of the window. He paused before answering and I could see the question inspired no conviction in him. 'Well yes, resettlement, in this sort of country, maybe.'

The plane descended, flew round a mountain, and up a rocky valley to Kombolcha, where an airstrip served for Dessie. Outside the airport building, the floorboards were cracked and rotting. A lammergeyer, the 'lamb vulture', swooped overhead, its black-and-white head darting between wings impossibly wide and still.

In Kombolcha I met a garage proprietor at the town's private hotel. We ate a meal of good pasta off English ironstone.

'I always come here,' said Kifle. 'Very good hotel. Many people come down from Dessie just to eat here.'

The manager, he explained, used to run the Ghion, which was just as good. But after the revolution it was nationalized, so he packed up his English china and brought it here, with his reputation and his loyal clientele.

Kifle said he would drive me up into Dessie. But first he had to pick up his brother from the veterinary clinic. We drove into a yard where Kifle's brother was castrating sheep on the grass. He looked up and waved, his hands tinted with iodine. He handed a clamp to his assistant, came over to us and offered me his forearm to shake.

We drove on up the valley. The road began to twist as it steepened.

Kifle's brother was talking about the centralized agricultural policies. 'All the best land they take for the co-operatives or state farms. . . . Dairy farmers often cannot get feed for their cattle. . . . These new microdams, they cost so much and only serve about 800 hectares – the valleys are so steep.'

As we approached Dessie the slopes became thick with eucalyptus. Kifle pointed at them, saying, 'Three years ago, this was all dead – no trees. Now, you can see, it is green.'

After the morning's cheerless litany, the trees took on a sudden poignancy: a little hope from the dead land.

Dessie was named when Yohannis IV saw a comet there towards the end of the nineteenth century. Comets are portents of good fortune in Ethiopia, and the name Dessie is translated as 'my joy'. But it has rarely been apt.

In 1943 Wilfred Thesiger was appointed by the Emperor as adviser to his son, Crown Prince Asfa Wossen. Asfa Wossen was Governor of Wollo province, and Dessie is its capital. For Thesiger, the year he spent in Dessie was the most frustrating of his life.

The town is built in the gully between two mountains, but the valley is deceptive. It hangs, at 8000 feet, above a much larger valley which itself borders the scarp, and tumbles into the deep wastes of the Danakil desert.

Thesiger was the first to explore the Danakil. Twenty-three years earlier, in June 1910, he had been born at the British Legation in Addis Ababa. As a boy he had witnessed the uncertainty of the interregnum after Menelik's death, and a victory parade below the city when he was six impressed on him 'a life-long craving for barbaric splendour'. There is nowhere that was more barbarous nor splendid than imperial Ethiopia.

So, in the early years of the Emperor's reign, he followed the Awash river along the Rift Valley, down to the Abhe salt flats where the water surrenders to the desert sun. In *The Life of My Choice* Thesiger records this six-month journey in affectionate detail: the hunting expeditions for bushbuck and nyala, his guide Omar's Arab cunning, the forests of Arussi and a moonlit dance by a Danakil woman.

Thesiger's account is haunted by the ambiguous shadow of these Danakil nomads, the Afar. His party encountered them frequently, and was often at risk from their merciless attacks. But to Thesiger they were also profoundly attractive, and their austere nobility seemed to articulate the failings of his English education.

In Dessie ten years later, Thesiger came up against Ethiopia's other persona: that impassive bureaucrat, xenophobic and evasive, who can imprison a foreigner better than any gaol. Thesiger spent a year in the town, never asked out, passing his days on an Arab stallion riding in the hills, shooting duck and snipe, and waiting for permission to tour the province. But it never came. So he resigned, and went off to the Empty Quarter.

Since the revolution, Thesiger has vowed never to set foot in Ethiopia again. His autobiography is a lament for a country which died with the Emperor. But I couldn't help feeling that his Ethiopia was something within him, and had vanished long before the revolution. Everything in his life seems to have been measured, almost always unfavourably, against the magical Ethiopian childhood, and the wild, brilliant days of the Danakil adventure.

One morning, at dawn, I walked out of the valley, up the western ridge above the town. I stood in a grove of young shoulder-high eucalyptus, with stems of a plastic green and leaves metallic blue. The brown roofs of Dessie stained the valley below like a pool of stagnant water. I found it hard to believe that this was the country's fourth largest city.

There is something of Gondar in Dessie's tin-shack architecture, the same rusty shadow of the Occupation. Italianate villas poke out of the slums, and above the shops, flanked by peeling jalousies, the windows stare down on streets once paced by Mussolini's troops.

In 1935 Haile Selassie waited in Dessie while the Italians marched south. He was photographed peeping over a machine gun, a tiny figure of great presence, defending his empire against the Blackshirts. When the photograph appeared in Europe, it helped to sway public opinion against Italy, and to ensure the failure of the Hoare–Laval Pact.

Ten days after the fall of Gondar, in April 1936, the Italians marched into Dessie and found banners stretched between the buildings, telling them in Amharic that 'The Hawk has flown.'

The Emperor had, in fact, gone north, skirting round the advancing army, on a pilgrimage to Lalibela. Three days he prayed there for his stricken empire, then wound back to Addis Ababa.

Now more than fifty years later, Dessie was again uneasy at the thought of enemies pushing south, through the mountains, down the same narrow route: Tigreans, *shifta*, all the counter-revolutionary threats to the Motherland.

Originally I had applied for permission to come to Dessie for two reasons. Lalibela was one of them.

Of all Ethiopia's remarkable testaments of faith, Lalibela is probably the greatest. Some hundred miles to the north of Dessie, it is an ancient religious community with eleven churches. Inside these churches, the detailing is elaborate: painted domes, mullioned windows, elaborate frieze work, monkey-head beams, arcades of square columns, not unusual features of Ethiopian architecture. But what is extraordinary is that they have not been built, but carved out of the rock. Nowhere is there any blemish, and the symmetry is near-perfect.

There is only one painting of King Lalibela, the thirteenth-century Zagwe ruler. It is in the British Museum and shows him cutting the rock with a pick, helped by angels. In a dream he had flown by night to Jerusalem, and decided he must have his own Holy City in the mountains.

The excavation took twenty-three years, and probably involved masons from Syria or Greece, and maybe India. Yet the details are indigenous.

Alvares was the first European to see the churches, in the sixteenth century. He wrote eight pages of rhapsodic description, but then gives up, pre-empting James Bruce's problems when describing Ethiopia's oddities:

> I weary of writing about these buildings because it seems to me I shall not be believed.

Since my arrival in Ethiopia I had considered every possible way to reach Lalibela, to meet the same shrugging response: it is closed because of the war. Sometimes the officials weren't even sure it was in government hands. In Dessie I thought I might somehow be able to elude the authorities, and thought of the Emperor's dash around the Italian lines. But he held more sway in the mountain villages, and I knew that the first peasants' association would hand me in. When I had travelled with Yared around Lake Tana, every village had asked to see my papers. I decided finally that I would not get there.

The closest I got was seeing the notorious Dean of Lalibela, down in Dessie to butter up officials. In the car park of the Ghion was his brand new V8 Land Rover, a gift of the Lutheran World Federation. In the hotel, people were quick to point him out and to say that he was a Party member, and that he carried a gun at all times.

So I set about investigating my other reason for coming to Dessie: Gishen Mariam, mountain-top monastery and site of the True Cross.

20

Sergio came from Naples and had just finished setting up a Primary Health Care Programme. We were driving to the Italian compound, late one evening.

'For me,' he said, 'sometimes the only good thing about being in Dessie is going to the lake. You know the lake at Haik?'

'Is that Haik Istifanos?'

'Yes, that's the monastery there.' He hit the steering wheel with the flat of his hand. 'Oh! If only we could go there now!'

'Why don't we?'

He waved his hand at the windscreen in a good Neapolitan gesture. 'The moon is too small!' Then, almost absent-mindedly, 'Anyway, we'd never get past the checkpoint at this time of night. We'll go there tomorrow.'

We took the infamous route north. In better days this road was Ethiopia's only link with her largest port at Massawa. But too many convoys had been intercepted by Tigrean guerrillas. So in the last couple of years, it had been closed from northern Wollo. Addis Ababa now only had two land routes to the outside world: the railway to Djibouti and the road across the Danakil to Assab.

From the checkpoint – manned by a large group of teenage soldiers – the road was rutted and single-track. It had been built by the Italians during the Occupation, and boasted a walled embankment. In one place this was breached, and I saw, far below, the shell of a military truck balanced on a terrace.

'That was two weeks ago,' said Sergio. 'Those Russian trucks – they're so old and dangerous.'

Murmurs of war echoed through the upper reaches of these mountains and seeped into the valleys, an invisible force like the wind – previous wars, current dissent, hidden behind impassive peasant faces. The checkpoint soldiers wore frowns and looked jumpy.

Earlier in the year, said Sergio, the Tigreans had pushed south and the nights were filled with the sound of artillery. The curfew was a little stricter, and there were the usual whispers about whether the government would survive. Embassies told their subjects not to go out of Dessie, and Sergio slept with a suitcase under his bed, ready to leave at a moment's notice.

One night at this time, a man went berserk and ran out into the street, shooting. A whole platoon of soldiers was needed to deal with him. Even then it took them some time.

'We could hear the gunfire going on and on – it sounded like a whole battle!' When the shooting finished, the madman was not the only one dead.

A week later, on a bright afternoon, Sergio was reading in his bedroom. He heard a muffled explosion above the compound. He went up to look and found, in a wide, sunny clearing in the shrubs, the scattered remains of five children. Sergio said it was probably an old British munitions dump from the war. Some British aid workers told me it was an Italian dump. Ethiopians hinted that it was government mines laid to protect the town.

More recently, since the massive government counter-offensive, there was a more comic incident. On the morning of Revolution Day, said Sergio, the streets filled quickly. The day was bright and warm after weeks of rain. It was a public holiday and there was to be a parade. But in the main square they found something much more entertaining: the large placard had been defaced and from the forehead of Mengistu sprouted two diabolic horns. Sergio and I agreed that to beat the curfew in such a prominent place, it had to be an inside job.

When we got to Lake Haik, a monk told us the abbot was away and had taken the key to the church. So we sat by the water and watched the pelicans, and Sergio told me how he longed to leave the mountains and go fishing on Lampedusa, a tiny island two hundred miles south of Sicily.

I found Hugo's artist friend and arranged to meet him at the Ghion, Dessie's government hotel. The waiters were servile and charmless, and wore monkey jackets that didn't fit.

Efrem was a self-taught painter and I was struck at once by his eloquence and sophistication. He made Dessie seem very provincial. He worked for the Red Cross, and counted most of Dessie's aid workers among his friends. But his conversation was littered with sardonic references to these *ferengi* 'visitors'.

'Let's not stay here,' I said. 'Can I see your work?'

We walked back through the town. The mountain rose straight up from the street, a sheer velvet shadow in the afternoon sun, dwarfing everything, threatening to engulf us.

'There is a joke,' said Efrem, pointing up to the high ridge. 'The people here say the *shifta* can line up along the top if they want, and piss down on us.'

Dessie's insecurity seemed pathological: an acute case of town-dwellers fearing the brigand. Everywhere I had been warned to beware of the *shifta,* yet never encountered them. No doubt they existed, but their danger, I imagined, was exaggerated. They were bogeymen, gypsies, like the Falashas suspect for their landlessness.

Efrem lived in a three-roomed house, mud walls, mud floor, his abstract mobiles hanging from the rafters. A square of red cloth stretched across a corner of the ceiling. This was his grandmother's house; she was ninety-seven and bed-bound.

Efrem had been born to the north of Dessie, close to the Tigré border. He was nine when his father, a local government official, was posted to Lalibela. His mother left, taking Efrem's sister with her. (Divorce is fairly acceptable in Ethiopia – to be on your fifth spouse is not unusual.)

'Lalibela opened my eyes,' he said. He used to wander round the churches and the labyrinth of connecting tunnels. And he watched the monks in all their guises: their meditations, festivals and services, their illumination and tempera painting. When he was fifteen he was given to his widowed grandmother by his father – again not an unusual practice – and came to live in Dessie.

Efrem had had no formal training, but at sixteen had discovered a compendium history of world painting in Dessie's public library, a gift from the United States. He knew each tiny reproduction of the great artists and trotted out an eclectic roll of favourites: Giotto, Turner, Monet, Mondrian. Friends in the aid agencies brought him paper and Winsor & Newton paints, and, when he wasn't working for the Ethiopian Red Cross, most of his time was spent at the easel.

Efrem prepared to show me his work. He propped the paintings, face down, against a chair and rigged up a Walkman with a pair of small speakers. He searched for a particular tape of American soul, and I realized that the presentation had been made before.

But his paintings were good: contemporary, liberal form, earthy colours and a sense of the highlands I recognized at once. They divided clearly into the two places of his childhood, Lalibela and Dessie: priests and churches and splashes of colour, then drab interiors or street scenes with bird-like figures.

He had had exhibitions in Addis Ababa, selling out to the diplomatic and aid communities. The previous year some of his pictures had been shown in Paris, with success. And in a few months he was going to London – his first time abroad – for an exhibition at the Africa Centre.

A maid came in and beckoned Efrem. 'Excuse me,' he said.

He left me looking at one of his church pictures. Two priests stood in a compound. He had captured their languor, the stripe of their *gabbis,* a stooping eucalyptus and the dull grey of the church's tin roof.

Efrem came back, wiping his hands. He said with a smile, 'She hates killing chickens. You'll stay for lunch?'

'Thank you.' I turned back to his paintings. 'What do Ethiopians think of your work?'

'Ha! I cannot give my pictures away here. People don't see the point of being a painter. The intelligent ones all try to become doctors or engineers. If you do well in school, that's what you want to do. But painting . . .' He tossed back his head in mock dismissal. 'They look at my work, and say, "Good, Efrem – but when are you going to finish it?"'

I was still trying hard to get to Gishen, criss-crossing the town with a sheaf of letters, on foot, by cart, buying favour from officials with sactimonius speeches. Now I was on a leafy knoll outside the office of the Archbishop of Wollo. Beside me was a group of *gabbied* priests and laymen clutching their own requests.

I was shown to the primate's office in a low wooden building. It was sparse and ill lit. He had just been driven the eight hours up from Addis and stared at a desk piled high with papers. A Lalibela cross stood among them, almost buried, like a favourite bloom half-strangled by weeds.

He stood to greet me, a tall man in episcopal black robes. A white beard hung from his chin and when he smiled his deep-set eyes folded into a web of crow's feet. I imagined him as an Old Testament figure, a dark-skinned Job, and found out later that he had spent time in prison during the Red Terror.

We talked for a while about my work, and he asked about the Church in my country. Every now and then the questioning stopped, and he would pick up a piece of paper from the desk, read it, tug his beard, then hand it to one of the lackeys who hovered in the room. The lackeys jumped and ran through the door like relay racers. Then I heard the commotion outside, the barking of orders, the chattering of minions: a secretary to type a letter, a runner to deliver it, and so it went on. The bishop himself was a still point, a paragon of clerical calm. But his word signalled the start of the Ethiopian farce, the comedy of manners: the hierarchy.

When it came to the question of getting to Gishen, the transport manager was called. He said that there might be a vehicle available tomorrow. But he added, 'Fuel short.' Apparently there'd been no deliveries to Dessie for some days. And I would need papers. I agreed to meet the transport manager the following morning at Security to sort it all out. The bishop blessed the expedition, and I thanked him, then walked back down to the town.

An hour or so out of Dessie, just north of Tabor, the road dropped through the plateau. This was the north-west route through Wollo, unsurfaced and closed during the rains. The EOC Land Cruiser clung to its curves, crossed rock-falls and river beds, and ran round beneath grim, overhanging cliffs. We came across a party of mules laden with bales of grain. Then they turned and ran back down the road, until we stopped. They squeezed past us, on the outside, their hooves kicking gravel down the precipice.

The road cut through a fan of debris. There were broken trees among the boulders.

'Only a few weeks the road has been opened,' said Abraham,

the driver. 'The stones are very big – you can see. This year there has been so much rain!'

The destruction, it was true, was on a massive scale, but now the stone was dry, and the residue itself looked like a frozen torrent.

The valley deepened and trickles of water appeared in its crutch, among the rocks. And our valley joined another, much larger, so steep that half was in shadow. Here there was a steady flow through the rocks, but shallow enough to drive across; downstream was the half-buried parapet of an Italian bridge.

This was the River Telayayen, which runs along the foot of the Gishen mountain. In Amharic, Telayayen means 'we are separated'. Once, Abraham told me, a small boy walked across the valley to a village on the opposite slope. The rains came and the water dashed down the dry bed in the annual flash-flood. For months the village was cut off. Each day the boy's mother stood and waved to her son across the river, crying, 'Telayayen!'

When Father Alvares came this way early in the sixteenth century, he was shown a locked gate that opened on to the lower slopes of Gishen. If he went through the gate, he was told, he would have to have his feet and hands cut off, and his eyes put out, and be left there to die. So he rode on, and the villagers showered him with rocks.

Now a track leaves the main road, and threads up past terraced fields towards the cliff-top monastery.

Abraham pointed up. 'There – Gishen!'

It was mid-afternoon and the light was at its sharpest. By leaning forward I could see the summit through the top of the windscreen – a line of cliffs framed against an impossibly blue sky.

For about ten miles the track climbed towards it, skirting the bigger spurs, hairpinning, gaining height. Abraham fought with the gears. And on the steepest corners the wheels struggled for grip, flicking stones behind, and sending them clanking against the wheel arches.

Beside the track, the bare flaking rock was studded with brighter nodules. I asked Abraham to stop, and found they were agates encased in copper-green shells.

Abraham dropped me off at the foot of the cliff. The track became a series of steps carved in the rock – 703 according to Thomas Pakenham who came here in the 1950s. The only access to the monastery is a narrow gap in the cliffs. The last steps run through the opening, along a ridge and up towards a crude gateway, half thatch, half stone. On each side the cliffs fall sheer to scree and dry, buff-brown fields.

Gishen is on an *amba*. *Ambas* are stubborn relics of the plateau, islands of flat land cut off by cliffs; they are isolated, virtually impregnable, and habitable – crops grow well on their flat summits (though water can be a problem); they are a microcosm of the highlands themselves.

Ethiopia's premier monastery, Debra Damo in northern Tigré is also on an *amba*, and can be reached only by being pulled up the cliff by a rope. Before Gishen, it was the royal prison – until the tenth century when Queen Judit somehow stormed the mountain and killed all four hundred princes.

Looking west from the gateway, over the abyss, the far ridges and summits rose like an archipelago through the haze. Just below the horizon, I picked out what I was looking for. Twenty or thirty miles away, maybe more, was the distinctive, slightly sloping profile of Magdala.

Towards the end of his nineteenth-century reign Theodore based himself at Magdala. These were the bad years when he would drink for days on the mountain top, then pitch prisoners off the edge. But the European hostages he saved.

At Easter 1868 Robert Napier (later Lord Napier of Magdala) arrived at the foot of the *amba*. To release the hostages he had marched from the coast with a large force of soldiers, who were weary and baffled by this strange country. One had written home, 'We were told that the interior of Abyssinia was a great table-land. But to me it looks more like a table turned upside down.'

But they had little difficulty storming Theodore's stronghold. As he saw the British soldiers breach the narrow col and swarm on to the *amba*, the emperor took one of the duelling pistols sent to him as a gift by Queen Victoria, and shot himself in the mouth.

Having escaped his stoning by the villagers below Gishen, Father Alvares rode on to find the royal court. Soon after his arrival a letter was delivered to the emperor. It was brought by a monk and a guard of two hundred men. The emperor read the letter, and when he saw it was signed by a prince, ordered the monk to be taken away. Alvares says the unfortunate envoy was 'flogged near to death every other day for two weeks'.

For the monk had come from Gishen where the royal princes were kept in strict isolation. Any contact with the outside world – even letters – was a severe offence.

Mogul princes were confined to the imperial palace in Delhi, Ottoman sultans strangled their brothers, but the Ethiopian solution seemed a good one to Alvares; idle princes were a perennial problem for Europe's royal houses. Unable to go up to Gishen, his account says no more than that the princes lived in great style, and were served by scions of the lesser nobility.

A hundred years after Alvares, Ahmed Gran and his Muslim army arrived at the foot of Gishen. They had sacked the churches at Lalibela, but had been told that its treasures had been taken to the *amba*. So the Muslims went to Gishen and laid siege. The chronicle says that they could see a thousand palaces and that the *amba* was home to 2300 Christian princes.

The Muslims tried to scale the cliffs but were bombarded with rocks. One night, impatient to crack the fortress, a party of seven of Gran's soldiers crept into the rocks beside the only entrance. Above the gate they could see the glow of a fire, and they knew that if it dimmed it would mean the guard was asleep. Much later the glow faded and one of the party took a dagger and crawled towards the sleeping guard. But one of the other Muslims coughed, the guard woke, and the Christians sent their attackers rolling back down the hill in a shower of rocks.

Months of sieging brought the natural fortress no closer to submission and Ahmed Gran said, 'There is nothing to be gained by fighting on this mountain.' He withdrew his troops and went campaigning in other regions. Only when he gained an alliance with the Falashas did Amba Gishen fall. It was never again used as a royal prison.

21

After the steep approach, the *amba* came as a shock. It felt like a summit, with cliffs and views down in every direction. Yet there were huts and eucalyptus groves, grazing cattle, and a farmer cracking a leather bird-scarer over a field of teff.

I found the abbot's quarters and presented my letters. I bent low and entered a round hut. Inside it was dark, but I could make out the shadowy robes of the father, and saw the flash of his teeth as he rose to greet me. Someone had told him I was coming.

'Thanks be to God, are you well?' He clasped my hand.

'I am well.'

'With God's help, you have arrived safely.'

'Thank you, I have arrived well.'

He released my hand and asked for tea to be brought. The floor was covered in fresh grass. Sheepskins lay on top of the grass, and the abbot reclined like a sultan against some cushions. He fiddled with a rosary of amber and stained wood. I sat on the grass with my back to the wall.

There was a long pause while the abbot smiled the boyish smile of the good priests. On the mud wall above him, from a torn poster, J. F. Kennedy smiled his democratic smile, and below in English was a notice announcing a film of his life, to be shown at Haile Selassie University. The date was February 1964.

'Philippos . . . Philippos . . .' mused the abbot. 'Like our Apostle!'

My exchanges with the clergy by now had a formal similarity. The first questions were always the same. But like the drawn-out Amharic greetings they were filled with such warmth that it didn't matter what was said. There were the usual questions about the 'Church in my country' and was I 'Roman or Protestant'.

Then there was my name, the bewilderment with 'Philip', until it was hellenized to 'Philippos' (the New Testament was translated to Ge'ez from the Greek). And this laid open all sorts of jokes about 'our Apostle', St Philip, who in Acts 8 converted the Ethiopian eunuch to Christianity.

The abbot propped himself up and asked me, 'Oh, Philippos, could you send blankets from your country? The monks get very cold in the night.'

'I'll try.' Then I asked him, 'How long have you been at Gishen?'

'Four years. I am forty-seven years old!'

He had been the abbot at another monastery not far away, no more than two days by mule. But this was the post he had always wanted. He remembered coming here for the *Maskal* festival, and the hundreds of pilgrims who walked up from Wuchale. He remembered too, in the last years before the revolution, a helicopter bringing the Imperial Family to the festival, flying up the valleys and landing on the *amba* like an outsize insect.

The abbot threw back his head and exclaimed, 'Haile Selassie – a great man! So clever and kind.' He laughed suddenly, and I couldn't tell if the remark had been in earnest, or what was meant. For he turned and stared through the doorway where the sun shone in a pool beneath the eaves.

Later I walked out to the furthest tip of the *amba*. Looking back, the transepts of the summit's cruciform are clear. They cross the main shaft as a remnant of more resistant rock, slightly higher, hung with eucalyptus, and regular. It was easy to imagine the hand of some divine mason.

But around it is the impossible landscape of the highlands. On all sides it falls into a warren of cavernous valleys, to rise again as the plateau somewhere else.

But the strange thing is that there are no peaks: the horizon is entirely flat. It is as if the rising land had been thwarted by an invisible ceiling, like the umbrella acacia trees in the Rift.

Nothing can really be understood about Ethiopia without seeing this landscape and realizing that, despite its rocky stillness, more Ethiopians live here than anywhere else. Looking closer at the far wall I could make out the dots of scattered homesteads. Since the first millennium BC, before the Axumite Empire, people have been pushing further up into the mountains, to the fringes of tillable land. Now the land is bald and exhausted, and the population still rising.

I had been told that the highland Ethiopians do not like villages. They tend to build their huts apart, cushioned from each other by their own land. They go to church and the market, and twice a week they fast. Then maybe a couple of times each year – *Maskal* and Christmas – they make a pilgrimage. And once every ten years or so the rains fail and there is a famine.

That is how it has always been. It is ungovernable land. Few roads cross it. It has never been successfully conquered – Muslims and Europeans were repelled by its geography as much as anything else. Even the Ethiopians themselves – imperial or communist – have never really controlled it. Successive emperors waged endless campaigns through its passes, and millions of Soviet dollars have been wasted trying to maintain its northern extremities.

Here on the end of the *amba*, the top of the cross, is the small church of St Mikhael. It was closed, so I sat on the wall and dangled my feet over the cliff. Beside me was a thorn tree and two or three blooms of yellow mullein. I watched a lammergeyer glide through the valley, before catching a thermal and soaring upwards.

Then I noticed a figure on a ledge just below. His rags were so soiled he seemed to merge into the rock. He wore a rimless hat hung with loose threads and I could hear him muttering – prayers or a song, I wasn't sure. He held a staff of twisted iron, slender as a spear, and topped with a cross. He was tapping his bare heels against the stone, his chin jutting out into the vast mountain space below us. He turned and saw me. Instantly he stopped his invocations, and managed a coy smile.

He said he was a *bahtawi*, a hermit living rough on the edge of the cliffs. But his words trickled out, mumbled with the awkwardness of a child. So I bowed and left him to his contemplations and went back to the abbot.

At the age of twenty-six, Dr Johnson's Rasselas, Prince of Abissinia, also took to solitary contemplations and began to find Happy Valley limiting. He escaped from his royal prison and went down the Nile to Egypt, looking for the secret of lasting happiness. But he didn't find it and went back to Ethiopia.

Johnson put his princes in a valley, but he clearly got the idea from Gishen. When he was twenty-six, Johnson had translated the journeys of Father Lobo, one of the last Portuguese missionaries to Ethiopia. Since then he had set himself up as something of an expert on the country, and in an essay on Ethiopian kingship said this:

> It was the custom formerly to keep the princes confined in the mountain Guexen, where the temper and manners of each prince are diligently observed.

Dr Johnson hated the sort of fantastic tales that usually came out of Ethiopia – he was among James Bruce's most caustic critics. *Rasselas* was strictly a moral tale to illustrate the sameness of humanity rather than its diversity. (It was also written to pay for his mother's funeral and completed in the evenings of a single week.)

How he must have scorned the rest of Gishen's mythology, the account in *Purchas His Pilgrimage* of the palaces and great library, the hordes of gold and jewels. And, if he knew about it, would have had little time for the 'Abyssinian Philosophy' and the idea that Milton cites in *Paradise Lost:*

> Nor, where Abassin kings their issue guard,
> Mount Amara (though by some supposed
> True Paradise) under the Ethiop line

Milton was tapping into an ancient tradition that had the site of the Earthly Paradise as a place of perpetual equinox: the Equator, 'the Ethiop line'. The specific link between Mount Amara – or its real name, Gishen – and Paradise is a weak one. It seems to rest on the belief of a huge mountain in the southern lands 'a whole day's journey high', combined with the fantastic splendour of Purchas's Gishen.

There is also a connection with Thomas Burnet's *The Sacred Theory of the Earth*. Why, he asks, is there no record of his antediluvian world, the First World? Burnet points to the destruction of the ancient libraries, Constantinople and Alexandria, or those at Buda and Fez 'in the hands of Mahometans'. But in the great

'Abyssine or Aethiopick library' – at Gishen – there, he says, must be proof of his theory, the secrets of the perfect world before the Flood.

But Ethiopia's link with Paradise goes back further. In Genesis the second of the four rivers that water the Garden of Eden is the 'Gihon . . . that compasseth the whole land of Ethiopia'. Gihon comes probably from *Jehon,* an ancient Egyptian name for the Nile. The traditional site for the biblical Paradise is between two of the other rivers, the Tigris and Euphrates, in Mesopotamia, a location dating to the days of the Jews in Babylon.

When locating Paradise became a serious pursuit for Europeans, and Genesis was taken literally, there was a problem getting the Nile to reach Mesopotamia. So they put it in a culvert and ran it under the Red Sea.

But before the exile there had been other sites – the high plains around Lake Van, Mount Saphon in Syria, Arabia Felix. *Eden* or *Edin* is simply an old Semitic word meaning a fertile area, the fantasy of those in dry lands for green fields.

At the time of the drought a few years before, the two small reservoirs on the *amba* had dried out completely.

'To get water,' said the abbot, 'we had to walk for two hours down the mountain. Now we have plenty of water, you see.'

He pointed at the pond and smiled. The water was the colour of slurry. An elaborate aqueduct brought to it catchment from the church roof, a corrugated iron gutter on high poles.

Then he showed me the generator which powers a system of fairy lights for the Maskal festival. Pakenham was appalled by it, and the glitzy *tabot* it lit up. But for the monks then it was a new toy, less than a year old, and he had to compromise his sacred regard for antiquity, and say how charming it was.

We walked through the compound of the extraordinary church of Igziyabher Ab. It is a fat white drum sprouting two stunted transepts. The wooden panels of its doors are painted separately in bright yellows, and orange and green. Below the tin roof, the bargeboard is carved in an ornate filigree, and on the whitewashed walls there are arabesques and a huge sneering *buda,* the evil spirit.

'Under here,' said the abbot, 'is the Cross.'

'But how did it get here?'

'Ah! I will show you.'

He led me up a wooden staircase that creaked and wobbled like an old ship. He lit a taper and showed me into a room heavy with dust and the smell of guano. There was a model of the church and religious crowns, wood-bound texts and loose vellum pages and racks of prayer sticks. There were rows and rows of vestments, countless coloured umbrellas (the standard gift of penance), and nowhere an inch of floor space.

The abbot sat me down and placed a book on my lap. It was bound in leather, but written in Ge'ez, and I was unable to read it. So he told me the story.

Dawit, grandson of the great Amda Tseyon, conqueror of the Muslims, succeeded to the throne in 1381. He had a dream in which he was told: 'Find the Cross and place it on the mountain that is itself shaped like a cross.' So he travelled to Metemma, and then down the Nile to Egypt. In Jerusalem he acquired the right half of the Cross and journeyed back to Ethiopia. But in Sennar, on the edge of the mountains, he fell from his mule and died. The Cross went back to Jerusalem.

His son Zara Yaqob was the greatest emperor since Ezana, the first Christian ruler. (In Europe rumours of his reign revived hopes of finding Prester John.) Having had the same dream, Zara Yaqob recovered the portion of the Cross and took it to his capital at Axum. But the earth shook when he put it down, and buildings cracked. The emperor then remembered the dream. He searched for the chosen mountain near Axum, at Debra Berhan, Managasha and Genet Le'ul. But wherever he placed the Cross, the earth shook.

After three years of vain questing, the emperor was visited by a saint who led him to Gishen, saying, 'That is the chosen mountain!'

So Zara Yaqob climbed up to the *amba*, and placed the Cross upon the ground and it was calm. So he buried it, and the blind and the lepers made pilgrimages there and were cured.

But I was told different versions by other people, and it seems that the festival of Maskal celebrates not Zara Yaqob's quest but the original discovery by Empress Helena in AD 326.

Exactly contemporary with the growth of Prester John's fame in Europe was the emergence of the Grail cycle. In these legends the Holy Grail is kept in a temple on the Mountain of Salvation. There lives the Grail King who presides at Mass and is the trusted keeper of the mysteries. But he is wounded, and with the wound the land around the mountain becomes barren, crippled by famine, the Waste Land.

The quest for the Grail is a quest for Paradise: if the king could be healed his land would flourish again, as the Garden of Earthly Delights, the Earthly Paradise. ('Paradise' is borrowed from the Persian *paradesh*, the walled gardens that surrounded royal palaces.)

The Grail King began to be associated with Prester John. Both ruled a land of miracles and plenty, both were priests and Christian kings ('Prester' was often taken to mean priest). So when Europe's Christians looked towards the land of Prester John, south and eastwards (the supposed direction of Paradise), they were looking for salvation, the Grail, knowing that there was a better place on earth, if only it could be found.

Myths of the Earthly Paradise show a great similarity. Compare the Hindu account with the Chinese 'Jade Mountain'. The Hindu Vedas point to Mount Meru in the centre of the earth, home of the gods, surrounded by a garden; in the garden is *Parijate,* the tree of heaven which Krishna stole (just as Prometheus stole fire from Mount Olympus). The Chinese look to the mountain of Kun-Lun, from which flow four rivers (in Eden they flow *into* the garden); on Kun-Lun is the Peach Tree of Immortality, and the mountain is the home of the gods. The Norse–Germanic Paradise is to the south, a warm region separated from the cold north by Ginnungagap, a great abyss; there on the Mountain of Asgard is the home of Wotan and the other gods, and the tree of immortality.

Then there is the Paradise that is returned to, the place of former glory or innocence, the Grail kingdom before the king's wound, Zion before the exile, Africa before the Europeans, Burnet's perfect antediluvian world, the collective expression of an individual's yearning for vanished joy, a child's joy.

In the West they looked south-east for Paradise, in the East they looked south-west. The Egyptians looked up the Nile to 'god's land' and Mohammed said, 'The Nile comes out of the garden of Paradise and if you were to examine it when it comes out, you would find in it the leaves of Paradise.' Dante pointed down towards the Equator.

If the myths tend to converge on Africa, the Ethiopia of the Ancient World, it could be because of the continent's fertility. Vegetable abundance is a common trait of Paradise. To the Ancient World, the African interior was the source of the Nile, the Land of Punt. Perhaps the Ethiopian highlands themselves, then forested and green, the closest of Africa's wetlands, and known by word of mouth, helped make a verdant symbol of the far continent.

But there is one other possible reason, one I would like to believe. If looking towards Paradise is also a longing to return, a looking back, there might be some trace in the collective memory, preserved by cultures from China to the Norselands: that the African Rift, as we now suppose from fossil evidence, is the scar of the First World, the place man noticed his own nakedness and lost the keys to Paradise.

Back in the hut, the abbot reclined again on his cushions and sheepskin. '*Tella*!' he said. 'You want *tella*!' *Tella* is a watery beer brewed locally throughout the highlands.

'You'll join me?'

'No, no!'

But I had to accept. A small woman in rags brought an earthenware jug. I drank from a glass stencilled: ETHIOPIAN REVOLUTION 1974–84.

We had watched the sun fall behind the plateau, a warm sun which picked up the distant, frayed course of the river. Now it was almost dark and the abbot was in high spirits. He leaned forward on his elbows and picked up the jug, his black soutane billowing behind him, his teeth flashing mischievously. 'More *tella*, Philippos!'

Then a man with bare legs came in from the darkness and unwrapped a gourd of wild honey. The abbot lit a taper from the fire and melted the wax seal. He scooped some honey into a bowl and passed it to me. He told his maid to wash and massage my feet (it seems that Gishen is not so prohibitive to women as the island monasteries of Lake Tana – the abbot's maid lived in the next hut). More people arrived, and we talked and joked. We drank more *tella* and ate honey and the fire filled the roof of the hut with smoke, and mingled with our laughter and the shrill cadence of spoken Amharic.

At about nine o'clock the abbot stood up. 'Now I must go to church.'

There was no moon when I crossed the *amba* a little later, but above the trees the sky was bright with hundreds of stars. The mountain air was clear and still, and I knew it would be a cold night. Approaching the church I heard the intermittent drumbeats of the *debtara*. Inside, there were children chasing each other round the ambulatory and monks with brass-topped prayer sticks leaning against the wall. The church was lit by candlelight and smelt of incense.

The church of Kiddus Maryam is stone-built, but in plan the same as all the circular wattle churches: two concentric sections around the walls of the square inner sanctum, the *maqdas*. In the *maqdas*, at the very centre of the church, is the *tabot*, the replica of the Ark. Only priests are allowed into the *maqdas* and its outer walls at Maryam are covered in crude frescoes, an iconostasis – to be looked at, rather than through. I found a space in front of a madonna and watched the priests prepare for the vigil. Tomorrow was the monthly feast of Kiddus Maryam, St Mary, the monastery's patron saint.

A distinguished-looking figure took his place beside me in black serge overcoat and white breeches. Before him came a barefoot retainer who unrolled a small prayer rug on the stone floor, and pulled up a stool. The old man sat down and placed three tallow candles on the carpet in front of him. Then he put on a pair of spectacles with a broken hinge, crossed his thin legs, and opened a prayer book.

A young deacon approached the lectern and started a reading.

I spotted the abbot standing in the outer section, slightly taller than those around, and bowed to him. But he made no acknowledgement. Gone were his comic high spirits, his toothy grins and teasing; such abandonment was allowed in his own hut. But now he was the abbot of an important monastery, conductor of the liturgy, guardian of the Cross. In his stern expression he held the respect of the novices and the simple families of the *amba*'s secular community; he knew they looked to him as the earthly manifestation of His power.

The service carried on with readings and chanted anaphora, and long formless periods of muttering and prayers. After some hours I heard the *debtara*'s drum announce the Song of Yared, and the start of the ritual dancing.

Ritual dancing was an ancient Jewish practice. But it was rejected by the early Christian Church. The early fathers found it too disturbing, too pagan, with its dangerous erotic rhythms, and only a few Gnostics persisted with it.

But in the Ethiopian Church it has survived as the most potent rite of worship. It is the spirit of the Old Testament – when the Ark was brought to Zion and the people of Israel played on harps and timbrels and cymbals, and David danced before the Lord (and Uzzah reached out to steady the Ark and was instantly killed). Without the *tabot* and a drum, the Ethiopians say a church is not a church. In these things are the awe and the ecstasy of the services, Judah and Africa, the twin roots of Ethiopian worship.

The dancers formed a circle around the drummer. The drum was beaten again and they flicked their sistra and shuffled inwards. The first low notes of a chant hummed from the group. Novices lit tapers and handed them round the church. Beside me sat the old man's servant. His master continued his prayers, ignoring the excitement. I imagined him as a nobleman from before the revolution, one of those who took to the hills, his land nationalized, his family in prison or in exile, living out his last years as a monk.

A tenor joined the chant and the tempo of the dance changed. A *debtara* hung the drum from his shoulder. He beat it with the flat of his palm and whirled round, shouting with each beat. Around him the circle swelled in a flurry of prayer sticks, and the singing got wilder and quicker. The drummer cried out. He hopped and spun like a dervish. His shadow in the candles flickered on the walls and between the dark rafters in the roof.

And then suddenly he stopped his drumming and lifted the strap over his head and there was just the last tinkling of the sistra, like something distant falling.

It was now very cold, and I could see the quick breath of the *debtara* as they put down their prayer sticks.

Later the doors of the *maqdas* opened and a priest appeared bearing a silvery madonna. The drum started again. The dancers shuffled into the outer section, clutching tapers, and the first funereal drumbeats quickened again.

The procession went round the church until I lost all sense of direction. I saw the still, glowing faces of the same monks, too old to take part. I felt the cold blasts of the night wind as we passed the open doors and the figures of the menstrual women who were forbidden entry. A fight broke out between two or three young boys, punching each other, rolling round the legs of the procession, until a couple of monks separated them and clipped their ears. And all the while the dancers vied with the drummer to step up the pace.

At the peak of the procession, a figure leapt suddenly into the fray. It was the shy hermit from the end of the *amba*. He was transformed by the ceremony, quivering, ecstatic as a shaman. He turned and his eyes shone among the tapers. He placed the flat of his hand against the pole-cross and dipped it through a perfect arc at each beat. He swayed and danced with flicks of his wrist and hips. Then he was lost among the *debtara* and all I could see was the cross dipping and dancing above their heads like a puppet.

The service went on all night. Soon after dawn I slipped out and watched the sun rise above the plateau. By the cliff I saw a woman come out of her hut and light a fire. I heard the hyrax scream from the rocks, and later I was told there were no mules, so I walked down the mountain.

Index